# The Commerce of
the Prairies

# The Commerce of the Prairies by Josiah Gregg

EDITED BY

MILO MILTON QUAIFE

University of Nebraska Press • Lincoln/London

The Bison Book edition of *The Commerce on the Prairies* by Josiah Gregg appeared as No. 24 in the Lakeside Classics, published in 1926, and is reprinted by arrangement with the Lakeside Press, R. R. Donnelley & Sons Co., Chicago, who are the sole proprietors of its special contents.

∞

Library of Congress Catalog Card Number 27–1450
International Standard Book Number 0–8032–5076–2

*First Bison Book printing October, 1967*

*Most recent printing shown by first digit below:*

6    7    8    9    10

*Manufactured in the United States of America*

# Contents

CHAPTER                                PAGE

HISTORICAL INTRODUCTION . . . . . . . . . . XI

PREFACE TO ORIGINAL EDITION . . . . . . . XXV

1. Origin of the Santa Fé Trade . . . . . . . 3

2. Organizing the Expedition . . . . . . . . 19

3. From Council Grove to The Caches . . . . 38

4. Encounters with Thirst and the Red Man . 59

5. From the Cimarron to Santa Fé . . . . . 77

6. An Historical Excursion . . . . . . . . 107

7. Geographical and Economic Conditions . . 130

8. The Return to Independence . . . . . . 155

9. A New Route to Santa Fé . . . . . . . . 171

10. Among the Comanches . . . . . . . . 191

11. Conclusion of the Journey . . . . . . . 212

12. From Santa Fé to Chihuahua . . . . . . 230

13. A Visit to Aguascalientes . . . . . . . 251

14. A Visit to the Silver Mines . . . . . . 273

15. Departure from Chihuahua . . . . . . . 290

16. From Santa Fé to Van Buren . . . . . . 304

INDEX . . . . . . . . . . . . . . . . . . . 331

# Historical Introduction

# Historical Introduction

IN the history of the American frontier there is no more interesting chapter than that which deals with the old Santa Fé Trail and its traffic. Although no such stream of travel ever poured over it as that which followed the Oregon Trail to California and the Pacific Northwest, its story is in many respects more picturesque and more interesting than is the story of the Oregon Trail; and although the field of prophecy is not the recognized domain of the historian, we venture the prediction that the Santa Fé Trail will yet find its place in fiction and on the silver screen, and that the magnates of moviedom will gather in more gold from the exploitation of its story than ever any of the merchants accumulated who a century ago pursued their venturesome calling of traders to Santa Fé.

However this may be, the Santa Fé Trail has been supremely fortunate in the matter of finding an historian adequately equipped to record its story. Dr. Josiah Gregg, whose narrative we reprint in the present volume of the *Lakeside Classics* series, spent almost ten years of his early manhood in the Santa Fé trade, in the course of which the wild, free life of the prairies wove a spell from whose domination he was never able to escape. A man of scholarly instincts and training, it was eminently fitting that he should assume the task of writing the history of the trade, and describing the life of the country he knew so well. Long since, his narrative became a classic of American historical literature. In its particular field it has no rival, and it will endure as long as Americans continue to cherish their country's past.

Gregg's *Commerce of the Prairies* was first published in two volumes simultaneously at New York and London in 1844. A second and a third edition appeared the following year, and others followed in 1850, 1855, and 1857. Meanwhile the work was translated into German, and three editions in this language were published in 1845-47. Almost fifty years after the Philadelphia edition of 1857, Gregg's work was again reprinted under the editorship of Dr. Reuben G. Thwaites, forming part of Volume XIX and all of Volume XX of that editor's *Early Western Travels 1748-1846* series.

In none of these numerous editions of Gregg's narrative was any information afforded concerning his career, other than the little the author himself supplies in the course of his narration. It remained for William E. Connelley, the capable secretary of the Kansas State Historical Society, and long an industrious worker in the field of western history, to rescue Gregg's personal story from the oblivion which had overtaken it. The fruits of his research were committed to print in 1921 in his article entitled "Dr. Josiah Gregg, Historian of the Old Santa Fé Trail," published in the *Proceedings* of the Mississippi Valley Historical Association for 1919–20. From this paper we have drawn the statements which follow, which constitute a fitting conclusion to this historical introduction.

The founder of the Gregg family in America was William Gregg, a Scotch-Irish immigrant, who removed from Ireland to Pennsylvania about the year 1682. He was of a Quaker family, which perhaps suffices to explain his coming to Pennsylvania. Jacob Gregg, a great-grandson of the immigrant of 1682, removed from Pennsylvania to North Carolina, and some years later he again migrated, this time to Arkansas. Neither the date of this removal nor the place of settlement in Arkansas is established, but it is a matter of family tradition that Josiah Gregg had relatives at or near Van Buren, which figures prominently in his narrative; there is some reason, therefore, for surmising that this was the place where Jacob Gregg made his final home.

Jacob's children had grown up before the removal from North Carolina. There were three sons: Harmon, David, and William, who, after various places of residence in Tennessee and Kentucky, finally became reunited in Illinois some time prior to the War of 1812.

Harmon Gregg was the father of Josiah, our author. He was born in Pennsylvania in February, 1774, and grew to manhood in that state. About the year 1796 he married Susannah Smelser, of Pennsylvania-German origin. This marriage occurred before the family migration to North Carolina. Eight children were born to the couple in the period 1797–1818. Of these Josiah was the fifth, born July 19, 1806, in Overton County, Tennessee.

About the year 1812 Harmon Gregg left Illinois for Missouri, accompanied, or possibly preceded, by his brother William. The latter settled in what is now Howard County. In December, 1814, the settlement was destroyed by Indians and William was among the slain. Harmon Gregg's family were inmates of Cooper's Fort (near the town of Glasgow) during the war, and Harmon Gregg, like every other man in the settlement, was a member of the local militia. He remained in the vicinity of Cooper's Fort until the autumn of 1825, when he removed to the Blue River country, settling about five miles northeast of modern Independence in Jackson County. He erected a house here, which was still standing as recently as twenty years ago, and this house was the home of Josiah Gregg, who never married. It was a log house, which at some subsequent date was covered with boards.

Josiah Gregg was a sickly child, predestined, it would seem, to fill a consumptive's grave.

# Historical Introduction

How he escaped this destiny is sufficiently set forth by Gregg himself in the pages which follow this introduction. His physical condition powerfully influenced the entire course of his life, as well before he took to the prairies as afterward. Frontier life was hard, and demanded men of physical stamina. Boys who lacked this qualification—who in the vernacular of the time were "weakly"—were expected to become storekeepers, lawyers, preachers, or doctors. Josiah Gregg, who was evidently of a scholarly turn of mind, elected the medical profession, and was sent by the family to a medical college in Philadelphia, where he remained several years. Neither the name of the school nor the date of Gregg's attendance have been preserved, but it is obvious from his writings and the facts of his later life that his studies must have included many things not pertaining to medicine.

Upon graduating, Gregg returned to Missouri and began the practice of medicine in Jackson County. His health became worse, however, until at length he was unable to mount his horse. The people of Jackson County were familiar with the Santa Fé trade, of which Independence about this time became the eastern terminus, and Gregg's own father had been a member of Becknell's expedition to Santa Fé in 1822. They knew of numerous instances where persons afflicted with tuberculosis had been benefited by a trip across the plains with the traders, and Gregg himself was, of course, cognizant of these facts. In the spring of 1831, therefore, he joined a caravan which was setting out for Santa Fé.

His activities during the next nine years are sufficiently set forth in his narrative. When he left the trade in 1840 he was still but thirty-four years old. Of his movements during the next few years we have no definite information, save that he made one more excursion into the plains and that his book was published in 1844. Although to large extent a personal narration it combines also the aspect of a general history, and it is certain that much time and labor were devoted to preparing it. This becomes more evident from an examination of the entire work than from the perusal of the portion of it here reprinted, which is mainly limited to the narration of Gregg's personal experiences. His historical sketch of New Mexico, for example, is said to have been the first in the English language. Although Gregg was a doctor by profession and a merchant by actual calling, he possessed historical ability of no mean order, as his narrative sufficiently evidences.

The Mexican War came on in the summer of 1846 and Gregg, whose literary reputation by now was well established, engaged in it in the capacity of newspaper correspondent. He was with General Taylor's army, accompanied a force sent by Taylor to Colonel Doniphan at Chihuahua, and returned with the latter officer to the sea coast. The war closed in 1848, and Gregg may have returned to his home in Missouri. At any rate, the following year he joined in the rush to California which followed upon the discovery of gold in that region.

If Gregg kept a journal of this enterprise, as seems probable, all knowledge of the fact has perished, nor do we even know what route he followed to reach the land of gold. At San Francisco he embarked upon an expedition to the Trinity River region of northern California. In October, 1849, he was at a mining camp called Rich Bar, whose precise location has not been identified. There were some forty miners gathered here. The store of provisions was insufficient to support them through the winter, and there was no possibility of obtaining fresh supplies. Information derived from the natives indicated that not more than eight days' travel to the westward there was a beautiful bay, surrounded by extensive prairies. There was much discussion of this information, ending in the resolve to send out two exploring parties in search of the bay, one to go overland from Rich Bar, the other to return to San Francisco and thence proceed by sea northward to the hoped-for destination. If the bay could be found, a city might be established which would serve as the port for the mines of the north, and incidentally enrich its founders.

Gregg was made leader of the overland expedition, for which choice he was well qualified by his earlier experience and by his knowledge of astronomy. Enthusiasm for the enterprise diminished as the day of departure drew near, however, and on November 5, 1849, Gregg set out from Rich Bar with only seven followers.

It proved to be his last expedition. The party was but poorly supplied with food and other necessaries, and it faced the task of traversing an unknown mountain region in winter. By November 13 the entire supply of provisions was exhausted and henceforth the sole reliance was upon hunting. As often under similar circumstances, the hardships endured gave rise to bad feeling among the explorers, and Gregg's requests for assistance in taking measurements and observations were answered with shameful abuse. On December 7 the explorers reached Trinidad Head, which they named Gregg Point. They soon turned southward, and although they kept together all discipline vanished, and each man looked out for himself.

On December 29 Humboldt Bay was discovered, and given the name of Trinity Bay. The original object of the exploration had been achieved, but the explorers were in no condition to take advantage of their discovery, or do anything in the way of carrying out the further project of founding a city. Their only thought was now to make their way to the settlements.

They finally separated into two parties of four men each. Gregg's party pushed southward along the coast in hope of reaching San Francisco, but growing steadily weaker, the men finally turned inland toward the Sacramento Valley. On the margin of a lake in what is now Lake County, California, Gregg fell from his horse unconscious and died a few hours later; his death was due to the combined effects of hardship, exposure, and starvation. Although but forty-four years of age, his companions in this last expedition repeatedly spoke of him as the "old" man. Evidently his appearance belied his years, for at forty-four he should have been still in the prime of vigorous manhood.

"So far as practical utility is concerned," says Connelley, "the discovery of Humboldt Bay by Dr. Gregg's party was its real discovery. The next spring it became generally known that this exploration had been made. Settlers went in by land and sea. A city was founded on this bay. . . . Other towns were laid out, and all the region round about was explored, the mines developed, and the country settled. So Dr. Gregg left a lasting monument of himself in California."

Of Gregg himself and his book, Mr. Connelley supplies this estimate:

"The great worth of the work was recognized at once. It became the authority on all subjects of which it treated; and not only has it retained the high place it immediately won, but its value has increased with a more extensive knowledge of its times. Much of the history of western Missouri, Kansas, New Mexico, northern Mexico, north Texas, and the entire territory embraced in the new state of Oklahoma must finally rest upon the great work of Dr. Gregg. It embraces accounts of the Indian tribes inhabiting that vast country, accounts which have stood the tests of the scientists of our own times. It contains acute delineations of the traits and characteristics of the Mexican people. It gave the first accurate statement of the geographical conformation of the country, the true course of its streams, the wild animals it contained, and its natural resources. The state of Oklahoma will need little better descriptions of its vast gypsum-beds than can be found in the pages of this book; and its salt deposits were carefully examined and adequately described. Dr. Gregg was the first to note the diminishing numbers of the buffalo, and he predicted their final extermination at no distant day. All this is beautifully told. His diction is masterful; his style is simple, chaste, elegant, pleasing, and sometimes eloquent. His descriptions are complete and full, and never tedious. The whole work is dignified and scholarly. The map which he drew for his book was pronounced by Dr. Elliott Coues (the highest authority) the best of its time. Upon its publication the book was immediately recognized as a masterpiece, and that verdict will ever stand.

# Historical Introduction

"Dr. Gregg was a merchant, with his own money invested in competition with many others who were engaged in the same business. He sought new fields for his enterprises; he explored countries and laid out new routes over which to carry on his trade. He held his own against the Mexicans, who were bent on despoiling him; and when they sent troops to compel him to return to a town upon one occasion, he was confident of his ability to defeat them with only his servants. He chose to return, however, and he faced the authorities with such resolute bearing that he was suffered to depart with their apologies. His fearlessness is the prominent characteristic of all his intercourse with the Mexicans and Indians; and the accounts of his adventures with the latter, had he preserved them, would fill volumes. In his conflicts with them he never quailed, never gave an inch, but stood his ground determined and grim as death. His iron will is typical of that unconquerable spirit that carried American conquest to the Pacific Ocean."

In editing the present edition of Gregg's classic it has been deemed best, from the viewpoint of the *Lakeside Classics* constituency, to reprint only those chapters which comprise his personal narrative, omitting those, about equal in number, which the author devoted to treatises on such subjects as the geography, minerals, animals, Indian tribes, etc., of the Southwest.

# Historical Introduction

In the chapters reprinted we have not hesitated to modernize the typographical details whenever, in our editorial judgment, such modification seemed called for. The scholar, therefore, into whose hands this volume may chance to come, will understand that it does not assume to be a *verbatim et literatim* reproduction of the original edition of the *Commerce of the Prairies*. The general reader, on the other hand, may rest assured that he has before him a faithful reproduction of the original, saving certain details of typography and, more rarely, of othography, which have been modernized to the end of producing a somewhat greater degree of readability than a verbatim reproduction of the original edition would afford.

M. M. QUAIFE.

# COMMERCE OF THE PRAIRIES:

OR THE

## Journal of a Santa Fé Trader,

DURING

EIGHT EXPEDITIONS ACROSS

## THE GREAT WESTERN PRAIRIES,

AND

A RESIDENCE OF NEARLY NINE YEARS

IN

## NORTHERN MEXICO.

### Illustrated with Maps and Engravings.

## BY JOSIAH GREGG.

IN TWO VOLUMES.

### VOL. I.

*1844*

## NEW YORK:

HENRY G. LANGLEY, 8 ASTOR HOUSE.

M DCCC XLIV.

# Preface to the Original Edition

IN adding another to the list of works which have already been published, appearing to bear more or less directly upon the subject matter of these volumes, I am aware that my labors make their appeal to the public under serious disadvantages. Topics which have occupied the pens of Irving and Murray and Hoffman, and more recently of Kendall,[1] the

[1] The works here referred to by Gregg were all of comparatively recent publication and well known to the reading public. Washington Irving's *Tour on the Prairies* was first published at Philadelphia in 1835. It has been reprinted with valuable annotation for use in the schools of Oklahoma as recently as 1926. Sir Charles Augustus Murray, a grandson of Lord Dunmore, the last colonial governor of Virginia, was master of the household of the Queen of England. In the years 1834–36 he traveled extensively over the United States, and his observations were embodied in a valuable two-volume work entitled *Travels in the United States*, which appeared at London in 1839. Charles Fenno Hoffman of New York City in 1833–34 made a tour into the West as far as Prairie du Chien and St. Louis and published his charming narrative, *A Winter in the West*, at New York and London in 1835. A few years later he issued another volume, *Wild Scenes in Forest and Prairie;* this, however, was a mere editorial compilation, and not a narrative of personal travel. George W. Kendall, a noted journalist of New Orleans, joined the Texan

graphic historiographer of the *Texan Santa Fé Expedition*, may fairly be supposed to have been so entirely exhausted that the entrance of a new writer in the lists, whose name is wholly unknown to the republic of letters and whose pretensions are so humble as mine, may be looked upon as an act of literary hardihood for which there was neither occasion nor excuse. In view of this foregone conclusion, I trust I may be pardoned for prefacing my literary offering with a few words in its justification—which will afford me an occasion to explain the circumstances that first led to my acquaintance with life upon the prairies and in northern Mexico.

For some months preceding the year 1831 my health had been gradually declining under a complication of chronic diseases which defied every plan of treatment that the sagacity and science of my medical friends could devise. This morbid condition of my system, which originated in the familiar miseries of dyspepsia and its kindred infirmities, had finally reduced me to such a state that for nearly a twelve-month I was not only disqualified for any systematic industry but so debilitated as rarely to be able to extend my walks beyond the narrow precincts of my chamber. In this hopeless condition, my physicians advised me to take a trip

Santa Fé Expedition in 1841 and after his return from a lengthy captivity in Mexico published at New York in 1844 his *Narrative of the Texan Santa Fé Expedition*.

across the prairies, and in the change of air and habits which such an adventure would involve to seek that health which their science had failed to bestow. I accepted their suggestion, and without hesitation proceeded at once to make the necessary preparations for joining one of the spring caravans which were annually starting from the United States for Santa Fé.

The effects of this journey were in the first place to reëstablish my health, and, in the second, to beget a passion for prairie life which I never expect to survive. At the conclusion of the season which followed my first trip I became interested as a proprietor in the Santa Fé trade, and continued to be so, to a greater or less extent, for the eight succeeding years. During the whole of the above periods I crossed the prairies eight different times; and with the exception of the time thus spent in traveling to and fro, the greater part of the nine years of which I speak were passed in northern Mexico.

Having been actively engaged and largely interested in the commerce of that country and across the prairies for so long a period, I feel that I have at least had opportunities for observation upon the subjects of which I have ventured to treat superior to those enjoyed by any writers who have preceded me. But not even an attempt has before been made to present any full account of the origin of the Santa Fé trade and modes of conducting it; nor of the early history and present condition of the people of New Mexico; nor of the Indian tribes by which the wild and unreclaimed regions of that department are inhabited. I think I may also assure my readers that most of the facts presented in my sketch of the natural history of the prairies, and of the Indian tribes who inhabit them, are now published for the first time. As I have not sought to make a treatise upon these subjects, I have not felt compelled, for the purpose of giving my papers symmetry and completeness, to enter to any extent upon grounds which have already been occupied by other travelers; but have contented myself with presenting such matters and observations as I thought least likely to have come before under the notice of my readers.

I am perfectly sensible, however, that in the selection of matter and in the execution of my work it is very far from being what it should be, and what in more capable hands it might have been. I only trust that with all its imperfections it may be found to contain some new and not unimportant facts, which may be thought in some measure to justify my appearance for once in the capacity of a book-maker; for which vocation, in all other respects, I am free to confess myself very poorly qualified.

This work has been prepared chiefly from a journal which I have been in the habit of keeping from my youth upward, and in which I was careful to preserve memoranda of my observations while engaged in the Santa Fé trade, though without the remotest intention of ever appropriating them to the present purpose. In addition, however, I have embraced every opportunity of procuring authentic information through others upon such matters as were beyond my own sphere of observation. From materials thus collected I have received much assistance in the preparation of the chapters from the sixth to the fifteenth inclusive of the first volume, which are chiefly devoted to the early history of New Mexico and the manners, customs, and institutions of its people. For favors thus conferred, I beg in particular to make my acknowledgments to Elisha Stanley, Esq., and Doctors Samuel B. Hobbs and David Waldo, whose names have been long and favorably associated with the Santa Fé trade.

Though myself cradled and educated upon the Indian border and familiar with the Indian character from my infancy, I am yet greatly indebted for information upon that subject to many intelligent Indian traders, and others resident upon our border, with whose ample experience I have been frequently favored.

Yet, while I recognize my indebtedness to others, I feel bound in self-defense to reclaim in a single case, at least, the waifs of my own pen, which have been dignified with a place in the pages of a contemporary writer. During the years 1841 and 1842 I contributed a number of letters upon the history and condition of the Santa Fé trade, etc., to the Galveston

# Original Preface

*Daily Advertiser* and the *Arkansas Intelligencer*, under the signatures of "J. G." and "G.," portions of which I have had occasion to insert in the present volumes. In Captain Marryat's recent work, entitled *Monsieur Violet*, I was not a little annoyed (when I presume I ought to have been flattered) to find large portions of this correspondence copied, much of it *verbatim*, without the slightest intimation or acknowledgment whatever of the source from whence they were procured. The public are already so familiar with the long series of literary larcenies of which that famous work was the product, that I should not have presumed to emphasize my own grievance at all here, but that the appearance of the same material, frequently in the same words, in these volumes, might, unless accompanied by some explanation, expose me to a charge of plagiarism among those who may never have seen my original letters, or who are not yet aware that *Monsieur Violet* was an offering which had evidently been intended for the altar of Mercury rather than of Minerva.[2]

---

[2] Captain Frederick Marryat was a well-known English writer who traveled widely in America in the years 1837–38, and produced thereafter his *Diary in America*, a work which still enjoys well-deserved repute. In 1843 his *Travels and Adventures of Monsieur Violet among the Snake Indians and Wild Tribes of the Great Western Prairies* was published in London in three volumes. What motive induced Marryat to produce this work is not easy to understand. Along with whole-

# Original Preface

In my historical sketches of New Mexico it might have been naturally expected that some notice would be taken of the Texan Santa Fé Expedition of 1841, the events of which are so closely connected with the history of that country. I declined, however, to enter upon the topic; for I considered that none who had seen Mr. Kendall's account of that ill-fated enterprise would have any inducement to consult these pages upon the subject; and for those who had not, I felt sure the best thing I could do was to direct their attention at once to its attractive pages.

The maps which accompany the present work will be found, I believe, substantially correct; or more so, at least, than any others of those regions which have been published.[3] They have been prepared for the most part from personal observations. Those portions of the country which I have not been able to observe myself have chiefly been laid down from manuscript maps kindly furnished me by

sale plagiarizing (such as Gregg here complains of) it combines wholesale fictionizing. Captain Marryat was a naval officer of undoubted bravery, and once fought a duel with Nathaniel P. Willis over a trivial literary matter. Yet although his plagiarisms in his *Monsieur Violet* were promptly exposed and denounced, his biographer makes no mention of his ever having resented or refuted the charges upon his honor.

[3] The correctness of this claim is attested by such recent authorities on the geography and exploration of the Southwest as Dr. Elliott Coues and William E. Connelley, Secretary of the Kansas Historical Society.

experienced and reliable traders and trappers, and also from the maps prepared under the supervision of United States surveyors.

The arrangement I have adopted seems to require a word of explanation. That the reader may the better understand the frequent notices, in the course of my personal narrative, of the Santa Fé trade, the first chapter has been devoted to the development of its early history. And though the results of my observations in northern Mexico and upon the prairies as well as on the border are sometimes interspersed through the narrative, I have to a great degree digested and arranged them into distinct chapters, occupying from the sixth to the fifteenth inclusive of the first volume, and the seven last chapters of the second.[4] This plan was resorted to with a view of giving greater compactness to the work and relieving the journal, as far as possible, from cumbrous details and needless repetitions.

J. G.

New York, June 12, 1844.

[4] Of these several chapters only the first two (Chapters 6 and 7 of Volume I) are included in the present reprint.

The Commerce of
the Prairies

# Chapter 1

## THE ORIGIN OF THE SANTA FÉ TRADE

THE overland trade between the United States and the northern provinces of Mexico seems to have had no very definite origin; having been rather the result of accident than of any organized plan of commercial establishment. For a number of years its importance attracted no attention whatever. From Captain Pike's narrative we learn that one James Pursley, after much wandering over the wild and then unexplored regions west of the Mississippi, finally fell in with some Indians on the Platte River, near its source in the Rocky Mountains; and obtaining information from them respecting the settlements of New Mexico, he set out in company with a party of these savages and descended in 1805 to Santa Fé, where he remained for several years—perhaps till his death. It does not appear, however, that he took with him any considerable amount of merchandise.[5]

[5] The narrative journal of *The Southwestern Expedition of Zebulon M. Pike* was reprinted as the annual *Lakeside Classics* offering for 1925. Pike's account of James Pursley, however (which contains practically all that is known concerning him), is found in the author's historical and statistical treatise on *New Spain,*

3

Although Captain Pike speaks of Pursley as the first American that ever crossed the desert plains into the Spanish provinces, it is nevertheless related by the same writer that, in consequence of information obtained by the trappers through the Indians relative to this isolated province, a merchant of Kaskaskia named Morrison had already dispatched, as early as 1804, a French Creole, by the name of Lalande, up Platte River, with directions to push his way into Santa Fé if the passage was at all practicable.[6] The ingenious emissary was perfectly successful in his enterprise; but the kind and generous treatment of the natives overcame at once his patriotism and his probity. He neither returned to his employer nor accounted for the proceeds of his adventure. His expansive intellect readily conceived the advantages of setting up in business for himself upon this borrowed capital; which he accordingly did, and remained there not only unmolested but honored and esteemed till his death, which occurred some fifteen or twenty years afterward—leaving a large family, and sufficient property to entitle him to the fame of *rico* among his neighbors.

which was not included in the volume as reprinted. For it the reader is referred to Elliott Coues (ed.), *The Expeditions of Zebulon Montgomery Pike* (New York, 1895), II, 756–58.

[6] For Pike's story of Baptiste Lalande see our *Southwestern Expedition of Zebulon M. Pike*, 131–33 and 156. For William Morrison see *ibid.*, 133.

The Santa Fé trade attracted very little notice, however, until the return of Captain Pike,[7] whose exciting descriptions of the new El Dorado spread like wildfire throughout the western country. In 1812 an expedition was fitted out under the auspices of Messrs. McKnight, Beard, Chambers, and several others (in all about a dozen) who, following the directions of Captain Pike across the dreary western wilds, finally succeeded in reaching Santa Fé in safety. But these new adventurers were destined to experience trials and disappointments of which they had formed no conception. Believing that the declaration of independence by Hidalgo in 1810 had completely removed those injurious restrictions which had hitherto rendered all foreign intercourse, except by special permission from the Spanish government, illegal, they were wholly unprepared to encounter the embarrassments with which despotism and tyranny invariably obstruct the path of the stranger. They doubtless were ignorant that the patriotic chief, Hidalgo, had already been arrested and executed, that the royalists had once more regained the ascendency, and that all foreigners, but particularly Americans, were now viewed with unusual suspicion. The result was that the luckless traders, immediately upon their

[7] At this point Gregg appends a long footnote sketch of Pike's southwestern expedition, which we omit to print.

arrival, were seized as spies, their goods and chattels confiscated, and themselves thrown into the *calabozos* of Chihuahua, where most of them were kept in rigorous confinement for the space of nine years; when the republican forces under Iturbide getting again in the ascendent, McKnight and his comrades were finally set at liberty. It is said that two of the party contrived early in 1821 to return to the United States in a canoe, which they succeeded in forcing down the Canadian fork of the Arkansas. The stories promulgated by these men soon induced others to launch into the same field of enterprise, among whom was a merchant of Ohio named Glenn, who at the time had an Indian trading-house near the mouth of the Verdigris River. Having taken the circuitous route up the Arkansas towards the mountains, this pioneer trader encountered a great deal of trouble and privation, but eventually reached Santa Fé with his little caravan before the close of 1821 in perfect safety.

During the same year, Captain Becknell of Missouri with four trusty companions went out to Santa Fé by the far western prairie route. This intrepid little band started from the vicinity of Franklin with the original purpose of trading with the Iatan or Comanche Indians; but having fallen in accidentally with a party of Mexican rangers when near the mountains, they were easily prevailed upon to accompany them to the new emporium, where notwithstanding the trifling amount of merchandise they were possessed of they realized a very handsome profit. The fact is, that up to this date New Mexico had derived all her supplies from the internal provinces by the way of Vera Cruz; but at such exorbitant prices that common calicoes and even bleached and brown domestic goods sold as high as two and three dollars per *vara* (or Spanish yard of thirty-three inches). Becknell returned to the United States alone the succeeding winter, leaving the rest of his company at Santa Fé.

The favorable reports brought by the enterprising Captain stimulated others to embark in the trade; and early in the following May Colonel Cooper and sons from the same neighborhood, accompanied by several others (their whole number about fifteen), set out with four or five thousand dollars' worth of goods, which they transported upon pack horses. They steered directly for Taos, where they arrived without any remarkable occurrence.

The next effort of Captain Becknell was attended with very different success. With a company amounting to near thirty men and perhaps five thousand dollars' worth of goods of various descriptions he started from Missouri about a month after Colonel Cooper. Being an excellent woodsman and anxious to avoid the circuitous route of the upper Arkansas country, he resolved this time, after having reached that point on the Arkansas

River since known as the Caches,[8] to steer more directly for Santa Fé, entertaining little or no suspicion of the terrible trials which awaited him across the pathless desert. With no other guide but the starry heavens and, it may be, a pocket-compass, the party embarked upon the arid plains which extended far and wide before them to the Cimarron River.

The adventurous band pursued their forward course without being able to procure any water, except from the scanty supply they carried in their canteens. As this source of relief was completely exhausted after two days' march, the sufferings of both men and beasts had driven them almost to distraction. The forlorn band were at last reduced to the cruel necessity of killing their dogs and cutting off the ears of their mules in the vain hope of assuaging their burning thirst with the hot blood. This only served to irritate the parched palates and madden the senses of the sufferers. Frantic with despair, in prospect of the horrible death which now stared them in the face, they scattered in every direction in search of that element which they had left behind them in such abundance, but without success.

Frequently led astray by the deceptive glimmer of the mirage, or false ponds, as those treacherous oases of the desert are called, and

[8] About five miles west of Dodge City, Kansas. In Chap. 3, *post*, Gregg gives an account of the origin of this term.

not suspecting (as was really the case) that they had already arrived near the banks of the Cimarron, they resolved to retrace their steps to the Arkansas. But they now were no longer equal to the task and would undoubtedly have perished in those arid regions had not a buffalo fresh from the river's side and with a stomach distended with water been discovered by some of the party just as the last rays of hope were receding from their vision. The hapless intruder was immediately dispatched and an invigorating draught procured from its stomach. I have since heard one of the parties to that expedition declare that nothing ever passed his lips which gave him such exquisite delight as his first draught of that filthy beverage.

This providential relief enabled some of the strongest men of the party to reach the river, where they filled their canteens and then hurried back to the assistance of their comrades, many of whom they found prostrate on the ground and incapable of further exertion. By degrees, following the course of the Arkansas for several days, thereby avoiding the arid regions which had occasioned them so much suffering, they succeeded in reaching Taos (sixty or seventy miles north of Santa Fé) without further difficulty. Although travelers have since suffered excessively with thirst upon the same desert, yet, having become better acquainted with the country, no other equally thrilling incidents have subsequently transpired.

It is from this period—the year 1822—that the virtual commencement of the Santa Fé Trade may be dated. The next remarkable era in its history is the first attempt to introduce wagons in these expeditions.[9] This was made in 1824 by a company of traders about eighty in number, among whom were several gentlemen of intelligence from Missouri, who contributed, by their superior skill and undaunted energy, to render the enterprise completely successful. A portion of this company employed pack-mules; among the rest were owned twenty-five wheeled vehicles, of which one or two were stout road-wagons, two were carts, and the rest dearborn carriages—the whole conveying some $25,000 or $30,000 worth of merchandise. Colonel Marmaduke, the present lieutenant governor of Missouri, having formed one of the party, has been pleased to place his diary at my disposal; but want of space necessarily compels me to pass over the many interesting and exciting incidents which it contains. Suffice it to say that the caravan reached Santa Fé with much less difficulty than must have been anticipated from a first experiment with wheeled vehicles. The route, indeed, appears to have presented fewer obstacles than any ordinary road of equal length in the United States.

[9] Two corrections may be noted in the author's narrative at this point. The terminus of Becknell's party was San Miguel instead of Taos; and it was equipped with wagons.

It was not until several years after this experiment, however, that adventurers with large capital began seriously to embark in the Santa Fé trade. The early traders, having but seldom experienced any molestations from the Indians, generally crossed the plains in detached bands, each individual rarely carrying more than two or three hundred dollars' worth of stock. This peaceful season, however, did not last very long; and it is greatly to be feared that the traders were not always innocent of having instigated the savage hostilities that ensued in after years. Many seemed to forget the wholesome precept that they should not be savages themselves because they dealt with savages. Instead of cultivating friendly feelings with those few who remained peaceful and honest, there was an occasional one always disposed to kill, even in cold blood, every Indian that fell into their power, merely because some of the tribe had committed some outrage either against themselves or their friends.

Since the commencement of this trade returning parties have performed the homeward journey across the plains with the proceeds of their enterprise, partly in specie and partly in furs, buffalo rugs, and animals. Occasionally these straggling bands would be set upon by marauding Indians, but if well armed and of resolute spirit they found very little difficulty in persuading the savages to let them pass unmolested; for, as Mr. Storrs very justly remarks in his representation presented by Colonel Benton in 1825 to the United States Senate,[10] the Indians are always willing to compromise when they find that they cannot rob "without losing the lives of their warriors, which they hardly ever risk, unless for revenge or in open warfare."

The case was very different with those who through carelessness or recklessness ventured upon the wild prairies without a sufficient supply of arms. A story is told of a small band of twelve men, who, while encamped on the Cimarron River in 1826 with but four serviceable guns between them, were visited by a party of Indians (believed to be Arapahoes), who made at first strong demonstrations of friendship and good will. Observing the defenseless condition of the traders they went away, but soon returned about thirty strong, each provided with a *lazo* and all on foot. The chief then began by informing the Americans that his men were tired of walking and must have horses. Thinking it folly to offer any resistance, the terrified traders told them if one animal apiece would satisfy them to go and catch them. This they soon did; but finding their requests so easily complied with, the Indians

[10] Senator Thomas H. Benton in 1825 introduced a bill in Congress to authorize the building of a road from Missouri through the Indian country to the confines of New Mexico. It became a law, being one of the last acts signed by President Monroe.

held a little parley together, which resulted in a new demand for more—they must now have two apiece. "Well, catch them!" was the acquiescent reply of the unfortunate band—upon which the savages mounted those they had already secured and swinging their *lazos* over their heads plunged among the stock with a furious yell and drove off the entire *caballada* of near five hundred head of horses, mules, and asses.

The fall of 1828 proved still more fatal to the traders on their homeward trip; for by this time the Indians had learned to form a correct estimate of the stock with which the return companies were generally provided. Two young men named McNees and Monroe, having carelessly lain down to sleep on the banks of a stream since known as McNee's Creek, were barbarously shot with their own guns, as it was supposed, in very sight of the caravan. When their comrades came up they found McNees lifeless and the other almost expiring. In this state the latter was carried nearly forty miles to the Cimarron River, where he died and was buried according to the custom of the prairies.[11]

[11] These funerals are usually performed in a very summary manner. A grave is dug in a convenient spot and the corpse, with no other shroud than its own clothes, and only a blanket for a coffin, is consigned to the earth. The grave is then usually filled up with stones or poles, as a safeguard against the voracious wolves of the prairies. Gregg.

Just as the funeral ceremonies were about to be concluded six or seven Indians appeared on the opposite side of the Cimarron. Some of the party proposed inviting them to a parley, while the rest, burning for revenge, evinced a desire to fire upon them at once. It is more than probable, however, that the Indians were not only innocent but ignorant of the outrage that had been committed, or they would hardly have ventured to approach the caravan. Being quick of perception, they very soon saw the belligerent attitude assumed by some of the company and therefore wheeled round and attempted to escape. One shot was fired, which wounded a horse and brought the Indian to the ground, when he was instantly riddled with balls! Almost simultaneously another discharge of several guns followed by which all the rest were either killed or mortally wounded except one, who escaped to bear to his tribe the news of their dreadful catastrophe!

These wanton cruelties had a most disastrous effect upon the prospects of the trade; for the exasperated children of the desert became more and more hostile to the pale faces, against whom they continued to wage a cruel war for many successive years. In fact, this same party suffered very severely a few days afterwards. They were pursued by the enraged comrades of the slain savages to the Arkansas River, where they were robbed of nearly a thousand

head of mules and horses. But the Indians
were not yet satisfied. Having beset a company of about twenty men who followed shortly
after, they killed one of their number and
subsequently took from them all the animals
they had in their possession. The unfortunate band were now not only compelled to
advance on foot, but were even constrained
to carry nearly a thousand dollars each upon
their backs to the Arkansas River, where it
was *cached* (concealed in the ground) till a
conveyance was procured to transfer it to the
United States.

Such repeated and daring outrages induced
the traders to petition the federal government
for an escort of United States troops. The request having been granted Major Riley,[12] with
three companies of infantry and one of rifle-
men, was ordered to accompany the caravan
which left in the spring of 1829. The escort
stopped at Chouteau's Island[13] on the Arkansas

[12] Bennett Riley was born in Virginia in 1787. He became an engineer in the army in 1813, captain in 1818,
and was breveted major in 1828. He served with distinction in the Mexican War and was made brigadier
general in 1847. In 1848 he was sent to California,
where he acted as last territorial governor. He died in
Buffalo in 1853.

[13] Chouteau's Island was at the upper crossing of the
Arkansas River, immediately above the present town of
Hartland, Kearny County, Kansas. Chouteau, a well-
known trader of St. Louis, was attacked near here
by Indians on one of his expeditions to the Rocky
Mountains about the year 1816. He took refuge on the

River, and the traders thence pursued their journey through the sand-hills beyond. They had hardly advanced six or seven miles when a startling incident occurred which made them wish once more for the company of the gallant Major and his well-disciplined troops. A vanguard of three men riding a few hundred yards ahead had just dismounted for the purpose of satisfying their thirst when a band of Kiowas,[14] one of the most savage tribes that infest the western prairies, rushed upon them from the immense hillocks of sand which lay scattered in all directions. The three men sprang upon their animals, but two only who had horses were enabled to make their escape to the wagons; the third, a Mr. Lamme, who was unfortunately mounted upon a mule, was overtaken, slain, and scalped before any one could come to his assistance. Somewhat alarmed at the boldness of the Indians, the traders dispatched an express to Major Riley, who immediately ordered

island, which was covered with a thick grove of cottonwood trees, and succeeded in beating off his assailants. This affair resulted in attaching his name to the island.

[14] The Kiowas enjoy the distinction of constituting alone a linguistic family of North American Indians. Their ancient habitat was the region of the Yellowstone and upper Missouri rivers, from which they were driven southward by rival tribes. Within the historic period they lived on the upper Arkansas and upper Canadian, ranging to the headwaters of Red River. They were confederates of the Comanches and enjoyed in the eyes of frontiersmen an evil repute for ferocity and cruelty.

his tents to be struck; and such was the rapidity of his movements that when he appeared before the anxious caravan every one was lost in astonishment. The reinforcement having arrived in the night, the enemy could have obtained no knowledge of the fact and would no doubt have renewed the attack in the morning, when they would have received a wholesome lesson from the troops, had not the reveille been sounded through mistake, at which they precipitately retreated. The escort now continued with the company as far as Sand Creek, when, perceiving no further signs of danger, they returned to the Arkansas to await the return of the caravan in the ensuing fall.

The position of Major Riley on the Arkansas was one of serious and continual danger. Scarce a day passed without his being subjected to some new annoyance from predatory Indians. The latter appeared, indeed, resolved to check all further concourse of the whites upon the prairies; and fearful of the terrible extremes to which their excesses might be carried, the traders continued to unite in single caravans during many years afterward, for the sake of mutual protection. This escort under Major Riley and one composed of about sixty dragoons commanded by Captain Wharton in 1834 constituted the only government protection ever afforded to the Santa Fé trade until 1843, when large escorts under Captain Cooke accompanied two different caravans as far as the Arkansas River.[15]

Of the composition and organization of these trading caravans I shall take occasion to speak from my own experience, in the following chapters.

[15] Philip St. George Cooke was a native of Virginia who graduated from West Point in 1827. During the ensuing decades he gained an extensive experience as an Indian fighter. He adhered to the Union in the Civil War and rose to the rank of brigadier general. On October 29, 1873, he was retired, after almost half a century of active service. He died at Detroit, March 20, 1895. He is the author of three volumes of history and adventure. An account of a later Santa Fé Trail expedition, undertaken by Cooke in 1843, was published for the first time in the June and September, 1925, issues of the *Mississippi Valley Historical Review*.

# Chapter 2

## ORGANIZING THE EXPEDITION

PEOPLE who reside at a distance, and especially at the North, have generally considered St. Louis as the emporium of the Santa Fé trade; but that city, in truth, has never been a place of rendezvous, nor even of outfit, except for a small portion of the traders who have started from its immediate vicinity. The town of Franklin [16] on the Missouri River, about a hundred and fifty miles farther to the westward, seems truly to have been the cradle of our trade; and, in conjunction with several neighboring towns, continued for many years to furnish the greater number of these adventurous traders. Even subsequently to 1831 many wagons have been fitted out and started from this interior section. But as the navigation of the Missouri River had considerably advanced towards the year 1831, and the advantages of some point of debarkation nearer

*150 mi. west of St. Louis*

[16] Franklin was founded in 1816, on the north bank of the Missouri River, opposite the modern town of Boonville. About ten years later the town was abandoned and soon thereafter its site was swept away by the hungry river. A charming historical sketch of the town by Jonas Viles, entitled "Old Franklin: a Frontier Town of the Twenties," is in the *Mississippi Valley Historical Review*, IX, 269-82.

the western frontier were very evident, whereby upwards of a hundred miles of troublesome
land-carriage over unimproved and often miry
roads might be avoided, the new town of Independence,[17] but twelve miles from the Indian
border and two or three south of the Missouri
River, being the most eligible point, soon began to take the lead as a place of debarkation,
outfit, and departure, which in spite of all
opposition it has ever since maintained. It is
to this beautiful spot, already grown up to be
a thriving town, that the prairie adventurer,
whether in search of wealth, health, or amusement, is latterly in the habit of repairing about
the first of May, as the caravans usually set
out some time during that month. Here they
purchase their provisions for the road, and
many of their mules, oxen, and even some of
their wagons—in short, load all their vehicles
and make their final preparations for a long
journey across the prairie wilderness.

As Independence is a point of convenient
access (the Missouri River being navigable at

[17] Independence, now a residential suburb of Kansas
City, was originally laid out in 1827 five miles east of
that place. Its importance as the starting point of the
trading caravans for Santa Fé is well stated by Gregg.
A few years subsequently it became an important center
of Mormon activities and until a few years since devout
Mormons fondly anticipated the fulfillment of one of
Joseph Smith's prophecies which indicated that here
would be the center of authority of the all-conquering
Church of Latter Day Saints.

all times from March till November), it has
become the general port of embarkation for
every part of the great western and northern
"prairie ocean." Besides the Santa Fé caravans, most of the Rocky Mountain traders and
trappers, as well as emigrants to Oregon, take
this town in their route. During the season
of departure, therefore, it is a place of much
bustle and active business.

Among the concourse of travelers at this
starting point, besides traders and tourists a
number of pale-faced invalids are generally to
be met with. The prairies have, in fact, become
very celebrated for their sanative effects—
more justly so, no doubt, than the more fashionable watering-places of the North. Most
chronic diseases, particularly liver complaints,
dyspepsias, and similar affections, are often
radically cured; owing, no doubt, to the
peculiarities of diet and the regular exercise
incident to prairie life, as well as to the purity
of the atmosphere of those elevated unembarrassed regions. An invalid myself, I can answer
for the efficacy of the remedy, at least in my
own case. Though, like other valetudinarians,
I was disposed to provide an ample supply
of such commodities as I deemed necessary for
my comfort and health, I was not long upon
the prairies before I discovered that most of
such extra preparations were unnecessary, or
at least quite dispensable. A few knick-knacks,
as a little tea, rice, fruits, crackers, etc., suffice

very well for the first fortnight, after which the invalid is generally able to take the fare of the hunter and teamster. Though I set out myself in a carriage, before the close of the first week I saddled my pony; and when we reached the buffalo range I was not only as eager for the chase as the sturdiest of my companions, but I enjoyed far more exquisitely my share of the buffalo than all the delicacies which were ever devised to provoke the most fastidious appetite.

The ordinary supplies for each man's consumption during the journey are about fifty pounds of flour, as many more of bacon, ten of coffee and twenty of sugar, and a little salt. Beans, crackers, and trifles of that description are comfortable appendages, but being looked upon as dispensable luxuries, are seldom to be found in any of the stores on the road. The buffalo is chiefly depended upon for fresh meat, and great is the joy of the traveler when that noble animal first appears in sight.

The wagons now most in use upon the prairies are manufactured in Pittsburg;[18] and are usually drawn by eight mules or the same number of oxen. Of late years, however, I have seen much larger vehicles employed, with ten

[18] These were the lineal successors of the famous Conestoga wagons of a slightly earlier period, about whose history a volume might well be written. For a brief sketch of the subject see M. M. Quaife, *Chicago's Highways Old and New* (Chicago, 1923), 142–43.

or twelve mules harnessed to each and a cargo of goods of about five thousand pounds in weight. At an early period the horse was more frequently in use, as mules were not found in great abundance; but as soon as the means for procuring these animals increased, the horse was gradually and finally discarded, except occasionally for riding and the chase.

Oxen having been employed by Major Riley for the baggage wagons of the escort which was furnished the caravan of 1829, they were found, to the surprise of the traders, to perform almost equal to mules. Since that time, upon an average about half the wagons in these expeditions have been drawn by oxen. They possess many advantages, such as pulling heavier loads than the same number of mules, particularly through muddy or sandy places; but they generally fall off in strength as the prairie grass becomes drier and shorter, and often arrive at their destination in a most shocking plight. In this condition I have seen them sacrificed at Santa Fé for ten dollars the pair; though in more favorable seasons they sometimes remain strong enough to be driven back to the United States the same fall. Therefore, although the original cost of a team of mules is much greater, the loss ultimately sustained by them is usually less, to say nothing of the comfort of being able to travel faster and more at ease. The inferiority of oxen as regards endurance is partially owing to the tenderness of their feet; for there are very few among the thousands who have traveled on the prairies that ever knew how to shoe them properly. Many have resorted to the curious expedient of shoeing their animals with moccasins made of raw buffalo-skin, which does remarkably well as long as the weather remains dry; but when wet, they are soon worn through. Even mules, for the most part, perform the entire trip without being shod at all; though the hoofs often become very smooth, which frequently renders all their movements on the dry grassy surface nearly as laborious as if they were treading on ice.

The supplies being at length procured and all necessary preliminaries systematically gone through, the trader begins the difficult task of loading his wagons. Those who understand their business take every precaution so to stow away their packages that no jolting on the road can afterwards disturb the order in which they had been disposed. The ingenuity displayed on these occasions has frequently been such that after a tedious journey of eight hundred miles the goods have been found to have sustained much less injury than they would have experienced on a turnpike road, or from the ordinary handling of property upon our western steamboats.

The next great difficulty the traders have to encounter is in training those animals that have never before been worked, which is frequently

attended by an immensity of trouble. There
is nothing, however, in the mode of harnessing
and conducting teams in prairie traveling
which differs materially from that practiced
on the public highways throughout the states,
the representations of certain travelers to the
contrary notwithstanding. From the amusing
descriptions which are sometimes given by this
class of writers one would be apt to suppose
that they had never seen a wagon or a team of
mules before, or that they had just emerged for
the first time from the purlieus of a large city.
The propensity evinced by these writers for
giving an air of romance to everything they
have either seen or heard would seem to imply
a conviction on their part that no statement of
unvarnished facts can ever be stamped with
the seal of the world's approbation—that a
work in order to prove permanently attractive
should teem with absurdities and abound in
exaggerated details. How far such an assump-
tion would be correct I shall not pause to
inquire.

At last all are fairly launched upon the broad
prairie—the miseries of preparation are over—
the thousand anxieties occasioned by weari-
some consultations and delays are felt no more.
The charioteer as he smacks his whip feels a
bounding elasticity of soul within him, which
he finds it impossible to restrain; even the
mules prick up their ears with a peculiarly
conceited air, as if in anticipation of that change

of scene which will presently follow. Harmony
and good feeling prevail everywhere. The hila-
rious song, the *bon mot*, and the witty repar-
tee go round in quick succession; and before
people have had leisure to take cognizance of
the fact, the lovely village of Independence
with its multitude of associations is already
lost to the eye.

It was on the 15th of May, 1831, and one of
the brightest and most lovely of all the days
in the calendar, that our little party set out
from Independence. The general rendezvous
at Council Grove was our immediate destination. It is usual for the traders to travel thus
far in detached parties, and to assemble there
for mutual security and defense during the
remainder of the journey. It was from thence
that the formation of the caravan was to be
dated and the chief interest of our journey
to commence: therefore, to this point we all
looked forward with great anxiety. The intermediate travel was marked by very few events
of any interest. As the wagons had gone before
us and we were riding in a light carriage we
were able to reach the Round Grove,[19] about
thirty-five miles distant, on the first day,
where we joined the rear division of the caravan, comprising about thirty wagons.

[19]Round Grove (called by Captain Cooke "Elm
Grove") was between Olathe and Gardner in Johnson
County, Kansas, in the high land at the head of Cedar
Creek.

On the following day we had a foretaste of those protracted, drizzling spells of rain, which at this season of the year so much infest the frontier prairies. It began sprinkling about dark and continued pouring without let or hindrance for forty-eight hours in succession; and as the rain was accompanied by a heavy north-wester and our camp was pitched in the open prairie without a stick of available timber within a mile of us, it must be allowed that the whole formed a prelude anything but flattering to valetudinarians. For my own part, finding the dearborn carriage in which I had a berth not exactly water-proof, I rolled myself in a blanket and lay snugly coiled upon a tier of boxes and bales, under cover of a wagon, and thus managed to escape a very severe drenching.

It may be proper to observe here for the benefit of future travelers that in order to make a secure shelter for the cargo against the inclemencies of the weather, there should be spread upon each wagon a pair of stout Osnaburg sheets, with one of sufficient width to reach the bottom of the body on each side, so as to protect the goods from driving rains. By omitting this important precaution many packages of merchandise have been seriously injured. Some preferred lining the exterior of the wagon-body by tacking a simple strip of sheeting all around it. On the outward trips especially a pair of Mackinaw blankets can be advantageously spread betwixt the two sheets, which effectually secures the roof against the worst of storms. This contrivance has also the merit of turning the blankets into a profitable item of trade by enabling the owners to evade the custom-house officers, who would otherwise seize them as contraband articles.

The mischief of the storm did not exhaust itself, however, upon our persons. The loose animals sought shelter in the groves at a considerable distance from the encampment, and the wagoners being loth to turn out in search of them during the rain, not a few, of course, when applied for were missing. This, however, is no uncommon occurrence. Travelers generally experience far more annoyance from the straying of cattle during the first hundred miles than at any time afterwards; because, apprehending no danger from the wild Indians (who rarely approach within two hundred miles of the border) they seldom keep any watch, although that is the very time when a cattle-guard is most needed. It is only after some weeks' travel that the animals begin to feel attached to the caravan, which they then consider about as much their home as the stock-yard of a dairy farm.

After leaving this spot the troubles and vicissitudes of our journey began in good earnest; for on reaching the narrow ridge which separates the Osage and Kansas waters (known as the Narrows), we encountered a region of very troublesome quagmires.[20]  On such occasions it is quite common for a wagon to sink to the hubs in mud while the surface of the soil all around would appear perfectly dry and smooth.  To extricate each other's wagons we had frequently to employ double and triple teams, with all hands to the wheels in addition —often led by the proprietors themselves up to the waist in mud and water.

Three or four days after this and while crossing the head branches of the Osage River we experienced a momentary alarm.  Conspicuously elevated upon a rod by the roadside we found a paper purporting to have been written by the Kansas agent, stating that a band of Pawnees were said to be lurking in the vicinity! The first excitement over, however, the majority of our party came to the conclusion that it was either a hoax of some of the company in advance or else a stratagem of the Kaws (or Kansas Indians), who, as well as the Osages, prowl about those prairies and steal from the caravans during the passage, when they entertain the slightest hope that their maraudings will be laid to others.  They seldom venture further, however, than to seize upon an occasional stray animal, which they frequently do with the view alone of obtaining a reward

[20] "The top of the ridge," says William E. Connelley, "was flat and the drainage poor.  The soil held water like a rubber blanket, and in wet weather the trail along the ridge was almost impassable."

from its owner for its return. As to the Pawnees, the most experienced traders were well aware that they had not been known to frequent those latitudes since the commencement of the Santa Fé trade. But what contributed as much as anything else to lull the fears of the timid was an accession to our forces of seventeen wagons which we overtook the same evening.

Early on the 26th of May we reached the long looked-for rendezvous of Council Grove, where we joined the main body of the caravan. Lest this imposing title suggest to the reader a snug and thriving village, it should be observed that on the day of our departure from Independence we passed the last human abode upon our route; therefore, from the borders of Missouri to those of New Mexico not even an Indian settlement greeted our eyes.

This point is nearly a hundred and fifty miles from Independence, and consists of a continuous strip of timber nearly half a mile in width, comprising the richest varieties of trees; such as oak, walnut, ash, elm, hickory, etc., and extending all along the valleys of a small stream known as Council Grove Creek, the principal branch of the Neosho River.[21] This

[21] Captain Cooke describes Council Grove as "a luxuriant, heavily timbered bottom of the Neosho or Grand River, containing about 160 acres. . . . It is a charming grove, where any grove would delight." *Miss. Valley Hist. Rev.*, IX, 78. At this site is today the town of Council Grove, the county seat of Morris County; it is about fifty miles southwest of Topeka.

stream is bordered by the most fertile bottoms and beautiful upland prairies, well adapted to cultivation: such, indeed, is the general character of the country from thence to Independence. All who have traversed these delightful regions look forward with anxiety to the day when the Indian title to the land shall be extinguished and flourishing white settlements dispel the gloom which at present prevails over this uninhabited region. Much of this prolific country now belongs to the Shawnees and other Indians of the border, though some portion of it has never been allotted to any tribe.

Frequent attempts have been made by travelers to invest the Council Grove with a romantic sort of interest, of which the following fabulous vagary, which I find in a letter that went the rounds of our journals, is an amusing sample: "Here the Pawnee, Arapaho, Comanche, Loup, and Eutaw Indians, all of whom were at war with each other, meet and smoke the pipe once a year." Now it is more than probable that not a soul of most of the tribes mentioned above ever saw the Council Grove. Whatever may be the interest attached to this place, however, on account of its historical or fanciful associations, one thing is very certain, that the novice, even here, is sure to imagine himself in the midst of lurking savages. These visionary fears are always a source of no little merriment to the veteran of the field, who does not hesitate to travel with a single wagon and a comrade or two, or even alone, from the Arkansas River to Independence.

The facts connected with the designation of this spot are simply these. Messrs. Reeves, Sibley, and Mathers, having been commissioned by the United States in the year 1825 to mark a road from the confines of Missouri to Santa Fé, met on this spot with some bands of Osages, with whom they concluded a treaty whereby the Indians agreed to allow all citizens of the United States and Mexico to pass unmolested, and even to lend their aid to those engaged in the Santa Fé trade; for which they were to receive a gratification of eight hundred dollars in merchandise. The commissioners on this occasion gave to the place the name of Council Grove.

But, although the route examined by the Commissioners named above was partially marked out as far as the Arkansas by raised mounds, it seems to have been of but little service to travelers, who continued to follow the trail previously made by the wagons, which is now the settled road to the region of the short buffalo grass.

The designation of Council Grove, after all, is perhaps the most appropriate that could be given to this place; for *we* there held a grand council, at which the respective claims of the different aspirants to office were considered, leaders selected, and a system of government agreed upon, as is the standing custom of these promiscuous caravans. One would have supposed that electioneering and party spirit would hardly have penetrated so far into the wilderness: but so it was. Even in our little community we had our office-seekers and their political adherents, as earnest and as devoted as any of the modern school of politicians in the midst of civilization. After a great deal of bickering and wordy warfare, however, all the candidates found it expedient to decline, and a gentleman by the name of Stanley, without seeking or even desiring the office, was unanimously proclaimed captain of the caravan. The powers of this officer were undefined by any constitutional provision, and consequently vague and uncertain: orders being only viewed as mere requests, they are often obeyed or neglected at the caprice of the subordinates. It is necessary to observe, however, that the captain is expected to direct the order of travel during the day and to designate the camping ground at night; with many other functions of a general character, in the exercise of which the company find it convenient to acquiesce. But the little attention that is paid to his commands in cases of emergency I will leave the reader to become acquainted with, as I did, by observing their manifestations during the progress of the expedition.

But after this comes the principal task of organizing. The proprietors are first notified by proclamation to furnish a list of their men and wagons. The latter are generally apportioned into four divisions, particularly when the company is large—and ours consisted of nearly a hundred wagons,[22] besides a dozen of dearborns and other small vehicles and two small cannons (a four and six pounder), each mounted upon a carriage. To each of these divisions a lieutenant was appointed, whose duty it was to inspect every ravine and creek on the route, select the best crossings, and superintend what is called in prairie parlance the "forming" of each encampment.

Upon the calling of the roll we were found to muster an efficient force of nearly two hundred men, without counting invalids or other disabled bodies, who, as a matter of course, are exempt from duty. There is nothing so much dreaded by inexperienced travelers as the ordeal of guard duty. But no matter what the condition or employment of the individual may be, no one has the smallest chance of evading the common law of the prairies. The amateur tourist and the listless loafer are precisely in the same wholesome predicament— they must all take their regular turn at the watch. There is usually a set of genteel idlers attached to every caravan, whose wits are forever at work in devising schemes for whiling

[22] About half of these wagons were drawn by ox-teams, the rest by mules. The capital in merchandise of the whole caravan was about $200,000. Gregg.

away their irksome hours at the expense of others. By embarking in these trips of pleasure they are enabled to live without expense; for the hospitable traders seldom refuse to accommodate even a loafing companion with a berth at their mess without charge. But then these lounging attachés are expected at least to do good service by way of guard duty. None are even permitted to furnish a substitute, as is frequently done in military expeditions, for he that would undertake to stand the tour of another besides his own would scarcely be watchful enough for the dangers of the prairies. Even the invalid must be able to produce unequivocal proofs of his inability, or it is a chance if the plea is admitted. For my own part, although I started on the sick list, and though the prairie sentinel must stand fast and brook the severest storm (for then it is that the strictest watch is necessary), I do not remember ever having missed my post but once during the whole journey.

The usual number of watches is eight, each standing a fourth of every alternate night. When the party is small the number is greatly reduced, while in the case of very small bands they are sometimes compelled for safety's sake to keep one watch on duty half the night. With large caravans the captain usually appoints eight sergeants of the guard, each of whom takes an equal portion of men under his command.

*[handwritten margin note: 2hrs of watch every other night.]*

The heterogeneous appearance of our company, consisting of men from every class and grade of society, with a little sprinkling of the softer sex, would have formed an excellent subject for an artist's pencil. It may appear, perhaps, a little extraordinary that females should have ventured across the prairies under such forlorn auspices. Those who accompanied us, however, were members of a Spanish family who had been banished in 1829 in pursuance of a decree of the Mexican congress and were now returning to their homes in consequence of a suspension of the decree. Other females, however, have crossed the prairies to Santa Fé at different times, among whom I have known two respectable French ladies, who now reside in Chihuahua.

The wild and motley aspect of the caravan can be but imperfectly conceived without an idea of the costumes of its various members. The most fashionable prairie dress is the fustian frock of the city-bred merchant furnished with a multitude of pockets capable of accommodating a variety of extra tackling. Then there is the backwoodsman with his linsey or leather hunting-shirt—the farmer with his blue jean coat—the wagoner with his flannel-sleeve vest—besides an assortment of other costumes which go to fill up the picture.

In the article of firearms there is also an equally interesting medley. The frontier hunter sticks to his rifle, as nothing could

36

induce him to carry what he terms in derision "the scatter-gun." The sportsman from the interior flourishes his double-barreled fowling-piece with equal confidence in its superiority. The latter is certainly the most convenient description of gun that can be carried on this journey; as a charge of buck-shot in night attacks (which are the most common) will of course be more likely to do execution than a single rifle-ball fired at random. The repeating arms have lately been brought into use upon the prairies and they are certainly very formidable weapons, particularly when used against an ignorant savage foe. A great many were furnished beside with a bountiful supply of pistols and knives of every description, so that the party made altogether a very brigand-like appearance.

During our delay at the Council Grove the laborers were employed in procuring timber for axle-trees and other wagon repairs, of which a supply is always laid in before leaving this region of substantial growths; for henceforward there is no wood on the route fit for these purposes; not even in the mountains of Santa Fé do we meet with any serviceable timber. The supply procured here is generally lashed under the wagons, in which way a log is not unfrequently carried to Santa Fé, and even sometimes back again.

# Chapter 3

OWING to the delays of organizing and other preparations, we did not leave the Council Grove camp till May 27th. Although the usual hour of starting with the prairie caravans is after an early breakfast, yet on this occasion we were hindered till in the afternoon. The familiar note of preparation, "Catch up! Catch up!" was now sounded from the captain's camp, and re-echoed from every division and scattered group along the valley. On such occasions a scene of confusion ensues which must be seen to be appreciated. The woods and dales resound with the gleeful yells of the light-hearted wagoners, who, weary of inaction and filled with joy at the prospect of getting under way, become clamorous in the extreme. Scarcely does the jockey on the race-course ply his whip more promptly at that magic word "Go" than do these emulous wagoners fly to harnessing their mules at the spirit-stirring sound of "Catch up." Each teamster vies with his fellows who shall be soonest ready; and it is a matter of boastful pride to be the first to cry out "All's set!"

The uproarious bustle which follows—the hallooing of those in pursuit of animals—the exclamation which the unruly brutes call forth from their wrathful drivers; together with the clatter of bells—the rattle of yokes and harness—the jingle of chains—all conspire to produce a clamorous confusion which would be altogether incomprehensible without the assistance of the eyes; while these alone would hardly suffice to unravel the labyrinthian maneuvers and hurly-burly of this precipitate breaking up. It is sometimes amusing to observe the athletic wagoner hurrying an animal to its post—to see him heave upon the halter of a stubborn mule, while the brute as obstinately sets back, determined not to move a peg till his own good pleasure thinks it proper to do so—his whole manner seeming to say, "Wait till your hurry's over!" I have more than once seen a driver hitch a harnessed animal to the halter and by that process haul his mulishness forward, while each of his four projected feet would leave a furrow behind; until at last the perplexed master would wrathfully exclaim, "A mule will be a mule any way you can fix it!"

"All's set!" is finally heard from some teamster—"All's set" is directly responded from every quarter. "Stretch out!" immediately vociferates the captain. Then the "Heps!" of drivers—the cracking of whips—the trampling of feet—the occasional creak of wheels—the rumbling of wagons—form a new scene of exquisite confusion, which I shall not attempt further to describe. "Fall in!" is heard from headquarters, and the wagons are forthwith strung out upon the long, inclined plain which stretches to the heights beyond Council Grove.

After fifteen miles' progress we arrived at the Diamond Spring [23] (a crystal fountain discharging itself into a small brook), to which in later years caravans have sometimes advanced before organizing. Near twenty-five miles beyond we crossed the Cottonwood Fork of the Neosho, a creek still smaller than that of Council Grove, and our camp was pitched immediately in its farther valley. [24]

When caravans are able to cross in the evening they seldom stop on the near side of a stream —first, because if it happens to rain during the night it may become flooded and cause both detention and trouble; again, though the stream be not impassable after rain, the banks become slippery and difficult to ascend. A third and still more important reason is that, even supposing the contingency of rain does not occur, teams will rarely pull as well in cold collars, as wagoners term it—that is, when fresh geared—as in the progress of a day's travel. When a heavy pull is just at hand in the morning wagoners sometimes resort to

[23] The Diamond Spring is about four miles north of the station of Diamond Springs on the Atchison, Topeka and Santa Fé Railroad. The spring still flows a bountiful supply of water.

[24] The camp was near the town of Durham, Marion County, Kansas.

the expedient of driving a circuit upon the prairie before venturing to take the bank.

We experienced a temporary alarm during the evening while we lay encamped at Cottonwood, which was rather more boisterous than serious in its consequences. The wagons had been "formed" across the neck of a bend in the creek, into which the cattle were turned, mostly in their yokes; for though when thoroughly trained teamsters usually unyoke their oxen every night, yet at first they often leave them coupled to save the trouble of reyoking them in their unruly state. A little after dark these animals started simultaneously with a thundering noise and rattle of the yokes towards the outlet protected by the wagons, but for which obstacle they might have escaped far into the prairie and have been irrecoverably lost, or at least have occasioned much trouble and delay to recover them. The cause of the fright was not discovered; but oxen are exceedingly whimsical creatures when surrounded by unfamiliar objects. One will sometimes take a fright at the jingle of his own yoke-irons, or the cough of his mate, and by a sudden flounce set the whole herd in a flurry. This was probably the case in the present instance; although some of our easily excited companions immediately surmised that the oxen had scented a lurking Pawnee.

Our route lay through uninterrupted prairie for about forty miles—in fact, I may say, for five hundred miles, excepting the very narrow fringes of timber along the borders of the streams. The antelope of the high prairies which we now occasionally saw is sometimes found as far east as Council Grove, and as a few old buffaloes have sometimes been met with about Cottonwood we now began to look out for this desirable game. Some scattering bulls are generally to be seen first, forming as it would appear the van or picket guards of the main droves with their cows and calves. The buffalo are usually found much farther east early in the spring than during the rest of the year on account of the long grass, which shoots up earlier in the season than the short pasturage of the plains.

Our hopes of game were destined soon to be realized; for early on the second day after leaving Cottonwood (a few miles beyond the principal Turkey Creek),[25] our eyes were greeted with the sight of a herd amounting to nearly a hundred head of buffalo quietly grazing in the distance before us. Half of our company had probably never seen a buffalo before (at least in its wild state); and the excitement that the first sight of these prairie beeves occasions among a party of novices beggars all description. Every horseman was off in a scamper; and some of the wagoners, leaving their teams

[25] Turkey Creek rises in McPherson County. The trail crossed three branches of this creek, a few miles south and east of the present town of McPherson.

to take care of themselves, seized their guns and joined the race afoot. Here went one with his rifle or yager—there another with his double-barreled shot-gun—a third with his holster pistols—a Mexican perhaps with his lance—another with his bow and arrows—and numbers joined without any arms whatever, merely for the pleasures of the chase—all helter-skelter —a regular John Gilpin race, truly neck or naught. The fleetest of the pursuers were soon in the midst of the game, which scattered in all directions, like a flock of birds upon the descent of a hawk.

A few beeves were killed during the chase; and as soon as our camp was pitched, the bustle of kindling fires and preparing for supper commenced. The new adventurers were curious to taste this prairie luxury; while we all had been so long upon salt provisions—now nearly a month—that our appetites were in exquisite condition to relish fresh meat. The fires had scarcely been kindled when the fumes of broiling meat pervaded the surrounding atmosphere; while all huddled about anxiously watching their cookeries and regaling their senses in anticipation upon the savory odors which issued from them.

For the edification of the reader, who has, no doubt, some curiosity on the subject, I will briefly mention that the kitchen and table wares of the traders usually consist of a skillet, a frying-pan, a sheet-iron camp-kettle, a coffee-pot, and each man with his tin cup and a butcher's knife. The culinary operations being finished, the pan and kettle are set upon the grassy turf, around which all take a lowly seat and crack their gleesome jokes while from their greasy hands they swallow their savory viands —all with a relish rarely experienced at the well-spread tables of the most fashionable and wealthy.

The insatiable appetite acquired by travelers upon the prairies is almost incredible, and the quantity of coffee drunk is still more so. It is an unfailing and apparently indispensable beverage, served at every meal—even under the broiling noon-day sun the wagoner will rarely fail to replenish a second time his huge tin cup.

Early the next day we reached the Little Arkansas,[26] which, although endowed with an imposing name, is only a small creek with a current but five or six yards wide. But, though small, its steep banks and miry bed annoyed us exceedingly in crossing. It is the practice upon the prairies on all such occasions for several men to go in advance with axes, spades, and mattocks and by digging the banks and erecting temporary bridges to have all in readiness by the time the wagons arrive. A bridge over a quagmire is made in a few minutes by cross-laying it with brush (willows are

[26] The crossing of the Little Arkansas was in the eastern edge of Rice County.

best, but even long grass is often employed as a substitute) and covering it with earth—across which a hundred wagons will often pass in safety.

We had now arrived at the point nearest to the border, I believe, where any outrages have been perpetrated upon the traders to Santa Fé. One of the early packing companies lost their animals on this spot and had to send back for a new supply.

Next day we reached Cow Creek,[27] where all the difficulties encountered at Little Arkansas had to be reconquered: but after digging, bridging, shouldering the wheels, with the usual accompaniment of whooping, swearing, and cracking of whips, we soon got safely across and encamped in the valley beyond. Alarms now began to accumulate more rapidly upon us. A couple of persons had a few days before been chased to the wagons by a band of —— buffalo; and this evening the encampment was barely formed when two hunters came bolting in with information that a hundred, perhaps, of the same enemy were at hand—at least this was the current opinion afterwards. The hubbub occasioned by this fearful news had scarcely subsided when another arrived on a panting horse, crying out, "Indians! Indians! I've just escaped from a couple, who pursued me to the very camp!" "To arms! to arms!" resounded

[27] Cow Creek rises in Rice County and flows into the Arkansas below the city of Hutchinson, Kansas.

from every quarter—and just then a wolf, attracted by the fumes of broiling buffalo bones, sent up a most hideous howl across the creek. "Some one in distress!" was instantly shouted. "To his relief!" vociferated the crowd —and off they bolted, one and all, arms in hand, hurly-burly—leaving the camp entirely unprotected; so that had an enemy been at hand indeed, and approached us from the opposite direction, they might have taken possession of the wagons. Before they had all returned, however, a couple of hunters came in and laughed very heartily at the expense of the first alarmist, whom they had just chased into the camp.

Half a day's drive after leaving this camp of false alarms brought us to the valley of Arkansas River. This point is about 270 miles from Independence. From the adjacent heights the landscape presents an imposing and picturesque appearance. Beneath a ledge of wavelike, yellow sandy ridges and hillocks spreading far beyond, descends the majestic river (averaging at least a quarter of a mile in width), bespeckled with verdant islets, thickly set with cottonwood timber. The banks are very low and barren with the exception of an occasional grove of stunted trees hiding behind a swamp or sand-hill, placed there as it were to protect it from the fire of the prairies, which in most parts keeps down every perennial growth. In many places, indeed, where there are no

270 mi. from Indep.

islands, the river is so entirely bare of trees that the unthinking traveler might approach almost to its very brink without suspecting its presence.

Thus far, many of the prairies have a fine and productive appearance, though the Neosho River (or Council Grove) seems to form the western boundary of the truly rich and beautiful country of the border. Up to that point the prairies are similar to those of Missouri—the soil equally exuberant and fertile; while all the country that lies beyond is of a far more barren character—vegetation of every kind is more stinted—the gay flowers more scarce, and the scanty timber of a very inferior quality. Indeed, the streams from Council Grove westward are lined with very little else than cottonwood, barely interspersed here and there with an occasional elm or hackberry.

Following up the course of this stream for some twenty miles, now along the valley and again traversing the points of projecting eminences, we reached Walnut Creek.[28] I have heard of a surgical operation performed at this point in the summer of 1826, which, though not done exactly *secundum artem*, might suggest some novel reflections to the man of science. A few days before the caravan had

[28] Walnut Creek rises north of Garden City, Kansas, and flows almost directly east into the Arkansas just below the town of Great Bend. Fort Zarat was later established at the mouth of Walnut Creek.

reached this place a Mr. Broadus, in attempting to draw his rifle from a wagon muzzle foremost, discharged its contents into his arm. The bone being dreadfully shattered, the unfortunate man was advised to submit to an amputation at once; otherwise, it being in the month of August and excessively warm, mortification would soon ensue. But Broadus obstinately refused to consent to this course till death began to stare him in the face. By this time, however, the whole arm had become gangrened, some spots having already appeared above the place where the operation should have been performed. The invalid's case was therefore considered perfectly hopeless and he was given up by all his comrades, who thought of little else than to consign him to the grave.

But being unwilling to resign himself to the fate which appeared frowning over him without a last effort, he obtained the consent of two or three of the party who undertook to amputate his arm merely to gratify the wishes of the dying man; for in such a light they viewed him. Their only case of instruments consisted of a handsaw, a butcher's knife, and a large iron bolt. The teeth of the saw being considered too coarse, they went to work and soon had a set of fine teeth filed on the back. The knife having been whetted keen and the iron bolt laid upon the fire, they commenced the operation, and in less time than it takes to tell it the arm was opened round to the bone, which was almost in an instant sawed off; and with the whizzing hot iron the whole stump was so effectually seared as to close the arteries completely. Bandages were now applied and the company proceeded on their journey as though nothing had occurred. The arm commenced healing rapidly and in a few weeks the patient was sound and well, and is perhaps still living to bear witness to the superiority of the hot iron over ligatures, in taking up arteries.

On the following day our route lay mostly over a level plain, which usually teems with buffalo and is beautifully adapted to the chase. At the distance of about fifteen miles the attention of the traveler is directed to the Pawnee Rock, so called, it is said, on account of a battle's having once been fought hard by between the Pawnees and some other tribe.[29] It is situated at the projecting point of a ridge and upon its surface are furrowed, in uncouth but legible characters, numerous dates and the names of various travelers who have chanced to pass that way.

We encamped at Ash Creek, where we again experienced sundry alarms in consequence of

[29] Pawnee Rock, one of the famous landmarks on the Santa Fé Trail, is in Barton County, Kansas, about twenty miles west of Great Bend. Pawnee Rock State Park, established by the state of Kansas in recent years, now includes the famous rock. It figures largely in the literature of the Santa Fé Trail, and gains its name from having been the great lookout of the Pawnee in their incursions against the Sioux.

Indian sign that was discovered in the creek valley, such as unextinguished fires, about which were found some old moccasins—a sure indication of the recent retreat of savages from the vicinity. These constant alarms, however, although too frequently the result of groundless and unmanly fears, are not without their salutary effects upon the party. They serve to keep one constantly on the alert and to sharpen those faculties of observation which would otherwise become blunted or inactive. Thus far, also, we had marched in two lines only; but after crossing the Pawnee Fork each of the four divisions drove on in a separate file, which became henceforth the order of march till we reached the border of the mountains. By moving in long lines as we did before, the march is continually interrupted; for every accident which delays a wagon ahead stops all those behind. By marching four abreast this difficulty is partially obviated, and the wagons can also be thrown more readily into a condition of defense in case of attack.

Upon encamping, the wagons are formed into a hollow square (each division to a side), constituting at once an enclosure (or *corral*) for the animals when needed, and a fortification against the Indians. Not to embarrass this cattle-pen, the camp fires are all lighted outside of the wagons. Outside of the wagons, also, the travelers spread their beds, which consist, for the most part, of buffalo-rugs and blankets.

# Commerce of the Prairies

Many content themselves with a single Mackinaw; but a pair constitutes the most regular pallet; and he that is provided with a buffalo-rug into the bargain is deemed luxuriously supplied. It is most usual to sleep out in the open air, as well to be at hand in case of attack as, indeed, for comfort; for the serene sky of the prairies affords the most agreeable and wholesome canopy. That deleterious attribute of night air and dews so dangerous in other climates is but little experienced upon the high plains: on the contrary, the serene evening air seems to affect the health rather favorably than otherwise. Tents are so rare on these expeditions that in a caravan of two hundred men I have not seen a dozen. In time of rain the traveler resorts to his wagon, which affords a far more secure shelter than a tent; for if the latter is not beaten down by the storms which so often accompany rain upon the prairies, the ground underneath is at least apt to be flooded. During dry weather, however, even the invalid prefers the open air.

Prior to the date of our trip it had been customary to secure the horses by hoppling them. The fore-hopple (a leather strap or rope manacle upon the fore-legs), being most convenient, was more frequently used; though the side-line (a hopple connecting a fore and hind leg) is the most secure; for with this an animal can hardly increase his pace beyond a hobbling walk; whereas, with the fore-hopple, a frighted horse will scamper off with nearly as much velocity as though he were unshackled. But better than either of these is the practice which the caravans have since adopted of tethering the mules at night around the wagons, at proper intervals, with ropes twenty-five or thirty feet in length tied to stakes fifteen to twenty inches long driven into the ground; a supply of which, as well as mallets, the wagoners always carry with them.

It is amusing to witness the disputes which often arise among wagoners about their staking ground. Each teamster is allowed by our common law a space of about a hundred yards immediately fronting his wagon, which he is ever ready to defend if a neighbor shows a disposition to encroach upon his soil. If any animals are found staked beyond the chartered limits, it is the duty of the guard to knock them up and turn them into the *corral*. Of later years the tethering of oxen has also been resorted to with advantage. It was thought at first that animals thus confined by ropes could not procure a sufficient supply of food; but experience has allayed all apprehension on the subject. In fact, as the camp is always pitched in the most luxuriantly clothed patches of prairie that can be selected, a mule is seldom able to dispatch in the course of one night all the grass within his reach. Again, when animals are permitted to range at liberty they are apt to mince and nibble at the tenderest blades and spend their time in roaming from point to point in search of what is most agreeable to their epicurean palates; whereas, if they are restricted by a rope they will at once fall to with earnestness and clip the pasturage as it comes.

Although the buffalo had been scarce for a few days, frightened off, no doubt, by the Indians whose sign we saw about Ash Creek, they soon became exceedingly abundant. The larger droves of these animals are sometimes a source of great annoyance to the caravans, as by running near our loose stock there is frequent danger of their causing *stampedes* (or general scamper), in which case mules, horses, and oxen have been known to run away among the buffalo as though they had been a gang of their own species. A company of traders in 1824 lost twenty or thirty of their animals in this way. Hunters have also been deprived of their horses in the same way. Leaping from them in haste in order to take a more determinate aim at the buffalo, the horse has been known to take fright and, following the fleeing game, has disappeared with saddle, bridle, pistols and all—most probably never to be heard of again. In fact, to look for stock upon these prairies would be emphatically to search for a needle in a haystack; not only because they are virtually boundless, but that being everywhere alive with herds of buffalo, from which horses cannot be distinguished at a distance, one knows not whither to turn in search after the stray animals.

We had lately been visited by frequent showers of rain, and upon observing the Arkansas River it was found to be rising, which seemed portentous of the troubles which the June freshet might occasion us in crossing it; and as it was already the 11th of this month, this annual occurrence was hourly expected. On some occasions caravans have been obliged to construct what is called a buffalo-boat, which is done by stretching the hides of these animals over an empty wagon-body. The June freshets, however, are seldom of long duration; and during the greatest portion of the year the channel is very shallow. Still, the bed of the river being in many places filled with quicksand, it is requisite to examine and mark out the best ford with stakes before one undertakes to cross. The wagons are then driven over, usually by double teams, which should never be permitted to stop else animals and wagons are apt to founder and the loading is liable to be damaged. I have witnessed a whole team down at once, rendering it necessary to unharness and drag each mule out separately: in fact, more than common exertion is sometimes required to prevent these dumpish animals from drowning in their fright and struggles through the water, though the current be but shallow at the place. Hence it is that oxen are much safer for fording streams than mules.

As for ourselves, we forded the river without serious difficulty.

Rattlesnakes are proverbially abundant upon all these prairies and as there is seldom to be found either stick or stone with which to kill them one hears almost a constant popping of rifles or pistols among the vanguard to clear the route of these disagreeable occupants, lest they should bite our animals. As we were toiling up through the sandy hillocks which border the southern banks of the Arkansas, the day being exceedingly warm, we came upon a perfect den of these reptiles. I will not say thousands, though this perhaps were nearer the truth—but hundreds, at least, were coiled or crawling in every direction. They were no sooner discovered than we were upon them with guns and pistols, determined to let none of them escape.

In the midst of this amusing scramble among the snakes, a wild mustang colt, which had somehow or other become separated from its dam, came bolting among our relay of loose stock to add to the confusion. One of our mules, evidently impressed with the impertinence of the intruder, sprang forward and attacked it with the apparent intention of executing summary chastisement; while another mule, with more benignity of temper than its irascible compeer, engaged most lustily in defense of the unfortunate little mustang. As the contest was carried on among the wagons, the teamsters soon became very uproarious; so that the whole, with the snake fracas, made up a capital scene of confusion. When the mule skirmish would have ended, if no one had interfered, is a question which remained undetermined; for some of our company, in view of the consequences that might result from the contest, rather inhumanly took sides with the assailing mule; and soon after they entered the lists a rifle ball relieved the poor colt from its earthly embarrassments and the company from further domestic disturbance. Peace once more restored, we soon got under way and that evening pitched our camp opposite the celebrated Caches, a place where some of the earliest adventurers had been compelled to conceal their merchandise.

The history of the origin of these Caches may be of sufficient interest to merit a brief recital. Beard, of the unfortunate party of 1812 alluded to in the first chapter, having returned to the United States in 1822, together with Chambers, who had descended the Canadian River the year before, induced some small capitalists of St. Louis to join in an enterprise, and then undertook to return to Santa Fé the same fall with a small party and an assortment of merchandise. Reaching the Arkansas late in the season, they were overtaken by a heavy snow storm and driven to take shelter on a large island. A rigorous winter ensued, which forced them to remain pent up in that place for three long months. During this time the greater portion of their animals perished; so that when the spring began to open they were unable to continue their journey with their goods. In this emergency they made a *cache* some distance above on the north side of the river, where they stowed away the most of their merchandise. From thence they proceeded to Taos, where they procured mules and returned to get their hidden property.

Few travelers pass this way without visiting these mossy pits, many of which remain partly unfilled to the present day. In the vicinity, or a few miles to the eastward perhaps, passes the hundredth degree of longitude west from Greenwich, which, from the Arkansas to Red River, forms the boundary between the United States and the Mexican, or rather the Texan, territory.

The term *cache*, meaning a place of concealment, was originally used by the Canadian French trappers and traders. It is made by digging a hole in the ground somewhat in the shape of a jug, which is lined with dry sticks, grass, or anything else that will protect its contents from the dampness of the earth. In this place the goods to be concealed are carefully stowed away; and the aperture is then so effectually closed as to protect them from the rains. In *caching* a great deal of skill is often required to leave no signs whereby the cunning savage might discover the place of deposit.

To this end the excavated earth is carried to some distance and carefully concealed, or thrown into a stream if one be at hand. The place selected for a cache is usually some rolling point, sufficiently elevated to be secure from inundations. If it be well set with grass, a solid piece of turf is cut out large enough for the entrance. The turf is afterward laid back, and taking root, in a short time no signs remain of its ever having been molested. However, as every locality does not afford a turfy site, the camp fire is sometimes built upon the place, or the animals are penned over it, which effectually destroys all traces of the cache.

This mode of concealing goods seems to have been in use from the time of the earliest French voyagers in America. Father Hennepin, during his passage down the Mississippi River in 1680, describes an operation of this kind in the following terms: "We took up the green Sodd, and laid it by, and digg'd a hole in the Earth where we put our Goods, and cover'd them with pieces of Timber and Earth, and then put in again the green Turf; so that 'twas impossible to suspect that any Hole had been digg'd under it, for we flung the Earth into the River." Returning a few weeks after, they found the cache all safe and sound.

# Chapter 4

ENCOUNTERS WITH THIRST AND THE RED MAN

OUR route had already led us up the course of the Arkansas River for over a hundred miles, yet the earlier caravans often passed from fifty to a hundred farther up before crossing the river; therefore nothing like a regular ford had ever been established. Nor was there a road, not even a trail, anywhere across the famous plain extending between the Arkansas and Cimarron rivers, a distance of over fifty miles, which now lay before us— the scene of such frequent sufferings in former times for want of water. It having been determined upon, however, to strike across this dreaded desert the following morning, the whole party was busy in preparing for the water scrape, as these droughty drives are very appropriately called by prairie travelers. This tract of country may truly be styled the grand prairie ocean; for not a single landmark is to be seen for more than forty miles—scarcely a visible eminence by which to direct one's course. All is as level as the sea, and the compass was our surest, as well as principal guide.

In view of this passage, as well as that of many other dry stretches upon the route, the traveler should be apprised of the necessity of providing a water-cask holding at least five gallons to each wagon, in which a supply for drinking and cooking may be carried along to serve in cases of emergency.

The evening before the embarking of a caravan upon this plain, the captain's voice is usually heard above the din and clatter of the camp ordering to "fill up the water kegs,"— a precaution which cannot be repeated too often as new adventurers are usually ignorant of the necessity of providing a supply sufficient to meet every contingency that may befall during two or more days' journey over this arid region. The cooks are equally engrossed by their respective vocations: some are making bread, others preparing viands, and all tasking their ingenuity to lay by such stores as may be deemed expedient for at least two days' consumption. On the following morning (June 14th), the words "Catch up" again resounded through the camp and the caravan was once more in motion.

For the first five miles we had a heavy pull among the sandy hillocks; but soon the broad and level plain opened before us. We had hardly left the river's side, however, when we experienced a delay of some hours in consequence of an accident which came very near proving fatal to a French doctor of our company. Fearful lest his stout, top-heavy dearborn should upset whilst skirting the slope of a hill, he placed himself below in order to sustain it with his hands. But in spite of all his exertions the carriage tumbled over, crushing and mashing him most frightfully. He was taken out senseless and but little hopes were at first entertained of his recovery. Having revived, however, soon after, we were enabled to resume our march; and in the course of time the wounded patient entirely recovered.

The next day we fortunately had a heavy shower, which afforded us abundance of water. Having also swerved considerably toward the south, we fell into a more uneven section of country, where we had to cross a brook swelled by the recent rain, into which one of the wagons was unfortunately overset. This, however, was not a very uncommon occurrence; for unruly oxen, when thirsty, will often rush into a pool in despite of the driver, dragging the wagon over every object in their way, at the imminent risk of turning it topsy-turvy into the water. We were now compelled to make a halt and all hands flocked to the assistance of the owner of the damaged cargo. In a few minutes about an acre of ground was completely covered with calicoes and other domestic goods, presenting altogether an interesting spectacle.

All were busily occupied at this work when some objects were seen moving in the distance, which at first were mistaken for buffalo; but were speedily identified as horsemen. Anxiety was depicted in every countenance. Could it be possible that the party of Capt. Sublette,[30] which was nearly a month ahead of us, had been lost in these dreary solitudes? Or was it the band of Capt. Bent,[31] who was expected to follow some time after us? This anxious suspense, however, lasted only for a few minutes; and the cry of "Indians!" soon made the welkin ring. Still they appeared to approach too slowly for the western prairie tribes. A

[30] William L. Sublette was born in Kentucky in 1799. In 1818 he located at St. Charles, Mo., and soon thereafter embarked in the fur trade. He had but slight connection with the Santa Fé trade, however, his activities being principally directed to the northwestern region. He died in 1845.

[31] Charles Bent was one of three brothers—Charles, William, and George—who were long prominent in the trade of the Southwest. In 1829 William Bent established Bent's Fort on the north bank of the Arkansas where the old route of the Santa Fé Trail there crossed that stream. It stood just west of the Otero-Bent County line, in latitude 38° 3′ and longitude 103° 25′. For almost a decade it held undisputed sway over a vast territory; thereafter competing interests entered the field. The three Bent brothers and two St. Vrains— Cerain and Marceline—were partners in trade for almost thirty years. Besides Fort Bent they had Fort St. Vrain on the South Platte and other trading establishments.

Charles Bent, here noted, was born in Charleston, Va., November 11, 1799. In September, 1846, General Kearny appointed him Governor of New Mexico, then newly conquered by the Americans. On January 19 following, in the course of a native revolt at Taos, he was killed. Of this revolt and its quelling Lewis H. Garrard has written entertainingly in his narrative, *Wahtoyah and the Taos Trail* . . . (Cincinnati, 1850).

little nearer, and we soon perceived that they carried a flag, which turned out to be that of the United States. This welcome sight allayed at once all uneasiness; as it is well known that most savages when friendly approach the whites with a hoisted flag, provided they have one. It turned out to be a party of about eighty Sioux, who were on a tour upon the prairies for the purpose of trading with, stealing from, or marauding upon the southwestern nations. Our communications were carried on entirely by signs; yet we understood them perfectly to say that there were immense numbers of Indians ahead upon the Cimarron River, whom they described by symbolic language to be Blackfeet and Comanches; a most agreeable prospect for the imagination to dwell upon!

We now moved on slowly and leisurely, for all anxiety on the subject of water had been happily set at rest by frequent falls of rain. But imagine our consternation and dismay when, upon descending into the valley of the Cimarron on the morning of the 19th of June, a band of Indian warriors on horse-back suddenly appeared before us from behind the ravines— an imposing array of death-dealing savages! There was no merriment in this! It was a genuine alarm—a tangible reality! These warriors, however, as we soon discovered, were only the van-guard of a countless host, who were by this time pouring over the opposite ridge, and galloping directly towards us.

The wagons were soon irregularly formed upon the hill-side: but in accordance with the habitual carelessness of caravan traders a great portion of the men were unprepared for the emergency. Scores of guns were empty, and as many more had been wetted by the recent showers, and would not go off. Here was one calling for balls—another for powder—a third for flints. Exclamations such as "I've broke my ramrod"—"I've spilt my caps"—"I've rammed down a ball without powder"—"My gun is choked; give me yours"—were heard from different quarters; while a timorous greenhorn would perhaps cry out, "Here, take my gun, you can out-shoot me!" The more daring bolted off to encounter the enemy at once, while the timid and cautious took a stand with presented rifle behind the wagons. The Indians who were in advance made a bold attempt to press upon us, which came near costing them dearly; for some of our fiery backwoodsmen more than once had their rusty but unerring rifles directed upon the intruders, some of whom would inevitably have fallen before their deadly aim had not a few of the more prudent traders interposed. The savages made demonstrations no less hostile, rushing with ready sprung bows upon a portion of our men who had gone in search of water; and mischief would, perhaps, have ensued had not the impetuosity of the warriors been checked by the wise men of the nation.

The Indians were collecting around us, however, in such great numbers that it was deemed expedient to force them away so as to resume our march, or at least to take a more advantageous position. Our company was therefore mustered and drawn up in line of battle; and accompanied by the sound of a drum and fife we marched towards the main group of the Indians. The latter seemed far more delighted than frightened with this strange parade and music, a spectacle they had no doubt never witnessed before, and perhaps looked upon the whole movement rather as a complimentary salute than a hostile array; for there was no interpreter through whom any communication could be conveyed to them. But, whatever may have been their impressions, one thing is certain—that the principal chief (who was dressed in a long red coat of strouding, or coarse cloth) appeared to have full confidence in the virtues of his calumet; which he lighted, and came boldly forward to meet our warlike corps, serenely smoking the pipe of peace. Our captain, now taking a whiff with the savage chief, directed him by signs to cause his warriors to retire. This most of them did, to rejoin the long train of squaws and papooses with the baggage, who followed in the rear and were just then seen emerging from beyond the hills. Having slowly descended to the banks of the stream, they pitched their wigwams or lodges; over five hundred of which soon bespeckled the ample valley before us and at once gave to its recently meager surface the aspect of an immense Indian village. The entire number of the Indians, when collected together, could not have been less than from two to three thousand —although some of our company insisted that there were at least four thousand souls. In such a case they must have mustered nearly a thousand warriors, while we were but little over two hundred strong. Still, our superior arms and the protection afforded by the wagons gave us considerably the advantage, even supposing an equality in point of valor. However, the appearance of the squaws and children soon convinced us that for the present at least they had no hostile intentions; so we also descended into the valley and formed our camp a few hundred yards below them. The capitanes, or head men of the whites and Indians, shortly after met and, again smoking the calumet, agreed to be friends.

Although we were on the very banks of the Cimarron,[32] even the most experienced traders of our party, whether through fright or ignorance, seemed utterly unconscious of the fact. Having made our descent far below the usual point of approach, and there being not a drop

---

[32] The Cimarron River is over 600 miles in length. It rises in the Raton Mountains, near the New Mexico-Colorado boundary, passes across southwestern Kansas, and joins the Arkansas in Oklahoma near latitude 36° 10′ N.

of water found in the sandy bed of the river, it was mistaken for Sand Creek and we accordingly proceeded without noticing it. Therefore, after our big talk was concluded and dinner dispatched we set out southward in search of the Cimarron. As we were starting, warriors, squaws, and papooses now commenced flocking about us, gazing at our wagons with amazement; for many of them had never, perhaps, seen such vehicles before. A few chiefs and others followed us to our next encampment; but these were sent away at night.

Our guards were now doubled as a night attack was apprehended; for although we were well aware that Indians never commit outrages with their families at hand, yet it was feared that they might either send them away or conceal them during the night. A little after dark these fears seemed about to be realized; as a party of thirty or forty Indians were seen coming up towards the encampment. Immediate preparations were made to attack them, when they turned out to be a band of squaws, with merely a few men as gallants— all of whom were summarily turned adrift without waiting to speculate upon the objects of their visit. The next morning a few others made their appearance, whom we treated in precisely the same manner, as a horse was missing which it was presumed the Indians had stolen.

We continued our march southward in search of the lost river. After a few miles' travel we encountered a ledge of sand-hills which obstructed our course and forced us to turn westward and follow their border for the rest of the day. Finding but little water that night and none at all the next day, we began by noon to be sadly frightened; for nothing is more alarming to the prairie traveler than a water-scrape. The impression soon became general that we were lost—lost on that inhospitable desert, which had been the theater of so many former scenes of suffering! and our course impeded by sand-hills! A council of the veteran travelers was called to take our emergency into consideration. It was at once resolved to strike in a northwesterly direction in search of the dry ravine we had left behind us, which was now supposed to have been the Cimarron.

We had just set out when a couple of Indians approached us, bringing the horse we had lost the night before; an apparent demonstration of good faith which could hardly have been anticipated. It was evidently an effort to ingratiate themselves in our favor and establish an intercourse—perhaps a traffic. But the outrages upon Major Riley, as well as upon a caravan not two years before, perpetrated probably by the same Indians, were fresh in the memory of all; so that none of us were willing to confide in their friendly professions. On inquiring by means of signs for the nearest water, they pointed to the direction we were traveling: and finally taking the lead, they led us by the shortest way to the valley of the long-sought Cimarron, which, with its delightful green-grass glades and flowing torrent (very different in appearance from where we had crossed it below), had all the aspect of an Elysian vale, compared with what we had seen for some time past. We pitched our camp in the valley, much rejoiced at having again made a port.

We were not destined to rest long in peace, however. About midnight we were all aroused by a cry of alarm the like of which had not been heard since the day Don Quixote had his famous adventure with the fulling-mills; and I am not quite sure but some of our party suffered as much from fright as poor Sancho Panza did on that memorable occasion. But Don Quixote and Sancho only heard the thumping of the mills and the roaring of the waters; while we heard the thumping of the Indian drums accompanied by occasional yells which our excited fancies immediately construed into notes of the fearful war-song.

After the whole company had been under arms for an hour or two, finding the cause of alarm approached no nearer, we again retired to rest. But a little before daylight we were again startled by the announcement, "The Indians are coming! They are upon the very camp!" In a moment every man was up in arms; and several guns were presented to salute the visitors, when, to our extreme mortification, they were found to be but eight or ten in number. They were immediately dispatched by signs and directed to remain away till morning, which they did.

On the following day we had been in motion but a few minutes when the Indians began flocking around us in large numbers, and by the time we encamped in the evening we had perhaps a thousand of these pertinacious creatures, males and females of all ages and descriptions, about us. At night every means, without resorting to violence, was employed to drive them away, but without entire success. At this time a small band of warriors took the round of our camp, and serenaded us with a monotonous song of *hee-o-hehs*, with the view, I suppose, of gaining permission to remain; hoping, no doubt, to be able to drive a fair business at pilfering during the night. In fact, a few small articles were already missing, and it was now discovered that they had purloined a pig of lead (between fifty and a hundred pounds weight) from one of the cannon-carriages where it had been carelessly left. This increased the uneasiness which already prevailed to a considerable extent; and many of us would imagine it already moulded into bullets, which we were perhaps destined to receive before morning from the muzzles of their fusils.

Some were even so liberal as to express a willingness to pardon the theft rather than give the Indians the trouble of sending it back in so hasty a manner. After a tedious night of suspense and conjecture it was no small relief to those whose feelings had been so highly wrought upon to find, on waking up in the morning, that every man still retained his scalp.

We started at a much earlier hour this morning, in hopes to leave our Indian tormentors behind; but they were too wide awake for us. By the time the wagoners had completed the task of gearing their teams, the squaws had geared their dogs and loaded them with their lodge poles and covers and other light plunder and were traveling fast in our wake. Much to our comfort, however, the greatest portion abandoned us before night; but the next day several of the chiefs overtook us again at noon, seeming anxious to renew the treaty of peace. The truth is, the former treaty had never been sealed—they had received no presents, which form an indispensable ratification of all their treaties with the whites. Some fifty or sixty dollars' worth of goods having been made up for them, they now left us, apparently satisfied; and although they continued to return and annoy us for a couple of days longer, they at last entirely disappeared.

It was generally supposed at the time that there was a great number of Comanches and Arapahoes among this troop of savages; but they were principally if not altogether Black-feet and Gros Ventres. We afterward learned that on their return to the northern mountains they met with a terrible defeat from the Sioux and other neighboring tribes, in which they were said to have lost more than half their number.

We now encountered a great deal of wet weather; in fact this region is famous for cold protracted rains of two or three days' duration. Storms of hail-stones larger than hens' eggs are not uncommon, frequently accompanied by the most tremendous hurricanes. The violence of the wind is sometimes so great that, as I have heard, two road-wagons were once capsized by one of these terrible thunder-gusts; the rain at the same time flooding the plain to the depth of several inches. In short, I doubt if there is any known region out of the tropics that can head the great prairies in getting up thunder-storms combining so many of the elements of the awful and sublime.

During these storms the guards were often very careless. This was emphatically the case with us, notwithstanding our knowledge of the proximity of a horde of savages. In fact, the caravan was subject to so little control that the patience of Capt. Stanley underwent some very severe trials; so much so that he threatened more than once to resign. Truly, there is not a better school for testing a man's temper than the command of a promiscuous caravan of independent traders. The rank of captain is, of course, but little more than nominal. Every proprietor of a two-horse wagon is apt to assume as much authority as the commander himself, and to issue his orders without the least consultation at head-quarters. It is easy, then, to conceive that the captain has anything but an enviable berth. He is expected to keep order while few are disposed to obey—loaded with execrations for every mishap, whether accidental or otherwise; and when he attempts to remonstrate he only renders himself ridiculous, being entirely without power to enforce his commands. It is to be regretted that some system of maritime law has not been introduced among these traders to secure subordination, which can never be attained while the commander is invested with no legal authority. For my own part, I can see no reason why the captain of a prairie caravan should not have as much power to call his men to account for disobedience or mutiny as the captain of a ship upon the high seas.

After following the course of the Cimarron for two days longer we at length reached a place called the Willow Bar,[33] where we took the usual mid-day respite of two or three hours, to afford the animals time to feed and our cooks to prepare dinner. Our wagons were regularly formed, and the animals turned loose to graze

[33] Near the boundary between Oklahoma and Colorado.

at leisure, with only a day-guard to watch them. Those who had finished their dinners lay stretched upon their blankets and were just beginning to enjoy the luxury of a siesta, when all of a sudden the fearful and oft-reiterated cry of "Indians!" turned this scene of repose into one of bustle and confusion.

From the opposite ridge, at the distance of a mile, a swarm of savages were seen coming upon us at full charge, and their hideous whoop and yell soon resounded through the valley. Such a jumbling of promiscuous voices I never expect to hear again. Every one fancied himself a commander and vociferated his orders accordingly. The air was absolutely rent with the cries of "Let's charge 'em, boys!"—"Fire upon 'em, boys!"—"Reserve! don't fire till they come nearer!"—while the voice of our captain was scarcely distinguishable in his attempts to prevent such rash proceedings. As the prairie Indians often approach their friends as well as enemies in this way, Captain Stanley was unwilling to proceed to extremities lest they might be peacefully inclined. But a popping salute and the whizzing of fusil balls over our heads soon explained their intentions. We returned them several rifle shots by way of compliment, but without effect, as they were at too great a distance.

A dozen cannoneers now surrounded our artillery, which was charged with canister. Each of them had, of course, something to say.

"Elevate her; she'll ground," one would suggest. "She'll over-shoot, now," rejoined another. At last, after raising and lowering the six-pounder several times, during which process the Indians had time to retreat beyond reach of shot, the match was finally applied and—bang! went the gun, but the charge grounded midway. This was followed by two or three shots with single ball, but apparently without effect; although there were some with sharp eyes who fancied they saw Indians or horses wounded at every fire. We came off equally unscathed from the conflict, barring a horse of but little value which ran away and was taken by the enemy. The Indians were about a hundred in number and supposed to be Comanches, though they might have been a band of warriors belonging to the party we had just left behind.

The novices were not a little discouraged at these frequent inroads of the enemy, although it is very seldom that any lives are lost in encounters with them. In the course of twenty years since the commencement of this trade I do not believe there have been a dozen deaths upon the Santa Fé route, even including those who have been killed off by disease as well as by the Indians.

On the following day we encamped near the Battle Ground, famous for a skirmish which a caravan of traders, in company with a detachment of Mexican troops under the command of

Col. Vizcarra, had in 1829 with a band of Gros Ventres. The united companies had just encamped on the Cimarron near the site of the burial catastrophe which occurred the preceding year. A party of about a hundred and twenty Indians soon after approached them on foot; but as the Americans were but little disposed to admit friendly intercourse between them, they passed into the camp of the Mexican commander, who received them amicably —a circumstance not altogether agreeable to the traders. As the Indians seemed disposed to remain till morning, Col. Vizcarra promised that they should be disarmed for the night; but the cunning wretches made some excuse to delay the surrender of their weapons, until the opportunity being favorable for a *coup de main*, they sprang to their feet, raised a fearful yell, and fired upon the unsuspecting party. Their aim seems chiefly to have been to take the life of the Mexican colonel; and it is said that a Taos Indian who formed one of the Mexican escort, seeing a gun leveled at his commander, sprang forward and received the ball in his own body, from the effects of which he instantly expired! The Indians were pursued for several miles into the hills and a considerable number killed and wounded. Of the Americans, not one received the slightest injury; but of the Mexican dragoons, a captain and two or three privates were killed.

# Chapter 5

FROM THE CIMARRON TO SANTA FÉ

IT was on the last day of June that we arrived at the Upper Spring,[34] which is a small fountain breaking into a ravine that declines toward the Cimarron some three or four miles to the north. The scarcity of water in these desert regions gives to every little spring an importance which, of course, in more favored countries it would not enjoy. We halted at noon on the brook below and then branched off towards the waters of the Canadian, in an average direction of about thirty degrees south of west. As the wagon-road passes upon the adjacent ridge a quarter of a mile to the south of this spring, some of us, to procure a draught of its refreshing water, pursued a path along the ravine, winding through dense thickets of underbrush matted with green-briers and grape-vines, which, with the wild-currant and plum-bushes, were all bent under their unripe fruit. The wildness of this place, with its towering cliffs, craggy spurs, and deep-cut crevices, became doubly impressive to us as we reflected that we were in the very midst of savage haunts. Often will the lonely traveler as he

[34] The Upper Spring was a short way beyond the boundary between Oklahoma and New Mexico.

plods his weary way in silence imagine in each click of a pebble the snap of a firelock, and in every rebound of a twig the whisk of an arrow. After regaling ourselves with a draught of the delicious beverage which gushed from the pure fountain, we ascended the rugged heights and now rejoined the caravan half a mile beyond.

We had now a plain and perfectly distinguishable track before us, and a party of *avant-couriers*, known in the technical parlance of the prairies as runners, soon began to make preparations for pushing forward in advance of the caravan into Santa Fé, though we were yet more than two hundred miles from that city. It is customary for these runners to take their departure from the caravans in the night in order to evade the vigilance of any enemy that might be lurking around the encampment. They are generally proprietors or agents; and their principal purpose is to procure and send back a supply of provisions, to secure good store-houses, and what is no less important, to obtain an agreeable understanding with the officers of the custom house.

The second day after the departure of the runners, as we lay encamped at McNee's Creek,[35] the Fourth of July dawned upon us. Scarce had gray twilight brushed his dusky

[35] For the tragedy which gave name to this creek see *ante*, p. 13. The creek is in Union County, New Mexico, and is now named Currampaw.

brow when our patriotic camp gave lively demonstrations of that joy which plays around the heart of every American on the anniversary of this triumphant day. The roar of our artillery and rifle platoons resounded from every hill, while the rumbling of the drum and the shrill whistle of the fife imparted a degree of martial interest to the scene which was well calculated to stir the souls of men. There was no limit to the huzzas and enthusiastic ejaculations of our people; and at every new shout the dales around sent forth a gladsome response. This anniversary is always hailed with heart-felt joy by the wayfarer in the remote desert; for here the strifes and intrigues of party-spirit are unknown: nothing intrudes in these wild solitudes to mar that harmony of feeling and almost pious exultation which every true-hearted American experiences on this great day.

The next day's march brought us in front of the Rabbit-Ear Mounds,[36] which might now be seen at a distance of eight or ten miles south of us, and which before the present track was established served as a guide to travelers. The first caravan of wagons that crossed these plains passed on the south side of these mounds, having abandoned our present route at the Cold Spring, where we encamped on the night of the 1st of July. Although the route we were

[36] Just north of Clayton, the county seat of Union County, New Mexico.

traveling swerves somewhat too much to the north, that pursued by the early caravans, as stated above, made still a greater circuit to the south, and was by far the most inconvenient.

As we were proceeding on our march we observed a horseman approaching, who excited at first considerable curiosity. His picturesque costume and peculiarity of deportment, however, soon showed him to be a Mexican *Cibolero* or buffalo-hunter. These hardy devotees of the chase usually wear leathern trousers and jackets and flat straw hats; while swung upon the shoulder of each hangs his *carcage* or quiver of bow and arrows. The long handle of their lance being set in a case and suspended by the side with a strap from the pommel of the saddle, leaves the point waving high over the head, with a tassel of gay parti-colored stuffs dangling at the tip of the scabbard. Their fusil, if they happen to have one, is suspended in a like manner at the other side, with a stopper in the muzzle fantastically tasseled.

The *Cibolero* saluted us with demonstrations of joy; nor were we less delighted at meeting with him; for we were now able to obtain information from Santa Fé, whence no news had been received since the return of the caravan the preceding fall. Traders and idlers, with equal curiosity, clustered around the new visitor; every one who could speak a word of

# Commerce of the Prairies

Spanish having some question to ask: "What prospects?"—"How are goods?"—"What news from the south?"—while the more experienced traders interested themselves chiefly to ascertain the condition of the custom house; and who were the present revenue officers; for unpropitious changes sometimes occur during the absence of the caravans.

But whatever joy we at first experienced was soon converted into mourning by a piece of most melancholy news—the tragical death of a celebrated veteran mountain adventurer. It has already been mentioned that Capt. Sublette and others had started near a month in advance of our company. We had frequently seen their trail and once or twice had received some vague information of their whereabouts through the Indians, but nothing satisfactory. Our visitor now informed us that a captain of this band had been assassinated by the Indians; and from his description we presumed it to be Capt. Smith, one of the partners—which was afterwards confirmed, with many particulars of the adventures of this company.

Capt. Smith and his companions were new beginners in the Santa Fé trade, but being veteran pioneers of the Rocky Mountains they concluded they could go anywhere; and imprudently set out without a single person in their company at all competent to guide them on the route. They had some twenty-odd wagons and about eighty men. There being a plain track to the Arkansas River, they did very well thus far; but from thence to the Cimarron not a single trail was to be found save the innumerable buffalo paths with which these plains are furrowed, and which are exceedingly perplexing to the bewildered prairie traveler. In a great many places, I have observed, they have all the appearance of immense highways over which entire armies would seem to have frequently passed. They generally lead from one watering-place to another; but as these reservoirs very often turn out to be dry, the thirsty traveler who follows them in search of water is liable to constant disappointment.

When Capt. Sublette's party entered this arid plain it was parched with drought; and they were doomed to wander about for several days with all the horrors of a death from thirst staring them continually in the face. In this perilous situation, Capt. Smith resolved at last to pursue one of these seductive buffalo paths, in hopes it might lead to the margin of some stream or pond. He set out alone; for besides the temerity which desperation always inspires, he had ever been a stranger to fear; indeed, he was one of the most undaunted spirits that had ever traversed the Rocky Mountains; and if but one-half of what has been told of him be true—of his bold enterprises—his perilous wanderings—his skirmishings with the savages—his hair-breadth escapes, etc.—he would surely be entitled to one of the most exalted seats in the Olympus of prairie mythology.[37] But, alas! unfortunate Captain Smith! after having so often dodged the arrow and eluded the snare of the wily mountain Indian, little could he have thought, while jogging along under a scorching sun, that his bones were destined to bleach upon those arid sands! He had already wandered many miles away from his comrades when, on turning over an eminence, his eyes were joyfully greeted with the appearance of a small stream meandering through the valley that spread before him. It was the Cimarron. He hurried forward to slake the fire of his parched lips, but imagine his disappointment at finding in the channel only a bed of dry sand! With his hands, however, he soon scratched out a basin a foot or two deep, into which the water slowly oozed from the saturated sand. While with his head bent down, in the effort to quench his burning thirst in the fountain, he was pierced by the arrows of a gang of Comanches who were lying in wait for him! Yet he struggled bravely to the last; and, as the Indians themselves have since related, killed two or three of their party before he was overpowered.

[37] Jedediah S. Smith, whose death Gregg describes, was one of the ablest and most enterprising men engaged in the Rocky Mountain fur trade. For an account of his career see Harrison C. Dale, *The Ashley-Smith Explorations and the Discovery of a Central Route to the Pacific, 1822–1829* (Cleveland, 1918).

Every kind of fatality seems to have attended this little caravan. Among other calamities, we also learned that a clerk in their company, named Minter, had been killed by a band of Pawnees before they crossed the Arkansas. This, I believe, is the only instance of loss of life among the traders while engaged in hunting: although the scarcity of accidents can hardly be said to be the result of prudence. There is not a day, from the time a caravan reaches the buffalo range, that hunters do not commit some indiscretion, such as straying at a distance of five and even ten miles from the caravan, frequently alone, and seldom in bands of more than two or three together. In this state they must frequently be spied by prowling savages; so that the frequency of escape, under such circumstances, must be partly attributed to the cowardice of the Indians. Indeed, generally speaking, the latter are very loth to charge upon even a single armed man, unless they can take him at a decided disadvantage. Therefore, it is at all times imprudent to fire at the first approach of Indians; for, seeing their guns empty, the savages would charge upon them; while very small bands of hunters have been known to keep large numbers of the enemy at bay by presenting their rifles but reserving their fire till assistance was at hand.

The companions of Capt. Smith, having descended upon the Cimarron at another point, appear to have remained ignorant of the terrible fate that had befallen him until they were informed of the circumstances by some Mexican traders, who had ascertained the facts from the murderous savages themselves. Not long after, this band of Capt. Sublette very narrowly escaped a total destruction. They had fallen in with that immense horde of Blackfeet and Gros Ventres with whom we afterwards met, and as the traders were literally but a handful among their thousands they fancied themselves for awhile in imminent peril of being virtually eaten up. But as Capt. Sublette possessed considerable experience he was at no loss how to deal with these treacherous savages; so that although the latter assumed a menacing attitude, he passed them without any serious molestation and finally arrived at Santa Fé in safety.

But to return to our *Cibolero*. He was desirous to sell us some provisions, which, by the by, were welcome enough; for most of the company were out of bread and meat was becoming very scarce, having seen but few buffalo since our first encounter with the Indians on the Cimarron. Our visitor soon retired to his camp hard by, and with several of his comrades afterwards brought us an abundance of dry buffalo beef and some bags of coarse oven-toasted loaves, a kind of hard bread much used by Mexican travelers. It is prepared by opening the ordinary leavened rolls and toasting them brown in an oven. Though exceedingly hard and insipid while dry, it becomes not only soft but palatable when soaked in water— or better still in hot coffee. But what we procured on this occasion was unusually stale and coarse, prepared expressly for barter with the Comanches, in case they should meet any: yet bread was bread, emphatically, with us just then.

A word concerning the *Ciboleros* may not be altogether uninteresting. Every year large parties of New Mexicans, some provided with mules and asses, others with *carretas* or truckle-carts and oxen, drive out into these prairies to procure a supply of buffalo beef for their families. They hunt like the wild Indians, chiefly on horseback and with bow and arrow, or lance, with which they soon load their carts and mules. They find no difficulty in curing their meat even in mid-summer, by slicing it thin and spreading or suspending it in the sun; or, if in haste, it is slightly barbecued. During the curing operation they often follow the Indian practice of beating or kneading the slices with their feet, which they contend contributes to its preservation.

Here the extraordinary purity of the atmosphere is remarkably exemplified. The caravans cure meat in the same simple manner, except the process of kneading. A line is stretched from corner to corner on each side of a wagon-body and strung with slices of beef, which remains from day to day till it is sufficiently cured to be stacked away. This is done without salt, and yet it very rarely putrefies. In truth, as blow-flies are unknown here, there is nothing to favor putrefaction. While speaking of flies I might as well remark that after passing beyond the region of the tall grass [38] between the Missouri frontier and Arkansas River, the horse-fly, also, is unknown. Judging from the prairies on our border we had naturally anticipated a great deal of mischief from these brute-tormentors; in which we were very agreeably disappointed.

But I have not yet done with the meat-curing operations. While in the midst of the

[38] In Kansas buffalo-grass was called "short grass" to distinguish it from the true prairie grass, or "long grass," to which it is in no way related. Prairie grass sometimes grows to a height of six feet, although on the prairie it seldom exceeds twelve inches. Originally it was not commonly found at elevations of more than 1,000 feet, but it is now slowly invading the uplands.

The region growing the buffalo-grass in Kansas is called the "short grass" or the "short grass country." The dividing line between the short grass country and the long grass was in the vicinity of Council Grove. Buffalo-grass does not form a continuous sod, but grows in patches. These lie close together, but there are always barren streaks between them, and they are not of any uniform size or shape. The grass cures in late summer, but it is not diminished in nutriment by this process. It furnished pasturage in all seasons. Buffaloes were found in large areas where the buffalo-grass did not grow, but they attained the greatest development in the buffalo-grass region. Information supplied by William E. Connelley.

buffalo range travelers usually take the precaution of laying up a supply of beef for exigencies in the absence of the prairie cattle. We had
somewhat neglected this provision in time of
abundance, by which we had come near being
reduced to extremities. Caravans sometimes
lie by a day or two to provide a supply of meat;
when numbers of buffalo are slaughtered and
the flesh jerked, or slightly barbecued, by
placing it upon a scaffold over a fire. The same
method is resorted to by Mexicans when the
weather is too damp or cloudy for the meat
to dry in the open air.

We were now approaching the Round
Mound, a beautiful round-topped cone rising
nearly a thousand feet above the level of the
plain by which it is for the most part surrounded. We were yet at least three miles from this
mound when a party set out on foot to ascend
it in order to get a view of the surrounding
country. They felt confident it was but a half
mile off—at most, three-quarters; but finding
the distance so much greater than they had
anticipated, many began to lag behind and
soon rejoined the wagons. The optical illusions
occasioned by the rarefied and transparent
atmosphere of these elevated plains are often
truly remarkable, affording another exemplification of its purity. One would almost
fancy himself looking through a spy-glass,
for objects frequently appear at scarce one-
fourth of their real distance—frequently much

magnified, and more especially elevated. I have often seen flocks of antelopes mistaken for droves of elks or wild horses, and when at a great distance even for horsemen; whereby frequent alarms are occasioned. I have also known tufts of grass or weeds, or mere buffalo bones scattered on the prairies, to stretch upward to the height of several feet, so as to present the appearance of so many human beings. Ravens in the same way are not infrequently taken for Indians, as well as for buffalo; and a herd of the latter upon a distant plain often appear so increased in bulk that they would be mistaken by the inexperienced for a grove of trees. This is usually attended with a continual waving and looming, which often so writhe and distort distant objects as to render them too indistinct to be discriminated. The illusion seems to be occasioned by gaseous vapors rising from the ground while the beaming rays of the sun are darting upon it.

But the most curious and at the same time the most perplexing phenomenon occasioned by optical deception is the *mirage*, or as familiarly called upon the prairies, the false ponds. Even the experienced traveler is often deceived by these upon the arid plains, where a disappointment is most severely felt. The thirsty wayfarer, after jogging for hours under a burning sky, at length espies a pond—yes, it must be water—it looks too natural for him to be mistaken. He quickens his pace, enjoying in anticipation the pleasure of a refreshing draught. But lo! as he approaches it recedes or entirely disappears; and when upon its apparent site, he is ready to doubt his own vision—he finds but a parched plain under his feet. It is not until he has been thus a dozen times deceived that he is willing to relinquish the pursuit: and then, perhaps, when he really does see a pond he will pass it unexamined for fear of another disappointment.

The philosophy of these false ponds seems generally not well understood. They have usually been attributed to refraction, by which a section of the bordering sky would appear below the horizon. But there can be no doubt that they are the effect of reflection upon a gas emanating perhaps from the sun-scorched earth and vegetable matter. Or it may be that a surcharge of carbonic acid precipitated upon the flats and sinks of those plains by the action of the sun produces the effect. At least, it appears of sufficient density, when viewed very obliquely, to reflect the objects beyond: and thus the opposite sky, being reflected in the pond of gas, gives the appearance of water. As a proof that it is the effect of reflection, I have often observed the distant trees and hilly protuberances which project above the horizon beyond distinctly inverted in the pond; whereas, were it the result of refraction, these would appear erect, only cast below the surface. Indeed, many are the singular atmospheric phenomena observable upon the plains which would afford a field of interesting research for the curious natural philosopher.

At last some of the most persevering of our adventurers succeeded in ascending the summit of the Round Mound, which commands a full and advantageous view of the surrounding country, in some directions to the distance of a hundred miles or more. Looking southward, a varied country is seen, of hills, plains, mounds, and sandy undulations; but on the whole northern side extensive plains spread out, studded occasionally with variegated peaks and ridges. Far beyond these to the northwestward, and low in the horizon, a silvery stripe appears upon an azure base resembling a list of chalk-white clouds. This is the perennially snow-capped summit of the eastern spur of the Rocky Mountains.

These immense bordering plains and even the hills with which they are interspersed are wholly destitute of timber, except a chance scattering tree upon the margins of the bluffs and ravines, which but scantily serves to variegate the landscape. Not even a buffalo was now to be seen to relieve the dull monotony of the scene; although at some seasons (and particularly in the fall) these prairies are literally strewed with herds of this animal. Then, thousands and tens of thousands might at times be seen from this eminence. But the buffalo is a migratory animal and even in the midst of the prairies where they are generally so very abundant we sometimes travel for days without seeing a single one; though no signs of hunter or Indian can be discovered. To say the truth, however, I have never seen them anywhere upon the prairies so abundant as some travelers have represented—in dense masses, darkening the whole country. I have only found them in scattered herds of a few scores, hundreds, or sometimes thousands in each, and where in the greatest numbers, dispersed far and wide; but with large intervals between. Yet they are very sensibly and rapidly decreasing. There is a current notion that the whites frighten them away; but I would ask, where do they go to? To be sure, to use a hunter's phrase, they frighten a few out of their skins; yet for every one killed by the whites more than a hundred, perhaps a thousand, fall by the hands of the savages. From these, however, there is truly nowhere to flee; for they follow them wheresoever they go: while the poor brutes instinctively learn to avoid the fixed establishments and, to some degree, the regular traveling routes of the whites.

As the caravan was passing under the northern base of the Round Mound it presented a very fine and imposing spectacle to those who were upon its summit. The wagons marched slowly in four parallel columns, but in broken lines, often at intervals of many rods between.

# Commerce of the Prairies

The unceasing crack, crack, of the wagoners' whips, resembling the frequent reports of distant guns, almost made one believe that a skirmish was actually taking place between two hostile parties: and a hostile engagement it virtually was to the poor brutes, at least; for the merciless application of the whip would sometimes make the blood spurt from their sides—and that often without any apparent motive of the wanton *carrettieri*, other than to amuse themselves with the flourishing and loud popping of their lashes!

The rear wagons are usually left without a guard; for all the loose horsemen incline to be ahead, where they are to be seen moving in scattered groups, sometimes a mile or more in advance. As our camp was pitched but a mile west of the Round Mound, those who lingered upon its summit could have an interesting view of the evolutions of "forming" the wagons, in which the drivers by this time had become very expert. When marching four abreast, the two exterior lines spread out and then meet at the front angle; while the two inner lines keep close together until they reach the point of the rear angle, when they wheel suddenly out and close with the hinder ends of the other two; thus systematically concluding a right-lined quadrangle, with a gap left at the rear corner for the introduction of the animals.

Our encampment was in a beautiful plain, but without water, of which, however, we had

had a good supply at noon. Our cattle, as was the usual custom, after having grazed without for a few hours, were now shut up in the pen of the wagons. Our men were all wrapt in peaceful slumber, except the guard, who kept their silent watch around the encampment; when all of a sudden, about the ominous hour of midnight, a tremendous uproar was heard, which caused every man to start in terror from his blanket couch with arms in hand. Some animal, it appeared, had taken fright at a dog and by a sudden start set all around him in violent motion: the panic spread simultaneously throughout the pen; and a scene of rattle, clash, and lumbering ensued which far surpassed everything we had yet witnessed. A general stampede (*estampida*, as the Mexicans say) was the result. Notwithstanding the wagons were tightly bound together, wheel to wheel, with ropes or chains, and several stretched across the gaps at the corners of the *corral*, the oxen soon burst their way out; and though mostly yoked in pairs, they went scampering over the plains, as though Tam O'Shanter's cutty-sark Nannie had been at their tails. All attempts to stop them were vain; for it would require Auld Clootie himself to check the headway of a drove of oxen when once thoroughly frightened. Early the following morning we made active exertions to get up a sufficient quantity of teams to start the caravan. At Rock Creek, a distance of six or seven miles, we were joined by those who had gone in pursuit of the stock. All the oxen were found except some half a dozen, which were never recovered. No mules were lost: a few that had broken through were speedily re-taken. The fact is that though mules are generally easiest scared, oxen are decidedly the worst when once started. The principal advantage of the latter in this respect is that Indians have but little inducement to steal them, and therefore few attempts would be made upon a caravan of oxen.

We were now entering a region of rough, and in some places rocky, road, as the streams which intervene from this to the mountains are all bordered with fine sandstone. These rugged passes acted very severely upon our wagons, as the wheels were by this time becoming loose and shackling, from the shrink of the wood occasioned by the extreme dryness and rarity of this elevated atmosphere. The spokes of some were beginning to reel in the hubs, so that it became necessary to brace them with false spokes, firmly bound with buffalo tug. On some occasions the wagon tires have become so loose upon the felloes as to tumble off while traveling. The most effective mode of tightening slackened tires (at least that most practiced on the plains, as there is rarely a portable forge in company), is by driving strips of hoop-iron around between the tire and felloe—simple wedges of wood are sometimes made to supply the place of iron. During halts I have seen a dozen wheels being repaired at the same time, occasioning such a clitter-clatter of hammers that one would almost fancy himself in a shipyard.

Emerging from this region of asperities, we soon passed the Point of Rocks, as a diminutive spur projecting from the north is called, at the foot of which springs a charming little fount of water. This is but thirty or forty miles from the principal mountains, along whose border similar detached ridges and hills are frequently to be seen. The next day, having descended from the table-plain, we reached the principal branch of the Canadian River,[39] which is here but a rippling brook hardly a dozen paces in width, though eighty miles from its source in the mountains to the north. The bottom being of solid rock, this ford is appropriately called by the Ciboleros *El Vado de Piedras.* The banks are very low and easy to ascend. The stream is called Rio Colorado by the Mexicans, and is known among Americans by its literal translation of Red River. This circumstance perhaps gave rise to the belief that it was the head branch

[39] The Canadian River is about 900 miles long. It rises in the northeastern quarter of New Mexico and runs eastward through northwest Texas and Oklahoma, and enters the Arkansas about forty-five miles above the city of Fort Smith. Its principal affluent is the Rio Nutria, or North Fork of the Canadian, a stream some 600 miles long.

of our main stream of this name:[40] but the nearest waters of the legitimate Red River of Natchitoches are still a hundred miles to the south of this road.

In descending to the Rio Colorado we met a dozen or more of our countrymen from Taos, to which town (sixty or seventy miles distant) there is a direct but rugged route across the mountains. It was a joyous encounter for among them we found some of our old acquaintances whom we had not seen for many years. During our boyhood we had spelled together in the same country school, and roamed the wild woods with a childish glee. They turned about with us and the remainder of our march was passed in answering their inquiries after their relatives and friends in the United States.

Before reaching the stream we encountered another party of visitors, being chiefly customhouse agents or clerks, who, accompanied by a military escort, had come out to guard the

[40] Previous to the year 1820, this *Rio Colorado* seems universally to have been considered as the principal source of *Red River*. But in the expedition of Major Long, during that year, he discovered this to be the head branch of the Canadian. The discovery cost him somewhat dearly too; for striking a branch of the Colorado near the mountains, he followed down its course, believing it to be of the main Red River. He was not fully undeceived until he arrived at its junction with the Arkansas; whereby he failed in a principal object of the expedition—the exploration of the true sources of "Red River of Natchitoches." Gregg.

caravan to the capital. The ostensible purpose of this escort was to prevent smuggling, a company of troops being thus dispatched every year with strict injunctions to watch the caravans. This custom appears since to have nearly grown out of use: and well might it be discontinued altogether, for any one disposed to smuggle would find no difficulty in securing the services of these preventive guards who, for a trifling *douceur*, would prove very efficient auxiliaries, rather than obstacles to the success of any such designs. As we were forming in the valley opposite where the escort was encamped Col. Vizcarra, the commandant, honored us with a salute from his artillery, which was promptly responded to by our little cannon.

Considering ourselves at last out of danger of Indian hostilities (although still nearly a hundred and forty miles from Santa Fé); and not unwilling to give our guard as much trouble as possible, we abandoned the organization of our caravan a few miles beyond the Colorado; its members wending their way to the capital in almost as many detached parties as there were proprietors. The road from this to San Miguel (a town nearly a hundred miles distant) leads in a southwestern direction along the base of, and almost parallel with, that spur of snow-clad mountains which has already been mentioned, bearing down east of the Rio del Norte.

# Commerce of the Prairies

This region is particularly celebrated for violent showers, hail-storms, and frightful thunder-gusts. The sudden cooling and contraction of the atmosphere which follows these falls of rain very often reverses the current of the lower stratum of air; so that a cloud which has just ceased pouring its contents and been wafted away is in a few minutes brought back and drenches the traveler with another torrent. I was deeply impressed with a scene I witnessed in the summer of 1832, about two days' journey beyond the Colorado, which I may be excused for alluding to in this connection. We were encamped at noon when a murky cloud issued from behind the mountains and, after hovering over us for a few minutes, gave vent to one of those tremendous peals of thunder which seem peculiar to those regions, making the elements tremble and leaving us so stunned and confounded that some seconds elapsed before each man was able to convince himself that he had not been struck by lightning. A sulphurous stench filled the atmosphere; but the thunderbolt had skipped over the wagons and lighted upon the *caballada*, which was grazing hard by; some of which were afterward seen stretched upon the plain. It was not a little singular to find an ox lying lifeless from the stroke, while his mate stood uninjured by his side and under the same yoke.

Some distance beyond the Colorado a party of about a dozen (which I joined) left the

wagons to go ahead to Santa Fé. Fifty miles
beyond the main branch of this stream we
passed the last of the Canadian waters, known
to foreigners as the Mora.[41] From thence to the
Gallinas,[42] the first of the Rio del Norte waters,
the road stretches over an elevated plain
unobstructed by any mountainous ridge. At
Gallinas Creek we found a large flock of sheep
grazing upon the adjacent plain; while a little
hovel at the foot of a cliff showed it to be a
*rancho*.[43] A swarthy *ranchero* soon made his
appearance, from whom we procured a treat
of goat's milk, with some dirty ewe's milk
curdle cheese to supply the place of bread.

Some twenty miles from this place we entered San Miguel, the first settlement of any
note upon our route. This consists of irregular
clusters of mud-wall huts and is situated in the
fertile valley of Rio Pecos, a silvery little river
which ripples from the snowy mountains of
Santa Fé—from which city this frontier village

[41] As *mora* means *mulberry*, and this fruit is to be
found at the mouth of this stream, one would suppose
that it had acquired its name from that fact did not the
Mexicans always call it *Rio de lo de Mora*, thus leaving
it to be inferred that the name had originated from
some individual called Mora, who had settled upon it.
Gregg.

[42] Called *Rio de las Gallinas* by *Mexicans*. Though
*Gallina* is literally *hen*, it is here also applied to the
*turkey* (usually with a surname, as *gallina de la tiena*).
It is therefore *Turkey River*. Gregg.

[43] This was the first dwelling in the city of Las Vegas,
whose beginning dates from the year 1835.

is nearly fifty miles to the southeast. The road makes this great southern bend [44] to find a pass-way through the broken extremity of the spur of mountains before alluded to, which from this point south is cut up into detached ridges and table-plains. This mountain section of the road, even in its present unimproved condition, presents but few difficult passes, and might with little labor be put in good order.

A few miles before reaching the city the road again emerges into an open plain. Ascending a table-ridge, we spied in an extended valley to the northwest occasional groups of trees skirted with verdant corn and wheat fields, with here and there a square block-like protuberance reared in the midst. A little farther and just ahead of us to the north irregular clusters of the same opened to our view. "Oh, we are approaching the suburbs!" thought I, on perceiving the cornfields and what I supposed to be brick-kilns scattered in every direction. These and other observations of the same nature becoming audible, a friend at my elbow said, "It is true those are heaps of unburnt bricks, nevertheless they are *houses*—this is the city of Santa Fé."

Five or six days after our arrival the caravan at last hove in sight, and wagon after wagon was seen pouring down the last declivity at about a mile distance from the city. To judge

[44] As does, also, the line of the Atchison, Topeka and Santa Fé Railroad.

from the clamorous rejoicings of the men and the state of agreeable excitement which the muleteers seemed to be laboring under, the spectacle must have been as new to them as it had been to me. It was truly a scene for the artist's pencil to revel in. Even the animals seemed to participate in the humor of their riders, who grew more and more merry and obstreperous as they descended towards the city. I doubt, in short, whether the first sight of the walls of Jerusalem was beheld by the crusaders with much more tumultuous and soul-enrapturing joy.

The arrival produced a great deal of bustle and excitement among the natives. "*Los Americanos!*"—"*Los carros!*"—"*La entrada de caravana!*" were to be heard in every direction; and crowds of women and boys flocked around to see the new-comers; while crowds of *léperos* hung about, as usual, to see what they could pilfer. The wagoners were by no means free from excitement on this occasion. Informed of the ordeal they had to pass, they had spent the previous morning in rubbing up; and now they were prepared, with clean faces, sleek-combed hair, and their choicest Sunday suit to meet the fair eyes of glistening black that were sure to stare at them as they passed. There was yet another preparation to be made in order to show off to advantage. Each wagoner must tie a brand new cracker to the lash of his whip; for on driving through the

streets and the *plaza publica* every one strives
to outvie his comrades in the dexterity with
which he flourishes this favorite badge of his
authority.

Our wagons were soon discharged in the
ware-rooms of the custom house; and a few
days' leisure being now at our disposal, we
had time to take that recreation which a
fatiguing journey of ten weeks had rendered so
necessary. The wagoners and many of the
traders, particularly the novices, flocked to
the numerous fandangoes which are regularly
kept up after the arrival of a caravan. But
the merchants generally were anxiously and
actively engaged in their affairs—striving who
should first get his goods out of the custom
house and obtain a chance at the hard chink of
the numerous country dealers, who annually
resort to the capital on these occasions.

Now comes the harvest for those idle interpreters who make a business of passing goods,
as they term it; for as but a small portion of
the traders are able to write the Spanish language, they are obliged to employ these legal
go-betweens, who pledge themselves for a
stipulated fee to make the arrangements and
translate the *manifiestos* (that is, bills of merchandise to be *manifested* at the custom
house), and to act the part of interpreters
throughout.

The inspection ensues, but this is rarely
carried on with rigid adherence to rules; for

an actuated sympathy for the merchants and a specific desire to promote the trade cause the inspector to open as few of such packages only as will exhibit the least discrepancy with the manifest.

The *derechos de arancel* (tariff imposts) of Mexico are extremely oppressive, averaging about a hundred per cent upon the United States' cost of an ordinary Santa Fé assortment. Those on cotton textures are particularly so. According to the *Arancel* of 1837 (and it was still heavier before), all plain-wove cottons, whether white or printed, pay twelve and a half cents duty per *vara*, besides the *derecho de consumo* (consumption duty), which brings it up to at least fifteen. But it is scarcely necessary to add that there are believed to be very few ports in the Republic at which these rigid exactions are strictly executed. An arrangement—a compromise—is expected, in which the officers are sure at least to provide for themselves. At some ports a custom has been said to prevail of dividing the legal duties into three equal parts: one for the officers—a second for the merchants—the other for the government.

For a few years Gov. Armijo of Santa Fé established a tariff of his own, entirely arbitrary, exacting five hundred dollars for each wagon-load, whether large or small, of fine or coarse goods! Of course this was very advantageous to such traders as had large wagons and costly assortments, while it was no less onerous to those with smaller vehicles or coarse heavy goods. As might have been anticipated, the traders soon took to conveying their merchandise only in the largest wagons, drawn by ten or twelve mules, and omitting the coarser and more weighty articles of trade. This caused the Governor to return to an *ad valorem* system, though still without regard to the *Arancel general* of the nation. How much of these duties found their way into the public treasury I will not venture to assert.

The arrival of a caravan at Santa Fé changes the aspect of the place at once. Instead of the idleness and stagnation which its streets exhibited before, one now sees everywhere the bustle, noise, and activity of a lively market town. As the Mexicans very rarely speak English the negotiations are mostly conducted in Spanish.

Taking the circuit of the stores, I found they usually contained general assortments much like those to be met with in the retail variety stores of the West. The stocks of the inexperienced merchants are apt to abound in unsalable goods—*mulas*, as the Mexicans figuratively term them.

Although a fair variety of dry goods, silks, hardware, etc., is to be found in this market, domestic cottons, both bleached and brown, constitute the great staple, of which nearly equal quantities ought to enter into a Santa Fé assortment. The demand for these goods is such that at least one-half of our stocks of merchandise is made up of them. However, although they afford a greater nominal per centum than many other articles, the profits are reduced by their freight and heavy duty. In all the southern markets where they enter into competition there is a decided preference given to the American manufactures over the British, as the former are more heavy and durable. The demand for calicoes is also considerable, but this kind of goods affords much less profit. The quantity in an assortment should be about equal to half that of domestics. Cotton velvets and drillings (whether bleached, brown, or blue, and especially the latter) have also been in much request. But all the coarser cotton goods, whether shirtings, calicoes, or drillings, etc., were prohibited by the *Arancel* of 1837, and still continue to be, with some modifications.

# Chapter 6

## AN HISTORICAL EXCURSION

HAVING resided for nearly nine years in northern Mexico and enjoyed opportunities for observation which do not always fall to the lot of a trader, it has occurred to me that a few sketches of the country—the first settlements—the early, as well as more recent struggles with the aboriginal inhabitants—their traditions and antiquities—together with some account of the manners and customs of the people, etc., would not be altogether unacceptable to the reader. The dearth of information which has hitherto prevailed on this subject is my best apology for traveling out of my immediate track and trespassing, as it were, upon the department of the regular historian.

The province of New Mexico, of which Santa Fé, the capital, was one of the first establishments, dates among the earliest settlements made in America. By some traditions it is related that a small band of adventurers proceeded thus far north shortly after the capture of the city of Mexico by Hernan Cortes. The historian Mariana speaks of some attempts having been made during the career of this renowned chieftain in America to conquer and take possession of these regions.[45] This, however, is somewhat doubtful; for it is hardly probable that the Spaniards, with all their mania for gold, would have pushed their conquests two thousand miles into the interior at so early a day, traversing the settlements of hostile savages and leaving unexplored intermediate regions, not only more beautiful but far more productive of the precious metals.

Herrera, writing of the events of 1550, mentions New Mexico as a known province lying north of New Galicia, though as yet hardly inhabited by the aborigines. It was probably called New Mexico from the resemblance of its inhabitants to those of the city of Mexico and its environs. They appear to have assimilated in their habits, their agriculture, their manufactures, and their houses; while those of the intermediate country (the Chichimecos, etc.) were in a much ruder state, leading a more wandering life and possessing much less knowledge of agriculture, arts, etc.

The only paper found in the archives at Santa Fé which gives any clue to the first settlement of New Mexico is the memorial of Don Juan de Oñate, a citizen of Zacatecas, dated September 21, 1595, of which I have been furnished with a copy through the politeness of Don Guadalupe Miranda, Secretary of State at Santa Fé. This petition prayed for

[45] New Mexico was first explored by Coronado, whose expedition took place in 1540–42.

the permission and assistance of the vice-regal government at Mexico to establish a colony on the Rio del Norte in the region already known as New Mexico; which having been granted, it was carried into effect, as I infer from the documents, during the following spring.

This appears to have been the first legal colony established in the province; yet we gather from different clauses in Oñate's memorial that an adventurer known as Captain Francisco de Leyva Bonillo had previously entered the province with some followers, without the king's permission, whom Oñate was authorized to arrest and punish. Some historians insist that New Mexico was first visited by a few missionaries in 1581; and there is a tradition in the country which fixes the first settlement in 1583—both having reference, no doubt, to the party of Leyva.

Oñate bound himself to take into New Mexico two hundred soldiers and a sufficiency of provisions for the first year's support of the colony; with abundance of horses, black cattle, sheep, etc., as also merchandise, agricultural utensils, tools, and materials for mechanics' purposes; and all at his own cost, or rather at the ultimate expense of the colonists.

This adventurer, in the course of his memorial, also stipulates for some extraordinary provisions on the part of the king: such as artillery and other arms, ammunitions, etc.—

six priests, with a full complement of books, ornaments, and church accouterments—a loan of $20,000 from the royal treasury—a grant of thirty leagues square of land wheresoever he might choose to select it, with all the vassals (Indians) residing upon it—his family to be ennobled wth the hereditary title of Marquis— the office of governor, with the titles of *Adelantado* and the rank of Captain-General for four generations—a salary of 8,000 ducats of Castile per annum—the privilege of working mines exempt from the usual crown-tax—permission to parcel out the aborigines among his officers and men; and besides other favors to his brothers and relatives, to have "Indians recommended to their charge," which, in other words, was the privilege of making slaves of them to work in the mines—with many other distinctions, immunities, and powers to himself sufficient to establish him in an authority far more despotic than any modern monarch of Europe would venture to assume. And although these exorbitant demands were not all conceded, they go to demonstrate by what incentives of pecuniary interest as well as of honors the Spanish monarchs sought the "*descubrimiento, pacificacion y conversion*," as they modestly termed it, of the poor aborigines of America.

The memorial referred to is extremely lengthy, being encumbered with numerous marginal notes, each containing the decree of assent or dissent of the Viceroy. All this, however, serves rather to illustrate the ancient manners and customs of the Spaniards in those feudal days—the formalities observed in undertaking an exploring and Christianizing enterprise—than to afford any historical data of the expedition.

In every part of this singular document there may be traced evidences of that sordid lust for gold and power which so disgraced all the Spanish conquests in America; and that crusading spirit which martyrized so many thousands of the aborigines of the New World under Spanish authority.

But to return to Oñate: In one article this adventurer or contractor, or whatever else we may choose to call him, inquires, "In case the natives are unwilling to come quietly to the acknowledgment of the true Christian faith, and listen to the evangelical word, and give obedience to the king our sovereign, what shall be done with them? that we may proceed according to the laws of the Catholic Church, and the ordinances of His Majesty. And what tributes that they may be Christianly borne, shall be imposed upon them, as well for the crown as for the adventurers?"—showing that these missionaries (as they were wont to call themselves) not only robbed the Indians of their country and treasure and made menial slaves of them, but exacted tribute beside—promulgated the gospel at the point of the bayonet and administered baptism by force of arms—compelling them to acknowledge the apostolic Roman Catholic faith, of which they had not the slightest idea. Cervantes, who wrote his *Don Quixote* about this time, no doubt intended to make a hit at this cruel spirit of religious bigotry, by making his hero command his captives to acknowledge the superiority of his Dulcinea's beauty over that of all others; and when they protest that they have never seen her, he declares that "the importance consists in this—that without seeing her, you have it to believe, confess, affirm, swear, and defend."

It is much to be regretted that there are no records to be found of the wars and massacres, the numberless incidents and wild adventures which one would presume to have occurred during the first three-quarters of a century of the colonization of New Mexico. It is probable, however, that, as the aborigines seem to have been at first of a remarkably pacific and docile character, the conqueror met with but little difficulty in carrying out his original plans of settlement. Quietly acquiescing in both the civil and religious authority of the invaders, the yoke was easily riveted upon them, as they had neither intelligence nor spirit to resist until goaded to desperation.

The colony had progressed very rapidly, the settlements extending into every quarter of the territory—villages, and even towns of considerable importance were reared in remote sections; of which there now remain but the ruins, with scarce a tradition to tell the fate of the once-flourishing population. Many valuable mines were discovered and worked, as tradition relates, the locations of which have been lost or (as the Mexicans say) concealed by the Indians, in order to prevent a repetition of the brutal outrages they had suffered in them. Whether this was the case or not, they surely had cause enough for wishing to conceal those with which they were acquainted; for in these very mines they had been forced to perform under the lash the most laborious tasks, till human strength could endure no more. Even then, perhaps, they would not have ventured upon resistance but for the instigations of an eloquent warrior from a distant tribe, who pretended to have inherited the power of Montezuma, of whose subjects all these Indians, even to the present day, consider themselves the descendants. Tecumseh-like, our hero united the different tribes and laid the plan of a conspiracy and general massacre of their oppressors; declaring that all who did not enter into the plot should share the fate of the Spaniards. I have been furnished, through the kindness of the Secretary of State before mentioned, with an account of this insurrection and consequent massacre of the Spanish population, taken from the journal of Don Antonio de Otermin, Governor and commandant at the time, which was preserved in the public archives at Santa Fé.

It appears that the night of the 13th of August, 1680, was the time fixed for a general insurrection of all the tribes and *Pueblos*.[46] At a stated hour the massacre of the Spanish population was to commence. Every soul was to be butchered without distinction of sex or age—with the exception of such young and handsome females as they might wish to preserve for wives! Although this conspiracy had evidently been in agitation for a great while, such strict secrecy had been maintained that nothing was known or even suspected till a few days before the appointed time. It is said that not a single woman was let into the secret, for fear of endangering the success of the cause; but it was finally disclosed by two Indian chiefs themselves to the Governor; and about the same time information of the conspiracy was received from some curates and officers of Taos.

Gov. Otermin, seeing the perilous situation of the country, lost no time in dispatching general orders for gathering the people of the south into the Pueblo of Isleta,[47] where the Lieutenant-Governor was stationed, and those of the north and adjacent districts into Santa

[46] A general term for all the *Catholic Indians* of New Mexico and their *villages*. Gregg.

[47] This was on an island in the Rio Grande River, not far from the site of the present Pueblo.

Fé. A considerable number collected in the fortifications of Isleta and many families from the surrounding jurisdictions were able to reach the capital; yet great numbers were massacred on the way; for the Indians, perceiving their plot discovered, did not await the appointed time, but immediately commenced their work of destruction.

General hostilities having commenced, every possible preparation was made for a vigorous defense of the capital. The population of the suburbs had orders to remove to the center and the streets were all barricaded. On the evening of the 10th two soldiers arrived from Taos, having with much difficulty escaped the vigilance of the Indians. They brought intelligence that the Pueblos of Taos had all risen; and that on arriving at La Cañada, they had found the Spaniards well fortified, although a great number of them had been assassinated in the vicinity. The Governor now sent out a detachment of troops to reconnoiter, instructing them to bring away the citizens who remained at La Cañada. They returned on the 12th with the painful information that they had found many dead bodies on their way, that the temples had been plundered and all the stock driven off from the *ranchos*.

The massacre of the Spaniards in many neighboring Pueblos was now unreservedly avowed by the Indians themselves; and as those who remained in Santa Fé appeared in the most imminent danger, the government buildings were converted into a fortification. By this time two friendly Indians who had been dispatched in the direction of Galisteo[48] came in with the intelligence that 500 warriors of the tribe called *Tagnos*[49] were marching towards the city, being even then only about a league distant. By conversing with the enemy the spies had been able to ascertain their temper and their projects. They seemed confident of success—"for the God of the Christians is dead," said they, "but our god, which is the sun, never dies"; adding that they were only waiting the arrival of the *Teguas*,[50] Taosas, and Apaches in order to finish their work of extermination.

Next morning the savages were seen approaching from the south. On their arrival they took up their quarters in the deserted houses of the suburbs with the view of waiting for their expected allies before they laid siege to the city. A parley was soon afterwards held with the chief leaders, who told the Spaniards that they had brought two crosses, of which they might have their choice: one was red, denoting war; the other was white and

[48] This was a Pueblo of the Tanos, a few miles west of Santa Fé. Its ruins are still to be seen near the present small place of the same name.

[49] The *Pecos* and several other populous *Pueblos* to the southward of Santa Fe were *Tagnos*. Gregg.

[50] These embraced nearly all the *Pueblos* between Santa Fé and Taos. Gregg.

professed peace, on the condition of their immediately evacuating the province. The Governor strove to concilate them by offering to pardon all the crimes they had committed provided they would be good Christians and loyal subjects thereafter. But the Indians only made sport of him and laughed heartily at his propositions. He then sent a detachment to dislodge them; but was eventually obliged to turn out in person, with all the efficient men he had. The battle continued the whole day, during which a great number of Indians and some Spaniards were killed. But late in the evening the Teguas, Taosas, and others were seen pouring down upon the city from the north, when the troops had to abandon the advantages they had gained and fly to the defense of the fortifications.

The siege had now continued for nine days, during which the force of the Indians had constantly been on the increase. Within the last forty-eight hours they had entirely deprived the city of water by turning off the stream which had hitherto supplied it; so that the horses and other stock were dying of thirst. The want of water and provisions becoming more and more insupportable every moment, and seeing no chance of rescue or escape, Governor Otermin resolved to make a sortie the next morning and die with sword in hand, rather than perish so miserably for want of supplies. At sunrise he made a desperate charge upon the enemy, whom, notwithstanding the inferiority of his forces, he was soon able to dislodge. Their ranks becoming entirely disordered, more than three hundred were slain and an abundance of booty taken, with forty-seven prisoners, who, after some examination as to the origin of the conspiracy, were all shot. The Spaniards, according to their account of the affair, only had four or five men killed, although a considerable number were wounded—the Governor among the rest.

The city of Santa Fé, notwithstanding a remaining population of at least a thousand souls, could not muster above a hundred able-bodied men to oppose the multitude that beset them, which had now increased to about three thousand. Therefore Governor Otermin, with the advice of the most intelligent citizens in the place, resolved to abandon the city. On the following day they accordingly set out, the greater portion afoot, carrying their own provisions; as there were scarcely animals enough for the wounded. Their march was undisturbed by the Indians, who only watched their movements till they passed Isleta, when nothing more was seen of them. Here they found that those who had been stationed at Isleta had also retreated to the south a few days before. As they passed through the country they found the Pueblos deserted by the Indians, and the Spaniards who pertained to them all massacred.

They had not continued on their march for many days when the caravan became utterly unable to proceed; for they were not only without animals but upon the point of starvation—the Indians having removed from the route everything that could have afforded them relief. In this emergency Otermin dispatched an express to the Lieutenant-Governor, who was considerably in advance, and received from his party a few carts with a supply of provisions. Towards the latter end of September the Governor and his companions in misfortune reached Paso del Norte (about 320 miles south of Santa Fé) where they found the advance party.

The Governor immediately sent an account of the disaster to the Viceroy at Mexico, soliciting reinforcements for the purpose of recovering the lost province, but none arrived till the following year. Meanwhile the refugees remained where they were, and founded, according to the best traditions, the town of El Paso del Norte, so called in commemoration of this retreat, or *passage from the north*.[51] This is in an extensive and fertile valley over which were scattered several Pueblos, all of whom remained friendly to the Spaniards, affording

[51] The town whose founding is here described was across the river from modern El Paso, Texas. The more probable significance of the name, which was in use long prior to 1680, is that here the Rio del Norte (Rio Grande) leaves the mountains for the plains country. See *post*, 242, footnote 97.

them an asylum with provisions and all the necessaries of life.

The following year Governor Otermin was superseded by Don Diego de Vargas Zapata, who commenced the work of reconquering the country. This war lasted for ten years. In 1688, Don Pedro Petrir de Cruzate entered the province and reduced the Pueblo of Zia, which had been famous for its brave and obstinate resistance. In this attack more than six hundred Indians of both sexes were slain, and a large number made prisoners. Among the latter was a warrior named Ojeda, celebrated for valor and vivacity, who spoke good Spanish. This Indian gave a graphic account of all that had transpired since the insurrection.

He said that the Spaniards, and especially the priests, had been assassinated in the most barbarous manner; and particularly alluded to the murder of the curate of Zia, whose fate had been singularly cruel. It appears that on the night of the outbreak, the unsuspecting *padre* being asleep in the convent, the Indians hauled him out, and having stripped him naked, mounted him upon a hog. Then lighting torches, they carried him in that state through the village and several times around the church and cemetery, scourging him all the while most unmercifully! Yet, not even contented with this, they placed the weak old man upon all fours, and mounting upon his back by turns, spurred him through the streets, lashing him without cessation till he expired!

The discord which soon prevailed among the different Pueblos greatly facilitated their second subjugation, which closely followed their emancipation. These petty feuds reduced their numbers greatly and many villages were entirely annihilated, of which history only furnishes the names.

In 1698, after the country had been for some time completely subdued again by the Spaniards, another irruption took place, in which many Pueblos were concerned; but through the energy of Governor Vargas Zapata it was soon quelled.[52]

Since this last effort the Indians have been treated with more humanity, each Pueblo being allowed a league or two of land and permitted to govern themselves. Their rancorous hatred for their conquerors, however, has never entirely subsided, yet no further outbreak took place till 1837, when they joined the Mexican insurgents in another bloody conspiracy. Some time before these tragic events took place it was prophesied among them that a new race was about to appear from the east to redeem them from the Spanish yoke. I heard this spoken of several months before the subject of the insurrection had been seriously agitated.

[52] This outbreak of the natives took place in the year 1696, instead of 1698 as stated by Gregg.

It is probable that the Pueblos built their hopes upon the Americans, as they seemed as yet to have no knowledge of the Texans. In fact, they have always appeared to look upon foreigners as a superior people, to whom they could speak freely of their discontent and their grievances. The truth is the Pueblos in every part of Mexico have always been ripe for insurrection. It is well known that the mass of the revolutionary chief Hidalgo's army had its origin among the Hispano-Mexican population. This grew chiefly out of the change of the federal government to that of *Centralismo* in 1835. A new governor, Col. Albino Perez, was then sent from the city of Mexico to take charge of this isolated department; which was not very agreeable to the sovereign people, as they had previously been ruled chiefly by native governors. Yet while the new form of government was a novelty and did not affect the pecuniary interests of the people it was acquiesced in; but it was now found necessary, for the support of the new organization, to introduce a system of direct taxation, with which the people were wholly unacquainted; and they would sooner have paid a *doblon* through a tariff than a *real* in this way.[53] Yet although the conspiracy had been brewing for some time, no indications of violence were

[53] The doubloon was a gold coin having a value of about sixteen American dollars; the real was a silver coin with a value of about one-eighth of a dollar.

demonstrated until, on account of some mis-
demeanor, an *alcalde* was imprisoned by the
*Prefecto* of the northern district, Don Ramon
Abreu. His honor of the staff was soon liber-
ated by a mob; an occurrence which seemed
as a watchword for a general insurrection.

These new movements took place about the
beginning of August, 1837, and an immense
rabble was soon gathered at La Cañada (a
town some twenty-five miles to the north of
Santa Fé) among whom were to be found the
principal warriors of all the northern Pueblos.
Governor Perez issued orders to the alcaldes
for the assembling of the militia; but all that
could be collected together was about a hundred and fifty men, including the warriors of the
Pueblo of Santo Domingo. With this inadequate force the Governor made an attempt to
march from the capital, but was soon surprised
by the insurgents, who lay in ambush near
La Cañada; when his own men fled to the enemy, leaving him and about twenty-five trusty
friends to make their escape in the best way
they could. Knowing that they would not be
safe in Santa Fé the refugees pursued their
flight southward, but were soon overtaken by
the exasperated Pueblos; when the Governor
was chased back to the suburbs of the city
and savagely put to death. His body was then
stripped and shockingly mangled; his head
was carried as a trophy to the camp of the
insurgents, who made a foot-ball of it among

themselves. I had left the city the day before this sad catastrophe took place, and beheld the Indians scouring the fields in pursuit of their victims, though I was yet ignorant of their barbarous designs. I saw them surround a house and drag from it the Secretary of State, Jesus Maria Alarid, generally known by the sobriquet of El Chico. He and some other principal characters, who had also taken refuge among the *ranchos*, were soon afterwards stripped and scourged and finally pierced through and through with lances, a mode of assassination styled in the vernacular of the country *á lanzadas*. Don Santiago Abreu, formerly Governor and decidedly the most famed character of New Mexico, was butchered in a still more barbarous manner. They cut off his hands, pulled out his eyes and tongue, and otherwise mutilated his body, taunting him all the while with the crimes he was accused of by shaking the shorn members in his face. Thus perished nearly a dozen of the most conspicuous men of the obnoxious party, whose bodies lay for several days exposed to the beasts and birds of prey.

On the 9th of August about two thousand of the insurgent mob, including the Pueblo Indians, pitched their camp in the suburbs of the capital. The horrors of a *saqueo* (or plundering of the city) were now anticipated by every one. The American traders were particularly uneasy, expecting every instant that their lives and property would fall a sacrifice to the ferocity of the rabble. But to the great and most agreeable surprise of all, no outrage of any importance was committed upon either inhabitant or trader. A great portion of the insurgents remained in the city for about two days, during which one of their boldest leaders, José Gonzalez of Taos, a good honest hunter but a very ignorant man, was elected for governor.

The first step of the revolutionists was to seize all the property of their proscribed or murdered victims, which was afterwards distributed among the victors by a decree of the *Asamblea general*—that being the title by which a council of all the alcaldes and the principal characters of the territory was dignified. The families of the unfortunate victims of this revolutionary movement were thus left destitute of everything; and the foreign merchants, who had given the officers credit to a large amount upon the strength of their reputed property and salaries, remained without a single resource with which to cover their demands. As these losses were chiefly experienced in consequence of a want of sufficient protection from the general government, the American merchants drew up a memorial setting forth their claims, which, together with a schedule of the various accounts due, was sent to the Hon. Powhattan Ellis, American minister at Mexico. These demands were certainly of a far more equitable character than many of those which some time after occasioned the French blockade; yet our government has given the unfortunate claimants no hope of redress. Even Mexico did not dispute the justness of these claims, but, on the contrary, she promptly paid to the order of General Armijo a note given by the late Governor Perez to Mr. Sutton, an American merchant, which Armijo had purchased at a great discount.

In the south the Americans were everywhere accused of being the instigators of this insurrection, which was openly pronounced another Texas affair. Their goods were confiscated or sequestered upon the slightest pretexts, or for some pretended irregularity in the accompanying documents; although it was evident that these and other indignities were heaped upon them as a punishment for the occurrence of events which it had not been in their power to prevent. Indeed, these ill-used merchants were not only innocent of any participation in the insurrectionary movements, but had actually furnished means to the government for the purpose of quelling the disturbances.

As I have observed before, the most active agents in this desperate affair were the Pueblo Indians, although the insurgent party was composed of all the heterogeneous ingredients that a Mexican population teems with. The

*rancheros* and others of the lowest class, however, were only the instruments of certain dis-
contented *ricos*, who, it has been said, were in
hope of elevating themselves upon the wreck
of their enemies. Among these was the present
Governor Armijo, an ambitious and turbulent
demagogue, who for some cause or other
seemed anxious for the downfall of the whole
administration.

As soon as Armijo received intelligence of
the catastrophe he hurried to the capital,
expecting, as I heard it intimated by his own
brother, to be elected governor; but, not having
rendered any personal aid, the mobocracy
would not acknowledge his claim to their suf-
frages. He therefore retired, Santa-Anna-like,
to his residence at Albuquerque to plot, in
imitation of his great prototype, some meas-
ures for counteracting the operation of his own
intrigues. In this he succeeded so well that
towards September he was able to collect a
considerable force in the Rio-Abajo, when he
proclaimed a *contra-revolucion* in favor of the
federal government. About the same time the
disbanded troops of the capital under Captain
Caballero made a similar *pronunciamento*, de-
manding their arms and offering their services gratis. The mobocratic dynasty had
gone so far as to deny allegiance to Mexico, and
to propose sending to Texas for protection:
although there had not been any previous
understanding with that Republic.

Armijo now marched to Santa Fé with all his force and Governor Gonzalez, being without an army to support him, fled to the north. After his triumphal entrance into the capital, Armijo caused himself to be proclaimed Governor and *Comandante General*, and immediately dispatched couriers to Mexico with a highly colored account of his own exploits, which procured him a confirmation of those titles and dignities for eight years.

In the meanwhile, news of the insurrection having reached Mexico, the *Escuadron de Vera Cruz* from Zacatecas, consisting of about two hundred dragoons with an equal number of regulars from the *Presidios* of Chihuahua under the command of Colonel Justinani, were ordered to New Mexico. Having arrived at Santa Fé these troops, together with Governor Armijo's little army, marched in January, 1838, to attack the rebels, who by this time had again collected in considerable numbers at La Cañada.

The greatest uneasiness and excitement now prevailed at the capital lest the rabble should again prove victorious, in which case they would not fail to come and sack the city. Foreign merchants had, as usual, the greatest cause for fear, as vengeance had been openly vowed against them for having furnished the government party with supplies. These, therefore, kept up a continual watch, and had everything in readiness for a precipitate flight to the United States. But in a short time their fears were completely dispelled by the arrival of an express with the welcome news of the entire defeat of the insurgents.

It appeared that when the army arrived within view of the insurgent force Armijo evinced the greatest perturbation. In fact, he was upon the point of retiring without venturing an attack, when Captain Muñoz, of the Vera Cruz dragoons, exclaimed: "What's to be done, General Armijo? If your Excellency will but permit me, I will oust that rabble in an instant with my little company alone." Armijo having given his consent, the gallant captain rushed upon the insurgents, who yielded at once and fled precipitately—suffering a loss of about a dozen men, among whom was the deposed Governor Gonzalez, who, having been caught in the town after the skirmish had ended, was instantly shot without the least form of trial.

# Chapter 7

## GEOGRAPHICAL AND ECONOMIC CONDITIONS

NEW MEXICO possesses but few of those natural advantages which are necessary to anything like a rapid progress in civilization. Though bounded north and east by the territory of the United States, south by that of Texas and Chihuahua, and west by Upper California, it is surrounded by chains of mountains and prairie wilds extending to a distance of 500 miles or more, except in the direction of Chihuahua, from which its settlements are separated by an unpeopled desert of nearly two hundred miles—and without a single means of communication by water with any other part of the world.

The whole nominal territory, including those bleak and uninhabitable regions with which it is intersected, comprises about 200,000 square miles—considered, of course, according to its original boundaries, and therefore independently of the claims of Texas to the Rio del Norte. To whichsoever sovereignty that section of land may eventually belong, that portion of it, at least, which is inhabited, should remain united. Any attempt on the part of Texas to make the Rio del Norte the line of demarkation would greatly retard her ultimate acquisition of the territory, as it would leave at least one-third of the population accustomed to the same rule, and bound by ties of consanguinity and affinity of customs, wholly at the mercy of the contiguous hordes of savages that inhabit the Cordilleras on the west of them. This great chain of mountains, which reaches the borders of the Rio del Norte not far above El Paso, would, in my opinion, form the most natural boundary between the two countries from thence northward.

There is not a single navigable stream to be found in New Mexico. The famous Rio del Norte is so shallow, for the most part of the year, that Indian canoes can scarcely float in it. Its navigation is also obstructed by frequent shoals and rippling sections for a distance of more than a thousand miles below Santa Fé. Opposite Taos, especially, for an uninterrupted distance of nearly fifteen miles it runs pent up in a deep *cañon*, through which it rushes in rapid torrents. This frightful chasm is absolutely impassable; and, viewed from the top, the scene is imposing in the extreme. None but the boldest hearts and firmest nerves can venture to its brink and look down its almost perpendicular precipice, over projecting crags and deep crevices, upon the foaming current of the river, which in some places appears like a small, rippling brook, while in others it winds its serpentine course silently but majestically along through a narrow little valley; with immense plains bordering and expanding in every direction, yet so smooth and level that the course of the river is not perceived till within a few yards of the verge. I have beheld this *cañon* from the summit of a mountain, over which the road passes some twenty miles below Taos, from whence it looks like the mere fissure of an insignificant ravine.

Baron Humboldt speaks of an extraordinary event as having occurred in 1752, of which he says the inhabitants of Paso del Norte still preserved the recollection in his day. "The whole bed of the river," says the learned historian, "became dry all of a sudden for more than thirty leagues above and twenty leagues below the Paso: and the water of the river precipitated itself into a newly-formed chasm, and only made its reappearance near the *Presidio* of San Eleazeario. . . . At length, after the lapse of several weeks, the water resumed its course, no doubt because the chasm and the subterraneous conductors had filled up." This, I must confess, savors considerably of the marvelous, as not the least knowledge of these facts appears to have been handed down to the present generation. During very great droughts, however, this river is said to have entirely disappeared in the sand in some places between San Elceario and the Presidio del Norte.

Notwithstanding the numerous tributary streams which would be supposed to pour their contents into the Rio del Norte, very few reach their destination before they are completely exhausted. Rio Puerco, so called from the extreme muddiness of its waters, would seem to form an exception to this rule. Yet this also, although at least a hundred miles in length, is dry at the mouth for a portion of the year. The creek of Santa Fé itself, though a bold and dashing rivulet in the immediate vicinity of the mountains, sinks into insignificance and is frequently lost altogether before it reaches the main river. Pecos and Conchos, its most important inlets, would scarcely be entitled to a passing remark but for the geographical error of Baron Humboldt, who set down the former as the head branch of Red River of Natchitoches. These streams may be considered the first constant-flowing inlets which the Rio del Norte receives from Santa Fé south—say for the distance of five hundred miles! It is then no wonder that this "Great River of the North" decreases in volume of water as it descends. In fact, above the region of tide-water, it is almost everywhere fordable during most of the year, being seldom over knee-deep, except at the time of freshets. Its banks are generally very low, often less than ten feet above low-water mark; and yet, owing to the disproportioned width of the channel (which is generally three or four hundred yards) it is not subject to inundations. Its only important rises are those of the annual freshets, occasioned by the melting of the snow in the mountains.

This river is only known to the inhabitants of northern Mexico as *Rio del Norte*, or North River, because it descends from that direction; yet in its passage southward, it is in some places called *Rio Grande*, on account of its extent; but the name of *Rio Bravo* (Bold or Rapid River) so often given to it on maps, is seldom if ever heard among the people. Though its entire length, following its meanders from its source in the Rocky Mountains to the Gulf of Mexico, must be considerably over two thousand miles, it is hardly navigable to the extent of two hundred miles above its mouth.

The head branch of Pecos, as well as the creeks of Santa Fé and Tezuque, are said to be fed from a little lake which is located on the summit of a mountain about ten miles east of Santa Fé. Manifold and marvelous are the stories related of this lake and its wonderful localities, which although believed to be at least greatly exaggerated, would no doubt induce numbers of travelers to visit this snowbound Elysium were it not for the laboriousness of the ascent. The following graphic account of a pleasure excursion to this celebrated "watering place" is from the memoranda of

Mr. E. Stanley, who spent many years in the New Mexican capital:

"The snow had entirely disappeared from the top of the highest mountains, as seen from Santa Fé, before the first of May, and on the eighteenth we set off on our trip. All were furnished with arms and fishing-tackle—well prepared to carry on hostilities both by land and water. Game was said to be abundant on the way—deer, turkeys, and even the formidable grizzly bear, ready to repel any invasion of his hereditary domain. Santa Fé Creek, we knew, abounded with trout, and we were in hopes of finding them in the lake, although I had been told by some Mexicans that there were no fish in it and that it contained no living thing except a certain nondescript and hideously misshapen little animal. We traveled up the course of the creek about eight miles, and then began to climb the mountain. Our journey now became laborious, the ascent being by no means gradual—rather a succession of hills—some long, others short—some declivitous, and others extremely precipitous. Continuing in this way for six or seven miles, we came to a grove of aspen, thick as cottonwoods in the Missouri bottoms. Through this grove, which extended for nearly a mile, no sound met the ear; no sign of life—not even an insect was to be seen; and not a breath of air was stirring. It was indeed a solitude to be felt. A mile beyond the grove brought us near the lake.

On this last level we unexpectedly met with occasional snow-banks, some of them still two or three feet deep. Being late, we sought out a suitable encampment, and fixed upon a little marshy prairie east of the lake. The night was frosty and cold and ice was frozen nearly an inch thick. Next morning we proceeded to the lake; when, lo—instead of beholding a beautiful sheet of water, we found an ugly little pond with an area of two or three acres—frozen over and one side covered with snow several feet deep. Thus all our hopes of trout and monsters were at an end; and the tracks of a large bear in the snow were all the game we saw during the trip."

Santa Fé, the capital of New Mexico, is the only town of any importance in the province. We sometimes find it written *Santa Fé de San Francisco* (Holy Faith of St. Francis), the latter being the patron or tutelary saint. Like most of the towns in this section of country, it occupies the site of an ancient Pueblo or Indian village, whose race has been extinct for a great many years. Its situation is twelve or fifteen miles east of the Rio del Norte, at the western base of a snow-clad mountain, upon a beautiful stream of small mill-power size, which ripples down in icy cascades and joins the river some twenty miles to the southwestward. The population of the city itself but little exceeds 3,000; yet, including several surrounding villages which are embraced in its corporate jurisdiction, it amounts to nearly 6,000 souls.[54]

The town is very irregularly laid out, and most of the streets are little better than common highways traversing scattered settlements which are interspersed with cornfields nearly sufficient to supply the inhabitants with grain. The only attempt at anything like architectural compactness and precision consists in four tiers of buildings whose fronts are shaded with a fringe of *portales* or *corredores* of the rudest possible description. They stand around the public square, and comprise the *Palacio*, or Governor's house, the Custom House, Barracks (with which is connected the fearful *Calabozo*), the *Casa Consistorial* of the *Alcaldes*, the *Capilla de los Soldados*, or Military Chapel, besides several private residences, as well as most of the shops of the American traders.

The population of New Mexico is almost exclusively confined to towns and villages, the suburbs of which are generally farms. Even most of the individual *ranchos* and *haciendas*

---

[54] The latitude of Santa Fé, as determined by various observations, is 35° 41' (though it is placed on most maps nearly a degree farther north); and the longitude about 106° west from Greenwich. Its elevation above the ocean is nearly 7,000 feet; that of the valley of Taos is over a mile and a half. The highest peak of the mountain (which is covered with perennial snow), some ten miles to the northeast of the capital, is reckoned about 5,000 feet above the town. Those from Taos northward rise still to a much greater elevation. Gregg.

have grown into villages—a result almost indispensable for protection against the marauding savages of the surrounding wilderness. The
principal of these settlements are located in the
valley of the Rio del Norte, extending from
nearly one hundred miles north to about one
hundred and forty south of Santa Fé.[55] The
most important of these, next to the capital,
is *El Valle de Taos*,[56] so called in honor of the
*Taosa* tribe of Indians, a remnant of whom still
forms a *Pueblo* in the north of the valley. No
part of New Mexico equals this valley in
amenity of soil, richness of produce, and beauty
of appearance. Whatever is thrown into its
prolific bosom, which the early frosts of autumn
will permit to ripen, grows to a wonderful
degree of perfection.

Wheat especially has been produced of a
superlative quality and in such abundance
that, as is asserted, the crops have often yielded
over a hundredfold. I would not have it
understood, however, that this is a fair sample of New Mexican soil; for in point of fact,
though many of the bottoms are of very fertile
character, the uplands must chiefly remain

[55] The settlements *up the river* from the capital are
collectively known as *Rio-Arriba*, and those *down the
river* as *Rio-Abajo*. The latter comprise over a third
of the population, and the principal wealth of New
Mexico. Gregg.

[56] The *Valley of Taos*, there being no *town* of this name.
It includes several villages and other settlements, the
largest of which are Fernandez and Los Ranchos. Gregg.

unproductive; owing, in part, to the sterility of the soil, but as much, no doubt, to want of irrigation; hence nearly all the farms and settlements are located in those valleys which may be watered by some constant-flowing stream.[57]

The first settler of the charming valley of Taos since the country was reconquered from the Indians is said to have been a Spaniard named Pando, about the middle of the eighteenth century. This pioneer of the north, finding himself greatly exposed to the depredations of the Comanches, succeeded in gaining the friendship of that tribe by promising his infant daughter, then a beautiful child, to one of their chiefs in marriage. But the unwilling maiden having subsequently refused to ratify the contract, the settlement was immediately attacked by the savages and all were slain except the betrothed damsel, who was led into captivity. After living some years with the Comanches on the great prairies, she was bartered away to the Pawnees, of whom she was eventually purchased by a Frenchman of St. Louis. Some very respectable families in that city are descended from her; and there are many people yet living

[57] For the generally barren and desolate appearance which the uplands of New Mexico present, some of them have possessed an extraordinary degree of fertility; as is demonstrated by the fact that many of the fields on the undulatory lands in the suburbs of Santa Fé have no doubt been in cultivation over two hundred years, and yet produce tolerable crops, without having been once renovated by manure. Gregg.

who remember with what affecting pathos the old lady was wont to tell her tale of woe. She died but a few years ago.

Salubrity of climate is decidedly the most interesting feature in the character of New Mexico. Nowhere—not even under the much-boasted Sicilian skies, can a purer or a more wholesome atmosphere be found. Bilious diseases—the great scourge of the valley of the Mississippi—are here almost unknown. Apart from a fatal epidemic fever of a typhoid character that ravaged the whole province from 1837 to 1839, and which, added to the small-pox that followed in 1840, carried off nearly ten per cent of the population, New Mexico has experienced very little disease of a febrile character; so that as great a degree of longevity is attained there, perhaps, as in any other portion of the habitable world. Persons withered almost to mummies are to be encountered occasionally, whose extraordinary age is only to be inferred from their recollection of certain notable events which have taken place in times far remote.

A sultry day, from Santa Fé north, is of very rare occurrence. The summer nights are usually so cool and pleasant that a pair of blankets constitutes an article of comfort seldom dispensed with. The winters are long, but not so subject to sudden changes as in damper climates; the general change of the thermometer throughout the year being from 10 to 75 above zero, of Fahrenheit. Baron Humboldt was led into as great an error with respect to the climate of New Mexico as to the rivers; for he remarks that near Santa Fé and a little farther north, "the Rio del Norte is sometimes covered for a succession of several years with ice thick enough to admit the passage of horses and carriages": a circumstance which would be scarcely less astounding to the New Mexicans than would the occurrence of a similar event in the harbor of New York be to her citizens.

The great elevation of all the plains about the Rocky Mountains is perhaps the principal cause of the extraordinary dryness of the atmosphere. There is but little rain throughout the year, except from July to October—known as the rainy season; and as the Missouri traders usually arrive about its commencement, the coincidence has given rise to a superstition, quite prevalent among the vulgar, that the Americans bring the rain with them. During seasons of drought, especially, they look for the arrival of the annual caravans as the harbinger of speedy relief.

There has never been an accurate census taken in New Mexico. Of the results of one which was attempted in 1832, the Secretary of State at Santa Fé speaks in the following terms: "At present (1841) we may estimate the Spanish or white population at about 60,000 souls or more, being what remains of 72,000, which the census taken eight or nine years ago showed there then existed in New Mexico." He supposes that this great diminution resulted from the ravages of the frightful diseases already alluded to. The decrease of population from these causes, however, is thus greatly overrated. The discrepancy must find its explanation in the original inaccuracy of the census referred to.

If we exclude the unsubjugated savages, the entire population of New Mexico, including the Pueblo Indians, cannot be set down, according to the best estimates I have been able to obtain, at more than 70,000 souls. These may be divided as follows: white creoles, say 1,000; Mestizos, or mixed creoles, 59,000; and Pueblos, 10,000. Of naturalized citizens, the number is inconsiderable—scarcely twenty; and if we except transient traders, there are not over double as many alien residents. There are no negroes in New Mexico, and consequently neither mulattoes nor *zambos*. In 1803, Baron Humboldt set down the population of this province at 40,200, so that according to this the increase for forty years has barely exceeded one per cent per annum.

Agriculture, like almost everything else in New Mexico, is in a very primitive and unimproved state. A great portion of the peasantry cultivate with the hoe alone—their ploughs (when they have any) being only used for mellow grounds, as they are too rudely constructed to be fit for any other service. Those

I have seen in use are mostly fashioned in this manner: a section of the trunk of a tree eight or ten inches in diameter is cut about two feet long, with a small branch left projecting upwards, of convenient length for a handle. With this a beam is connected to which oxen are yoked. The block, with its fore end sloped downwards to a point, runs flat and opens a furrow similar to that of the common shovel-plough. What is equally worthy of remark is that these ploughs are often made exclusively of wood, without one particle of iron or even a nail to increase their durability.

The *labores* and *milpas* (cultivated fields) are often, indeed most usually, without any enclosure. The owners of cattle are obliged to keep herdsmen constantly with them, else graze them at a considerable distance from the farms; for if any trespass is committed upon the fields by stock, the proprietor of the latter is bound to pay damages: therefore, instead of the cultivator's having to guard his crop from the cattle as with us, the owners of these are bound to guard them from the crops. Only a chance farm is seen fenced with poles scattered along on forks, or a loose hedge of brush. Mud fences, or walls of very large *adobes*, are also occasionally to be met with.

The necessity of irrigation has confined, and no doubt will continue to confine, agriculture principally to the valleys of the constant-flowing streams. In some places the crops are frequently cut short by the drying up of the streams. (Where water is abundant, however, art has so far superseded the offices of nature in watering the farms that it is almost a question whether the interference of nature in the matter would not be a disadvantage.) On the one hand the husbandman need not have his grounds overflowed if he administers the water himself, much less need he permit them to suffer from drought. He is therefore more sure of his crop than if it were subject to the caprices of the weather in more favored agricultural regions.

One *acequia madre* (mother ditch) suffices generally to convey water for the irrigation of an entire valley, or at least for all the fields of one town or settlement. This is made and kept in repair by the public, under the supervision of the alcaldes; laborers being allotted to work upon it as with us upon our county roads. The size of this principal ditch is, of course, proportioned to the quantity of land to be watered. It is conveyed over the highest part of the valley, which, on these mountain streams, is for the most part next to the hills. From this, each proprietor of a farm runs a minor ditch in like manner, over the most elevated part of his field. Where there is not a superabundance of water, which is often the case on the smaller streams, each farmer has his day, or portion of a day, allotted to him for irrigation; and at no other time is he permitted to extract water from the *acequia madre*. Then the cultivator, after letting the water into his minor ditch, dams this, first at one point and then at another, so as to overflow a section at a time, and with his hoe depressing eminences and filling sinks he causes the water to spread regularly over the surface. Though the operation would seem tedious, an expert irrigator will water in one day his five or six-acre field, if level, and everything well arranged; yet on uneven ground he will hardly be able to get over half of that amount.[58]

All the *acequias* for the valley of the Rio del Norte are conveyed from the main stream, except where a tributary of more convenient water happens to join it. As the banks of the river are very low and the descent considerable, the water is soon brought upon the surface by a horizontal ditch along an inclined bank, commencing at a convenient point of constant-flowing water—generally without dam, except sometimes a wing of stones to turn the current into the canal.

[58] There is no land measure here corresponding to our acres. Husbandmen rate their fields by the amount of wheat necessary to sow them; and thus speak of a *fanega* of land—*fanega* being a measure of about two bushels—meaning an extent which two bushels of wheat will suffice to sow. Tracts are usually sold by the number of *leguas* (leagues), or *varas* front of irrigable lands; for those back from the streams are considered worthless. The *vara* is nearly 33 English inches; 5,000 of which constitute the Mexican league—under two miles and two-thirds. Gregg.

The staple productions of the country are emphatically Indian corn and wheat. The former grain is most extensively employed for making *tortillas*—an article of food greatly in demand among the people, the use of which has been transmitted to them by the aborigines. The corn is boiled in water with a little lime: and when it has been sufficiently softened, so as to strip it of its skin, it is ground into paste upon the *metate*,[59] and formed into a thin cake. This is afterwards spread on a small sheet of iron or copper called *comal* (*comalli*, by the Indians) and placed over the fire, where in less than three minutes it is baked and ready for use. The thinness of the tortilla is always a great test of skill in the maker, and much rivalry ensues in the art of preparation. The office of making tortillas has from the earliest times pertained chiefly to the women, who appear to be better adapted to this employ than the other sex, both as regards skill and dexterity in preparing this particular food for the table. I perfectly agree with the historian Clavigero,[60] however, in the opinion that "although this species of

[59] From the Indian word *metatl*, a hollowed oblong stone used as a grinding-machine. Gregg.

[60] Francisco Xavier Clavigero was born in Mexico in 1731 and, entering the Jesuit order, became a teacher of history in the Jesuit College in Mexico. Following the expulsion of the order in 1767 he went to Italy. In 1780 his history of Mexico was published, and in 1789 (two years after his death) his history of California.

corn-bread may be very wholesome and substantial, and well-flavored when newly-made,
it is unpleasant when cold.''

A sort of thin mush called *atole,* made of
Indian meal, is another sort of diet the preparation of which is from the aborigines; and
such is its nationality that in the north it is
frequently called *el café de los Mexicanos* (the
coffee of the Mexicans). How general soever
the use of coffee among Americans may appear,
that of *atole* is still more so among the lower
classes of Mexicans. They virtually breakfast,
dine, and sup upon it. Of this, indeed, with
*frijoles* and *chile* (beans and red pepper), consists their principal food. The extravagant
use of red pepper among the Mexicans has become truly proverbial. It enters into nearly
every dish at every meal, and often so predominates as entirely to conceal the character
of the viands. It is likewise ground into a
sauce, and thus used even more abundantly
than butter. *Chile verde* (green pepper), not
as a mere condiment, but as a salad, served up
in different ways, is reckoned by them one of
the greatest luxuries. But however much we
may be disposed to question their taste in this
particular, no one can hesitate to do homage
to their incomparable chocolate, in the preparation of which the Mexicans surely excel every
other people.

Besides these, many other articles of diet
peculiar to the country, and adopted from the

aborigines, are still in use—often of rich and exquisite flavor, and though usually not much relished at first by strangers, they are for the most part highly esteemed after a little use.

The rancheros and all the humbler classes of people very seldom use any table for their meals, an inconvenience which is very little felt, as the dishes are generally served out from the kitchen in courses of a single plate to each guest, who usually takes it upon his knees. Knives and forks are equally dispensed with, the viands being mostly hashed or boiled so very soft as to be eaten with a spoon. This is frequently supplied by the *tortilla*, a piece of which is ingeniously doubled between the fingers so as to assist in the disposal of anything, be it ever so rare or liquid. Thus it may well be said, as in the story of the oriental monarch, that these rancheros employ a new spoon for every mouthful: for each fold of the tortilla is devoured with the substance it conveys to the mouth.

The very singular custom of abstaining from all sorts of beverages during meals has frequently afforded me a great deal of amusement. Although a large cup of water is set before each guest, it is not customary to drink it off till the repast is finished. Should any one take it up in his hand while in the act of eating, the host is apt to cry out, "Hold, hold! there is yet more to come." I have never been able to ascertain definitely the meaning of this peculiarity;

but from the strictness with which it is observed, it is natural to suppose that the use of any kind of drink whilst eating is held extremely unwholesome.[61] The New Mexicans use but little wine at meals, and that exclusively of the produce of the Paso del Norte.

But to return to the productions of the soil. Cotton is cultivated to no extent, although it has always been considered as indigenous to the country; while the ancient manufactures of the aborigines prove it to have been especially so in this province. Flax is entirely neglected, and yet a plant resembling in every respect that of the *linum usitatissimum*, is to be found in great abundance in many of the mountain valleys. The potato (*la papa*), although not cultivated in this country till very lately, is unquestionably an indigenous plant, being still found in a state of nature in many of the mountain valleys—though of small size, seldom larger than filberts: whence it appears that this luxury had not its exclusive origin in South America, as is the current opinion of the present day. Universal as the use of tobacco is among these people, there is very little of it grown, and that chiefly of a light and weak species, called by the natives *punche*, which is also indigenous, and still to be met with growing

[61] What also strikes the stranger as a singularity in that country is that the females rarely ever eat with the males—at least in the presence of strangers—but usually take their food in the kitchen by themselves. Gregg.

wild in some places. What has in a great measure contributed to discourage people from attending to the cultivation of the tobacco plant is the monopoly of this indispensable by the federal government; for although the tobacco laws are not enforced in New Mexico (there being no *Estanquillo*, or public store-house), yet the people cannot carry it anywhere else in the Republic for sale without risk of its being immediately confiscated. A still more powerful cause operating against this, as well as every other branch of agriculture in New Mexico, is the utter want of navigable streams as a cheap and convenient means of transportation to distant markets.

Famous as the republic of Mexico has been for the quality and variety of its fruits, this province, considering its latitude, is most singularly destitute in this respect. A few orchards of apples, peaches, and apricots are occasionally met with, but these are of very inferior quality, being only esteemed in the absence of something better. A few small vineyards are also to be found in the valley of the Rio del Norte, but the grape does not thrive as at El Paso. The mode of cultivating the grape in these parts is somewhat peculiar, and might, I have no doubt, be practiced to great advantage in other countries. No scaffold or support of any kind is erected for the vines, which are kept pruned so as to form a sort of shrubbery. Every fall of the year these are completely covered with earth, which protects them during the winter. Upon the opening of spring the dirt is scraped away and the vines pruned again. This being repeated from year to year, the shrubs soon acquire sufficient strength to support the heavy crops of improved and superiorly-flavored grapes which they finally produce.

Indigenous wild fruits are not quite so scarce, a clear evidence that the lack of cultivated fruit is not so much the fault of nature as the result of indolence and neglect on the part of the people. The prickly pear is found in greatest abundance and of several varieties: and though neither very wholesome nor savory, it is nevertheless frequently eaten.

There is but little timber in New Mexico, except in the mountains and along the watercourses; the table-plains and valleys are generally all open prairie. The forest growths, moreover, of all the north of Mexico present quite a limited variety of timber, among which a species of pitch-pine mostly predominates. The tree which appears to be most peculiar to the country is a kind of scrub pine called *piñon*, which grows generally to the height of twenty or thirty feet, with leaves ever-green and pine-like, but scarcely an inch long. From the surface of this tree exudes a species of turpentine resembling that of the pitch-pine, but perhaps less resinous. The wood is white and firm and much used for fuel. The most remarkable appendage of this tree is the fruit it bears, which is also known by the same name. This is a little nut about the size of a kidney-bean, with a rich oily kernel in a thin shell, enclosed in a chestnut-like bur. It is of pleasant flavor and much eaten by the natives, and considerable quantities are exported annually to the southern cities. It is sometimes used for the manufacture of a certain kind of oil, said to be very good for lamps.

The *mezquite* tree, vulgarly called *muskeet* in Texas, where it has attained some celebrity, grows in some of the fertile valleys of Chihuahua to the height of thirty and forty feet, with a trunk of one to two feet in diameter. The wood makes excellent fuel, but it is seldom used for other purposes as it is crooked, knotty, and very coarse and brittle, more resembling the honey-locust (of which it might be considered a scrubby species) than the mahogany, as some people have asserted. The fruit is but a diminutive honey-locust in appearance and flavor, of the size and shape of a flattened bean-pod, with the seeds disposed in like manner. This pod, which, like that of the honey-locust, encloses a glutinous substance, the Apaches and other tribes of Indians grind into flour to make their favorite *pinole*. The mezquite seems undoubtedly of the *Acacia Arabica* species; as some physicians who have examined the gum which exudes from the tree pronounce it genuine Arabic.

On the water-courses there is little timber to be found except cottonwood, scantily scattered along their banks. Those of the Rio del Norte are now nearly bare throughout the whole range of the settlements, and the inhabitants are forced to resort to the distant mountains for most of their fuel. But nowhere, even beyond the settlements, are there to be seen such dense cottonwood bottoms as those of the Mississippi Valley. Besides the common cottonwood there is another to be found upon the mountain streams of New Mexico, which has been called willow-leaf or bitter cottonwood (*populus angustifolia?*) and has been reckoned by some a species of cinchona, yet for no other reason, perhaps, than that the bark possesses efficacious tonic qualities. Attached to the seeds of this tree is also a cotton similar to that of the sweet cottonwood, or *populus angulata*.

Among the wild productions of New Mexico is the *palmilla*—a species of palmetto, which might be termed the *soap-plant*—whose roots, as well as those of another species known as *palma* (or palm), when bruised, form a saponaceous pulp called *amole*, much used by the natives for washing clothes, and said to be even superior to soap for scouring woolens.

But by far the most important indigenous product of the soil of New Mexico is its pasturage. Most of the high table-plains afford the finest grazing in the world, while, for want of water, they are utterly useless for most other purposes. That scanty moisture which suffices to bring forth the natural vegetation is insufficient for agricultural productions, without the aid of irrigation. The high prairies of all northern Mexico differ greatly from those of our border in the general character of their vegetation. They are remarkably destitute of the gay flowering plants for which the former are so celebrated, being mostly clothed with different species of a highly nutritious grass called *grama*, which is of a very short and curly quality. The highlands, upon which alone this sort of grass is produced, being seldom verdant till after the rainy season sets in, the *grama* is only in perfection from August to October. But being rarely nipped by the frost until the rains are over, it cures upon the ground and remains excellent hay—equal if not superior to that which is cut and stacked from our western prairies. Although the winters are rigorous, the feeding of stock is almost entirely unknown in New Mexico; nevertheless, the extensive herds of the country, not only of cattle and sheep, but of mules and horses, generally maintain themselves in excellent condition upon the dry pasturage alone through the cold season, and until the rains start up the green grass again the following summer.[62]

[62] At this point in Gregg's narrative follow eight chapters of a general descriptive and social nature which we omit to reprint. Our Chapter 8 which follows is Chapter 1, Volume two, of the work as originally printed.

# Chapter 8

I DO not propose to detain the reader with an account of my journeyings between Mexico and the United States during the seven years subsequent to my first arrival at Santa Fé. I will here merely remark that I crossed the plains to the United States in the fall of 1833 and 1836, and returned to Santa Fé with goods each succeeding spring. It was only in 1838, however, that I eventually closed up my affairs in northern Mexico and prepared to take my leave of the country, as I then supposed, forever. But in this I was mistaken, as will appear in the sequel.

The most usual season for the return of the caravans to the United States is the autumn, and not one has elapsed since the commencement of the trade which has not witnessed some departure from Santa Fé with that destination. They have also crossed occasionally in the spring, but without any regularity or frequency and generally in very small parties. Even the fall companies, in fact, are small when compared with the outward-bound caravans; for besides the numbers who remain permanently in the country, many of those who trade southward return to the United States *via*

Matamoros or some other southern port. The return parties of autumn are therefore comparatively small, varying in number from fifty to a hundred men. They leave Santa Fé some four or five weeks after their arrival—generally about the first of September. In these companies there are rarely over thirty or forty wagons; for a large portion of those taken out by the annual caravans are disposed of in the country.

Some of the traders who go out in the spring return the ensuing fall, because they have the good fortune to sell off their stock promptly and to advantage: others are compelled to return in the fall to save their credit; nay, to preserve their homes, which, especially in the earlier periods, have sometimes been mortgaged to secure the payment of the merchandise they carried out with them. In such cases their goods were not unfrequently sold at great sacrifice to avoid the penalties which the breaking of their engagements at home would involve. New adventurers, too, are apt to become discouraged with an unanticipated dullness of times, and not unfrequently sell off at wholesale for the best price they can get, though often at a serious loss. But those who are regularly engaged in this trade usually calculate upon employing a season—perhaps a year, in closing an enterprise—in selling off their goods and making their returns.

156

# Commerce of the Prairies

The wagons of the return caravans are generally but lightly laden: one to two thousand pounds constitute the regular return cargo for a single wagon; for not only are the teams unable to haul heavy loads, on account of the decay of pasturage at this season, but the approaching winter compels the traders to travel in greater haste; so that this trip is usually made in about forty days. The amount of freight, too, from that direction is comparatively small. The remittances, as has already been mentioned, are chiefly in specie or gold and silver bullion. The gold is mostly dust, from the placer or gold mine near Santa Fé: the silver bullion is all from the mines of the south—chiefly from those of Chihuahua. To these returns may be added a considerable number of mules and asses—some buffalo rugs, furs, and wool,—which last barely pays a return freight for the wagons that would otherwise be empty. Coarse Mexican blankets, which may be obtained in exchange for merchandise, have been sold in small quantities to advantage on our border.

On the 4th of April, 1838, we departed from Santa Fé. Our little party was found to consist of twenty-three Americans, with twelve Mexican servants. We had seven wagons, one dearborn, and two small field pieces, besides a large assortment of small arms. The principal proprietors carried between them about $150,000 in specie and bullion, being for the most part the proceeds of the previous year's adventure.

We moved on at a brisk and joyous pace until we reached Ocate Creek, a tributary of the Colorado,[63] a distance of a hundred and thirty miles from Santa Fé, where we encountered a very sudden bereavement in the death of Mr. Langham, one of our most respected proprietors. This gentleman was known to be in weak health, but no fears were entertained for his safety. We were all actively engaged in assisting the more heavily laden wagons over the miry stream, when he was seized with a fit of apoplexy and expired instantly. As we had not the means of giving the deceased a decent burial, we were compelled to consign him to the earth in a shroud of blankets. A grave was accordingly dug on an elevated spot near the north bank of the creek, and on the morning of the 13th, ere the sun had risen in the east, the mortal remains of this most worthy man and valued friend were deposited in their last abode, without a tomb-stone to consecrate the spot, or an epitaph to commemorate his virtues. The deceased was from St. Louis, though he

[63] Ocate Creek, in Mora County, New Mexico, is in fact a tributary of one of the affluents of the Canadian, a stream to which the Mexicans applied the name Colorado. Readers of *The Southwestern Expedition of Zebulon M. Pike* will hardly need to be reminded of the ignorance which prevailed among Americans in the early nineteenth century concerning the geography and the river courses of the Southwest.

had passed the last eleven years of his life in Santa Fé, during the whole of which period he had seen neither his home nor his relatives.

The melancholy rites being concluded, we resumed our line of march. We now continued for several days without the occurrence of any important accident or adventure. On the 19th we encamped in the Cimarron Valley, about twelve miles below Willow Bar. The very sight of this desolate region, frequented as it is by the most savage tribes of Indians, was sufficient to strike dismay into the hearts of our party; but as we had not as yet encountered any of them, we felt comparatively at ease. Our mules and horses were staked as usual around the wagons, and every man, except the watch, betook himself to his blanket, in anticipation of a good night's rest. The hour of midnight had passed away, and nothing had been heard except the tramping of the men on guard, and the peculiar grating of the mules' teeth, nibbling the short grass of the valley. Ere long, however, one of our sentinels got a glimpse of some object moving stealthily along, and as he was straining his eyes to ascertain what sort of apparition it could be, a loud Indian yell suddenly revealed the mystery. This was quickly followed by a discharge of firearms, and the shrill note of the Pawnee whistle, which at once made known the character of our visitors. As usual, the utmost confusion prevailed in our camp: some, who had been snatched from the land of dreams, ran their heads against the wagons—others called out for their guns while they had them in their hands. During the height of the bustle and uproar, a Mexican servant was observed leaning with his back against a wagon and his fusil elevated at an angle of forty-five degrees, cocking and pulling the trigger without ceasing, and exclaiming at every snap, "*Carajo, no sirve!*"— "Curse it, it's good for nothing."

The firing still continued—the yells grew fiercer and more frequent; and everything betokened the approach of a terrible conflict. Meanwhile a number of persons were engaged in securing the mules and horses which were staked around the encampment; and in a few minutes they were all shut up in the *corral*—a hundred head or more in a pen formed by seven wagons. The enemy failing in their principal object—to frighten off our stock, they soon began to retreat; and in a few minutes nothing more was to be heard of them. All that we could discover the next morning was, that none of our party had sustained any injury, and that we had not lost a single animal.

The Pawnees have been among the most formidable and treacherous enemies of the Santa Fé traders. But the former have also suffered a little in turn from the caravans. In 1832 a company of traders were approached by a single Pawnee chief, who commenced a parley with them, when he was shot down by a Pueblo Indian of New Mexico who happened to be with the caravan. Though this cruel act met with the decided reprobation of the traders generally, yet they were of course held responsible for it by the Indians.

On our passage this time across the prairie ocean which lay before us, we ran no risk of getting bewildered or lost, for there was now a plain wagon trail across the entire stretch of our route, from the Cimarron to the Arkansas River.

This track, which has since remained permanent, was made in the year 1834. Owing to continuous rains during the passage of the caravan of that year, a plain trail was then cut in the softened turf, on the most direct route across this arid desert, leaving the Arkansas about twenty miles above the Caches. This has ever since been the regular route of the caravans; and thus a recurrence of those distressing sufferings from thirst, so frequently experienced by early travelers in that inhospitable region, has been prevented.

We forded the Arkansas without difficulty and pursued our journey to the Missouri border with comparative ease; being only now and then disturbed at night by the hideous howlings of wolves, a pack of which had constituted themselves into a kind of guard of honor and followed in our wake for several hundred miles —in fact to the very border of the settlements.

They were at first attracted no doubt by the remains of buffalo which were killed by us upon the high plains, and afterwards enticed on by an occasional fagged animal, which we were compelled to leave behind, as well as by the bones and scraps of food which they picked up about our camps. Not a few of them paid the penalty of their lives for their temerity.

Had we not fortunately been supplied with a sufficiency of meat and other provisions, we might have suffered of hunger before reaching the settlements; for we saw no buffalo after crossing the Arkansas River. It is true that owing to their disrelish for the long dry grass of the eastern prairies the buffalo are rarely found so far east in autumn as during the spring; yet I never saw them so scarce in this region before. In fact, at all seasons they are usually very abundant as far east as our point of leaving the Arkansas River.

Upon reaching the settlements I had an opportunity of experiencing a delusion which had been the frequent subject of remark by travelers on the prairies before. Accustomed as we had been for some months to our little mules and the equally small-sized Mexican ponies, our sight became so adjusted to their proportions that when we came to look upon the commonest hackney of our frontier horses it appeared to be almost a monster. I have frequently heard exclamations of this kind from the new arrivals: "How the Missourians have improved their breed of horses!" "What a huge gelding!" "Did you ever see such an animal!" This delusion is frequently availed of by the frontiersmen to put off their meanest horses to these deluded travelers for the most enormous prices.

On the 11th of May we arrived at Independence, after a propitious journey of only thirty-eight days.[64] We found the town in a thriving condition, although it had come very near being laid waste a few years before by the Mormons, who had originally selected this section of the country for the site of their New Jerusalem. In this they certainly displayed far more taste and good sense than they are generally supposed to be endowed with:[65] for the rich and beautiful uplands in the vicinity of Independence might well be denominated the garden spot of the Far West. Their principal motive for preferring the border country, however, was no doubt a desire to be in the immediate vicinity of the Indians, as the

[64] At this point in the original narrative is appended a footnote table of distances and camp-sites from Independence to Santa Fé, which we omit to reprint.

[65] The sketch of early Mormonism which follows is animated by the prejudice entertained by Gregg's fellow-gentile Missourians toward the obnoxious sect. It is in many respects inadequate, viewed as a history of Mormonism in Missouri, yet it is valuable from the viewpoint of reflecting contemporary gentile opinion on the subject.

reclamation of the lost tribes of Israel was a part of their pretended mission.

Prior to 1833 the Mormons, who were then flocking in great swarms to this favored region, had made considerable purchases of lots and tracts of land both in the town of Independence and in the adjacent country. A general depot, profanely styled the Lord's Store, was established, from which the faithful were supplied with merchandise at moderate prices; while those who possessed any surplus of property were expected to deposit it in the same for the benefit of the mass. The Mormons were at first kindly received by the good people of the country, who looked upon them as a set of harmless fanatics, very susceptible of being moulded into good and honest citizens. This confidence, however, was not destined to remain long in the ascendant, for they soon began to find that the corn in their cribs was sinking like snow before the sun-rays, and that their hogs and their cattle were by some mysterious agency rapidly disappearing. The new-comers also drew upon themselves much animadversion in consequence of the immorality of their lives, and in particular their disregard for the sacred rites of marriage.

Still they continued to spread and multiply, not by conversion but by immigration, to an alarming extent; and in proportion as they grew strong in numbers they also became more exacting and bold in their pretensions. In a little paper printed at Independence under their immediate auspices everything was said that could provoke hostility between the Saints and their worldly neighbors, until at last they became so emboldened by impunity as openly to boast of their determination to be the sole proprietors of the Land of Zion; a revelation to that effect having been made to their prophet.

The people now began to perceive that at the rate the intruders were increasing they would soon be able to command a majority of the country, and consequently the entire control of affairs would fall into their hands. It was evident, then, that one of the two parties would in the course of time have to abandon the country; for the old settlers could not think of bringing up their families in the midst of such a corrupt state of society as the Mormons were establishing. Still the nuisance was endured very patiently, and without any attempt at retaliation, until the Saints actually threatened to eject their opponents by main force. This last stroke of impudence at once roused the latent spirit of the honest backwoodsmen, some of whom were of the pioneer settlers of Missouri, and had become familiar with danger in their terrific wars with the savages. They were therefore by no means appropriate subjects for yielding what they believed to be their rights. Meetings were held for the purpose of devising means of redress, which only tended to increase the insolence of the Mormons. Finally a mob was collected which proceeded at once to raze the obnoxious printing establishment to the ground, and to destroy all the materials they could lay hands upon. One or two of the Mormon leaders who fell into the hands of the people were treated to a clean suit of tar and feathers, and otherwise severely punished. The Prophet Joseph, however, was not then in the neighborhood. Having observed the storm-clouds gathering apace in the frontier horizon he very wisely remained in Ohio, whence he issued his flaming mandates.

These occurrences took place in the month of October, 1833, and I reached Independence from Santa Fé while the excitement was raging at its highest. The Mormons had rallied some ten miles west of the town, where their strongest settlements were located. A hostile encounter was hourly expected: nay, a skirmish actually took place shortly after, in which a respectable lawyer of Independence, who had been an active agent against the Mormons, was killed. In short, the whole country was in a state of dreadful fermentation.

Early on the morning after the skirmish just referred to, a report reached Independence that the Mormons were marching in a body towards the town, with the intention of sacking and burning it. I had often heard the cry of "Indians!" announcing the approach of hostile savages, but I do not remember ever to have witnessed so much consternation as prevailed at Independence on this memorable occasion. The note of alarm was sounded far and near, and armed men eager for the fray were rushing in from every quarter. Officers were summarily selected without deference to rank or station: the spirit-stirring drum and the ear-piercing fife made the air resound with music, and a little army of as brave and resolute a set of fellows as ever trod a field of battle was, in a very short time, paraded through the streets. After a few preliminary exercises they started for a certain point on the road where they intended to await the approach of the Mormons. The latter very soon made their appearance, but surprised at meeting with so formidable a reception they never even attempted to pull a trigger, but at once surrendered at discretion. They were immediately disarmed, and subsequently released upon condition of their leaving the country without delay.

It was very soon after this affair that the much talked of phenomenon of the meteoric shower (on the night of November 12th) occurred. This extraordinary visitation did not fail to produce its effects upon the superstitious minds of a few ignorant people, who began to wonder whether, after all, the Mormons might not be in the right; and whether this was not a sign sent from heaven as a remonstrance for the injustice they had been guilty of towards that chosen sect.[66] Some time afterward a terrible misfortune occurred which was in no way calculated to allay the superstitious fears of the ignorant. As some eight or ten citizens were returning with the ferryboat which had crossed the last Mormons over the Missouri River into Clay County, the district selected for their new home, the craft filled with water and sank in the middle of the current; by which accident three or four men were drowned. It was owing, perhaps, to the craziness of the boat, yet some persons suspected the Mormons of having scuttled it by secretly boring auger-holes in the bottom just before they had left it.

After sojourning a few months in Clay County, to the serious annoyance of the inhabitants (though, in fact, they had been kindly received at first), the persecuted Latter Day Saints were again compelled to shift their quarters farther off. They now sought to establish themselves in the new county of Caldwell, and founded their town of Far West, where they lingered in comparative peace for a few years. As the county began to fill up

[66] In northern Mexico, as I learned afterwards, the credulity of the superstitious was still more severely tried by this celestial phenomenon. Their Church had been deprived of some important privileges by the Congress but a short time before, and the people could not be persuaded but that the meteoric shower was intended as a curse upon the nation in consequence of that sacrilegious act. Gregg.

with settlers, however, quarrels repeatedly broke out, until at last in 1838 they found themselves again at open war with their neighbors. They appear to have set the laws of the state at defiance, and to have acted so turbulently throughout that Governor Boggs deemed it necessary to order out a large force of state militia to subject them: which was easily accomplished without bloodshed. From that time the Mormons have harbored a mortal enmity towards the Governor: and the attempt which was afterwards made to assassinate him at Independence is generally believed to have been instigated, if not absolutely perpetrated, by that deluded sect.[67]

Being once more forced to emigrate, they passed into Illinois, where they founded the famous City of Nauvoo.[68] It would seem that their reception from the people of this state was even more strongly marked with kindness and indulgence than it had been elsewhere, being generally looked upon as the victims of persecution on account of their religious belief;

[67] Governor Boggs was shot at his house in Independence in 1841, supposedly by a Mormon fanatic, but the individual accused of the crime was acquitted and the identity of the criminal was never established. By anti-Mormons Joseph Smith, the leader of the Mormon sect, was accused, probably unjustly, of having instigated the crime.

[68] This occurred some time prior to the attempted assassination of Governor Boggs. Nauvoo, the Mormon capital in Illinois, was made a stake of the church in the autumn of 1839.

yet it appears that the good people of Illinois have since become about as tired of them as were any of their former neighbors. It seems very clear then, that fanatical delusion is not the only sin which stamps the conduct of these people with so much obliquity, or they would certainly have found permanent friends somewhere; whereas it is well known that a general aversion has prevailed against them wherever they have sojourned.

Before concluding this chapter it may be proper to remark that the Mormons have invariably refused to sell any of the property they had acquired in Missouri, but have on the contrary expressed a firm determination to reconquer their lost purchases. Of these, a large lot, situated on an elevated point at Independence, known as the Temple Lot, upon which the Temple of Zion was to have been raised, has lately been profaned by cultivation, having been converted into a corn-field! [69]

[69] Over the legal title of this property the Utah branch of Mormonism and its principal rival faction, the Reorganized Church of Latter Day Saints, waged a notable legal contest, which was won by the latter. Within a few years past the Reorganized Church has formally established its headquarters at Independence. It is non-polygamous, claims to be the true Mormon church (a claim which in so far as property rights are concerned has been upheld by the United States courts), and has about 100,000 members. The Brighamite or Utah faction of Mormonism is supposed to have upwards of half a million present-day adherents.

# Chapter 9

A N unconquerable propensity to return to prairie life inclined me to embark in a fresh enterprise. The blockade of the Mexican ports by the French also offered strong inducements for undertaking such an expedition in the spring of 1839; for as Chihuahua is supplied principally through the seaports, it was now evident that the place must be suffering from great scarcity of goods. Being anxious to reach the market before the ports of the Gulf were reopened, we deemed it expedient to abandon the regular route from Missouri for one wholly untried, from the borders of Arkansas, where the pasturage springs up nearly a month earlier. It is true that such an attempt to convey heavily laden wagons through an unexplored region was attended with considerable risk; but as I was familiar with the general character of the plains contiguous to the north, I felt little or no apprehension of serious difficulties, except from what might be occasioned by regions of sandy soil. I have often been asked since, why we did not steer directly for Chihuahua, as our trade was chiefly destined for that place, instead of taking the circuitous route *via* Santa

Fé. I answer, that we dreaded a journey across the southern prairies on account of the reputed aridity of the country in that direction, and I had no great desire to venture directly into a southern port in the present state of uncertainty as to the conditions of entry.

Suitable arrangements having been made, and a choice stock of about $25,000 worth of goods shipped to Van Buren on the Arkansas River,[70] we started on the evening of the 21st of April, but made very little progress for the first eight days. While we were yet but ten or fifteen miles from Van Buren an incident occurred which was attended with very melancholy results. A young man named Hays, who had driven a wagon for me for several months through the interior of Mexico and thence to the United States in 1838, having heard that this expedition was projected, was desirous of engaging again in the same employ. I was equally desirous to secure his services, as he was well-tried and had proved himself an excellent fellow on those perilous journeys. But soon after our outset, and without any apparent reason, he expressed an inclination to abandon the trip. I earnestly strove to dissuade him from his purpose and supposed I had succeeded. What was my surprise, then, upon my return after a few hours' absence in advance of the company, to learn that he had secretly

[70] Van Buren is near the western boundary of Arkansas, a few miles northeast of Fort Smith.

absconded! I was now led to reflect upon some of his eccentricities, and bethought me of several evident indications of slight mental derangement. We were, however, but a few miles from the settlements of the whites and in the midst of the civilized Cherokees, where there was little or no danger of his suffering; therefore, there seemed but little occasion for serious uneasiness on his account. As it was believed he had shaped his course back to Van Buren I immediately wrote to our friends there to have search made for him. However, nothing could be found of him till the next day, when his hat and coat were discovered upon the bank of the Arkansas near Van Buren, which were the last traces ever had of the unfortunate Hays! Whether intentionally or accidentally, he was evidently drowned.

On the 28th of April we crossed the Arkansas River a few miles above the mouth of the Canadian Fork.[71] We had only proceeded a short distance beyond, when a Cherokee shopkeeper came up to us with an attachment for debt against a free mulatto whom we had engaged as teamster. The poor fellow had no alternative but to return with the importunate creditor, who committed him at once to the care of "Judge Lynch" for trial. We ascertained afterwards that he had been sentenced to take the benefit of the bankrupt law after the manner of the Cherokees of that neighborhood.

[71] In modern Muskogee County, Oklahoma.

This is done by stripping and tying the victim to a tree; when each creditor, with a good cowhide or hickory switch in his hand, scores the amount of the bill due upon his bare back. One stripe for every dollar due is the usual process of whitewashing; and as the application of the lash is accompanied by all sorts of quaint remarks, the exhibition affords no small merriment to those present, with the exception, no doubt, of the delinquent himself. After the ordeal is over the creditors declare themselves perfectly satisfied: nor could they, as is said, ever be persuaded thereafter to receive one red cent of the amount due, even if it were offered to them. As the poor mulatto was also in our debt, and was perhaps apprehensive that we might exact payment in the same currency, he never showed himself again.

On the 2d of May we crossed the North Fork of the Canadian about a mile from its confluence with the main stream.[72] A little westward of this there is a small village of Creek Indians, and a shop or two kept by American traders. An Indian who had quarreled with his wife came out and proposed to join us, and to our great surprise carried his

[72] Near the town of Eufaula, McIntosh County, Oklahoma. The Canadian River crosses central Oklahoma from west to east in wide-sweeping curves. From Van Buren near the Arkansas-Oklahoma boundary, Gregg's party pursued a generally westerly course across the central part of the latter state, most of the way ascending the valley of the Canadian.

proposal into execution. The next morning his repentant consort came to our camp and set up a most dismal weeping and howling after her truant husband, who, notwithstanding, was neither to be caught by tears nor softened by entreaties, but persisted in his determination to see foreign countries. His name was Echu-eleh-hadjo (or Crazy-deer-foot), but for brevity's sake, we always called him Chuly. He was industrious and possessed many clever qualities, though somewhat disposed to commit excesses whenever he could procure liquor, which fortunately did not occur until our arrival at Santa Fé. He proved to be a good and willing hand on the way, but as he spoke no English our communication with him was somewhat troublesome. I may as well add here that while in Santa Fé he took another freak and joined a volunteer corps, chiefly of Americans, organized under one James Kirker to fight the Navajo and Apache Indians; the government of Chihuahua having guaranteed to them all the spoils they should take. With these our Creek found a few of his red brethren—Shawnees and Delawares, who had wandered thus far from the frontier of Missouri. After this little army was disbanded, Chuly returned home, as I have been informed, with a small party who crossed the plains directly from Chihuahua.

We had never considered ourselves as perfectly *en chemin* till after crossing the Arkansas

River; and as our little party experienced no further change, I may now be permitted to introduce them collectively to the reader. It consisted of thirty-four men, including my brother John Gregg and myself. These men had all been hired by us except three, two of whom were eastern-bred boys—a tailor and a silver-smith—good-natured, clever little fellows, who had thought themselves at the jumping-off place when they reached Van Buren, but now seemed nothing loth to extend their peregrinations a thousand miles or so farther, in the hope of doing the Spaniards, as the Mexicans are generally styled in the West, out of a little surplus of specie. The other was a German peddler, who somewhat resembled the Dutchman's horse, "put him as you vant, and he ish alvays tere"; for he did nothing during the whole journey but descant on the value of a chest of trumperies which he carried, and with which he calculated, as he expressed it, to "py a plenty of te Shpanish toller." The trip across the prairies cost these men absolutely nothing, inasmuch as we furnished them with all the necessaries for the journey in consideration of the additional strength they brought to our company.

It is seldom that such a variety of ingredients are found mixed up in so small a compass. Here were the representatives of seven distinct nations, each speaking his own native language, which produced at times a very respectable jumble of discordant sounds. There was one Frenchman whose volubility of tongue and curious gesticulations contrasted very strangely with the frigidity of two phlegmatic wanderers from Germany; while the calm eccentricity of two Polish exiles, the stoical look of two sons of the desert (the Creek already spoken of, and a Chickasaw), and the pantomimic gestures of sundry loquacious Mexicans contributed in no small degree to heighten the effects of the picture. The Americans were mostly backwoodsmen, who could handle the rifle far better than the whip, but who nevertheless officiated as wagoners.

We had fourteen road-wagons, half drawn by mules, the others by oxen (eight of each to the team); besides a carriage and a Jersey wagon. Then we had two swivels mounted upon one pair of wheels; but one of them was attached to a movable truckle, so that upon stopping it could be transferred to the other side of the wagons. One of these was a long brass piece made to order, with a caliber of but an inch and a quarter, yet of sufficient metal to throw a leaden ball to the distance of a mile with surprising accuracy. The other was of iron and a little larger. Besides these, our party was well supplied with small arms. The Americans mostly had their rifles and a musket in addition, which they carried in their wagons, always well charged with ball and buckshot. Then my brother and myself were each provided with one of Colt's repeating rifles and a pair of pistols of the same so that we could, if necessary, carry thirty-six ready-loaded shots apiece; which alone constituted a capacity of defense rarely matched even on the prairies.

Previous to our departure we had received a promise from the war department of an escort of U. S. dragoons, as far as the borders of the Mexican territory; but upon sending an express to Gen. Arbuckle[73] at Fort Gibson to that effect we were informed that in consequence of some fresh troubles among the Cherokees it was doubtful whether the force could be spared in time. This was certainly no very agreeable news, inasmuch as the escort would have been very serviceable in assisting to search out a track over the unexplored wilderness we had to pass. It was too late, however, to recede; and so we resolved at all hazards to pursue our journey.

We had advanced beyond the farthest settlements of the Creeks and Seminoles and pitched our camp on a bright balmy evening in the border of a delightful prairie, when some of the young men, attracted by the prospect of game,

[73] Matthew Arbuckle was born in Greenbrier County, West Virginia, in 1776. He entered the United States army as an ensign in 1799 and ultimately rose (in 1830) to the rank of brevet brigadier general. He died at Fort Smith, June 11, 1851. For over twenty years he was in command of the military forces in eastern Oklahoma, with stations at Fort Gibson and Fort Smith.

shouldered their rifles and wended their steps through the dense forest which lay contiguous to our encampment. Among those that went forth there was one of the downeasters already mentioned, who was much more familiar with the interior of a city than of a wilderness forest. As the shades of evening were beginning to descend, and all the hunters had returned except him, several muskets and even our little field-pieces were fired, but without effect. The night passed away and the morning dawned upon the encampment, and still he was absent. The firing was then renewed; but soon after he was seen approaching, very sullen and dejected. He came with a tale of perilous adventures and hair-breadth escapes upon his lips which somewhat abated the storm of ridicule by which he was at first assailed. It seemed that he had heard our firing on the previous evening, but believed it to proceed from a contrary direction—a very common mistake with persons who have become bewildered and lost. Thus deceived and stimulated by the fear of Indians (from a party of whom he supposed the firing to proceed) he continued his pathless wanderings till dark, when, to render his situation still more critical, he was attacked by a "painter"—*anglice* panther—which he actually succeeded in beating off with the breech of his gun, and then betook himself to the topmost extremity of a tree, where, in order to avoid a similar intrusion, he passed the remainder of the night. From a peculiar odor with which the shattered gun was still redolent, however, it was strongly suspected that the terrific painter was not many degrees removed in affinity from a—polecat.

We had just reached the extreme edge of the far famed Cross Timbers when we were gratified by the arrival of forty dragoons, under the command of Lieut. Bowman, who had orders to accompany us to the supposed boundary of the United States. On the same evening we had the pleasure of encamping together at a place known as Camp Holmes, a wild romantic spot in latitude 35° 5', and but a mile north of the Canadian River. Just at hand there was a beautiful spring, where in 1835 Colonel Mason[74] with a force of U. S. troops had a big talk and still bigger smoke with a party of Comanche and Witchita Indians. Upon the same site Col. Chouteau[75] had also

[74] Richard B. Mason was a native of Virginia who at the age of twenty entered the army as a lieutenant in 1817. He rose to the rank of colonel in 1846 and brigadier general in 1848. He was the first military and civil governor of California. He died at St. Louis in 1850.

[75] This was Auguste Pierre Chouteau, eldest son of Pierre Chouteau of the noted family of St. Louis traders. He was born at St. Louis in 1786, was educated at West Point, and became an ensign in the First U. S. Infantry in 1806. In 1809 he resigned his commission to engage in the fur trade. Following the close of the War of 1812 he engaged in a partnership with Julius De Munn for trading with the Indians of the upper Platte and

caused to be erected not long after a little stockade fort, where a considerable trade was subsequently carried on with the Comanches and other tribes of the southwestern prairies. The place had now been abandoned, however, since the preceding winter.

From the Arkansas River to Chouteau's Fort,[76] our route presented an unbroken succession of grassy plains and fertile glades, intersected here and there with woody belts and numerous rivulets, most of which, however, are generally dry except during the rainy season. As far as Camp Holmes we had a passable wagon road, which was opened upon the occasion of the Indian treaty before alluded to, and was afterwards kept open by the Indian traders. Yet, notwithstanding the road, this stretch gave us more trouble—presented more rugged passes, miry ravines, and steep ascents —than all the rest of our journey put together.

We had not been long at the fort before we received a visit from a party of Comanches,

upper Arkansas River region. This venture ended disastrously, through the hostile attitude of the natives. Most of the further trading career of Chouteau was spent farther south in the present state of Oklahoma. In 1835 he established a post at Camp Holmes, near the mouth of Little River in modern Hughes County. In 1838 he built a new post in southern Cleveland County, about five miles northeast of the town of Purcell. Here he was trading at the time of his death at Fort Gibson, as related by Gregg, in the winter of 1838–39.

[76] This was the post, noted above, near Purcell in southern Cleveland County.

who having heard of our approach came to greet us with a welcome, on the supposition that it was their friend Chouteau returning to the fort with fresh supplies of merchandise. Great was their grief when we informed them that their favorite trader had died at Fort Gibson the previous winter. On visiting their wigwams and inquiring for their *capitan*,[77] we were introduced to a corpulent, squint-eyed old fellow, who certainly had nothing in his personal appearance indicative of rank or dignity. This was Tabba-quena (or the Big Eagle), a name familiar to all the Comanche traders. As we had frequently heard that he spoke Spanish fluently, we at once prepared ourselves for a social chit-chat; but, on accosting him in that tongue, and inquiring whether he could talk Spanish, he merely replied "*Poquito*," putting at the same time his fore-finger to his ear to signify that he merely understood a little—which proved true to a degree, for our communication was chiefly by signs. We were now about to launch upon an unknown region—our route lay henceforth across that unexplored wilderness of which I have so frequently spoken, without either pilot or trail to guide us for nearly 500 miles. We had to depend entirely upon our knowledge of the geographical position of the country for

[77] Most of the prairie Indians seem to have learned this Spanish word, by which, when talking with the whites, all their chiefs are designated. Gregg.

which we were steering, and the indications of a compass and sextant. This was emphatically a pioneer trip; such a one also as had, perhaps, never before been undertaken—to convey heavily laden wagons through a country almost wholly untrod by civilized man, and of which we, at least, knew nothing. We were therefore extremely anxious to acquire any information our visitors might be able to give us; but Tabba-quena being by no means experienced in wagon tactics, could only make us understand by gestures, mixed with a little wretched Spanish, that the route up the Canadian presented no obstacles according to his mode of traveling. He appeared, however, very well acquainted with the whole Mexican frontier from Santa Fé to Chihuahua and even to the Gulf, as well as with all the prairies. During the consultation he seemed occasionally to ask the opinions of other chiefs who had huddled around him. Finally, we handed him a sheet of paper and a pencil, signifying at the same time a desire that he would draw us a map of the prairies. This he very promptly executed; and although the draft was somewhat rough, it bore, much to our astonishment, quite a map-like appearance, with a far more accurate delineation of all the principal rivers of the plains—the road from Missouri to Santa Fé, and the different Mexican settlements than is to be found in many of the engraved maps of those regions.

Tabba-quena's party consisted of about sixty persons, including several squaws and papooses, with a few Kiowa chiefs and warriors, who, although of a tribe so entirely distinct, are frequently found domiciled among the Comanches. As we were about to break up the camp they all started for Fort Gibson for the purpose, as they informed us, of paying a visit to the "Capitan Grande"—a Spanish phrase used by many prairie tribes and applied, in their confused notions of rank and power, not only to the president of the United States himself, but to the seat of the federal government. These they are again apt to confound with Fort Gibson and the commanding officer of that station.

On the 18th of May we set out from Chouteau's Fort. From this forward our wagons were marched in two lines and regularly formed at every camp, so as to constitute a fortification and a *corral* for the stock. This is different from the forming of the large caravans. The two front wagons are driven up, side by side, with their tails a little inclined outward. About half of the rest are drawn up in the same manner, but each stopped with the forewheel a little back of the hind-wheel of the next ahead. The remainder are similarly brought up, but inclined inward behind so as nearly to close again at the rear of the pen; leaving a gap through which to introduce the stock. Thus the *corral* remains of an ovate form. After the drivers become expert the whole is performed in a very short time.

On the following day we were again joined by old Tabba-quena and another Comanche chief with five or six warriors and as many squaws, including Tab's wife and infant son. As we were jogging along in the afternoon I held quite a long conversation in our semi-mute language with the squinting old chief. He gave me to understand as well as he could that his comrades[78] had proceeded on their journey to see the Capitan Grande, but that he had concluded to return home for better horses. He boasted in no measured terms of his friendship for the Americans, and promised to exert his influence to prevent the turbulent and unruly spirits of his nation from molesting us. But he could not disguise his fears in regard to the Pawnees and Osages, who, he said, would be sure to run off with our stock while we were asleep at night. When I informed him that we kept a strict night-watch, he said, "*Esta bueno*" (that's good), and allowed that our chances for safety were not so bad after all.

These friendly Indians encamped with us that night and on the following morning the old chief informed us that some of his party had a few "mules para *swap*" (mules to trade; for having learned the word *swap* of some

[78] Some of these (principally Kiowas, as I afterwards learned) reached Fort Gibson, and received a handsome reward of government presents for their visit. **Gregg.**

American traders, he very ingeniously tacked it at the tail of his little stock of Spanish). A barter for five mules was immediately concluded upon, much to our advantage, as our teams were rather in a weak condition. Old Tab and his party then left us to join his band, which, he said, was located on the Faux Ouachitta River,[79] and we never saw aught of them more.

After leaving the fort we generally kept on the ridge between the Canadian and the North Fork, crossing sometimes the tributary brooks of the one and sometimes those of the other. Having traveled in this manner for about eighty miles, we entered one of the most charming prairie vales that I have ever beheld, and which in the plenitude of our enthusiasm we named Spring Valley, on account of the numerous spring-fed rills and gurgling rivulets that greeted the sight in every direction; in whose limpid pools swarms of trout and perch were carelessly playing. Much of the country, indeed, over which we had passed was somewhat of a similar character—yet nowhere quite so beautiful. I must premise, however, that westward of this it is only the valleys immediately bordering the streams that are at all

[79] The Washita River rises in northern Texas and flows southwesterly across western Oklahoma to its junction with the Red midway of the southern boundary of that state. It closely parallels the general course of the Canadian, being the first stream of consequence southward of that stream.

fit for cultivation: the high plains are too dry and sandy. But here the soil was dark and mellow, and the rich vegetation with which it was clothed plainly indicated its fertility. Spring Valley gently inclines towards the North Fork, which was at the distance of about five miles from our present route. It was somewhere along the border of this enchanting vale that a little picket fort was erected in 1822 by an unfortunate trader named McKnight, who was afterwards betrayed and murdered by the faithless Comanches. The landscape is beautifully variegated with stripes and fringes of timber: while the little herds of buffalo that were scattered about in fantastic groups imparted a degree of life and picturesqueness to the scene, which it was truly delightful to contemplate.

It was three days previous that we had first met with these prairie cattle. I have often heard backwoodsmen speak of the buck ague, but commend me to the buffalo fever of the prairies for novelty and amusement. Very few of our party had ever seen a buffalo before in its wild state; therefore at the first sight of these noble animals the excitement surpassed anything I had ever witnessed before. Some of our dragoons in their eagerness for sport had managed to frighten away a small herd that were quietly feeding at some distance, before our still hunters, who had crawled towards them, had been able to get within rifle-shot of them. No sooner were the movements of our mounted men perceived than the whole extent of country, as far as the eye could reach, became perfectly animate with living objects, fleeing and scampering in every direction. From the surrounding valleys sprang up numerous herds of these animals which had hitherto been unobserved, many of which in their indiscriminate flight passed so near the wagons that the drivers, carried away by the contagious excitement of the movement, would leave the teams and keep up a running fire after them. I had the good fortune to witness the exploits of one of our northern greenhorns who, mounted upon a sluggish mule and without any kind of weapon, amused himself by chasing every buffalo that came scudding along, as if he expected to capture him by laying hold of his tail. Plying spur and whip, he would gallop after one division till he was left far behind, and then turn to another and another, with the same earnestness of purpose, until they had all passed out of sight. He finally came back disheartened and sullen, with his head hanging down like one conscious of having done something supremely ridiculous; but still cursing his lazy mule, which, he said, might have caught the buffalo, if it had had a mind to.

The next day, the buffalo being still more numerous, the chase was renewed with greater zest. In the midst of the general hurly-burly which ensued three persons on foot were perceived afar off, chasing one herd of buffalo and then another until they completely disappeared. These were two of our cooks, the one armed with a pistol, the other with a musket, accompanied by Chuly (the Creek), who was happily provided with a rifle. We traveled several miles without hearing or seeing anything of them. At last, when we had almost given them up for lost, Frank, the French cook, came trudging in, and his rueful countenance was no bad index of the doleful tale he had to relate. Although he had been chasing and shooting all day he had, as he expressed it, "no killet one," till eventually he happened to stumble upon a wounded calf, which he boldly attacked; but as ill luck would have it, the youngster took it into his head to give him battle. "Foutre de varment! he butt me down," exclaimed the exasperated Frenchman.—"Sacré! me plentee scart; but me kill him for all." Chuly and the other cook came in soon after in equally dejected spirits; for in addition to his ill luck in hunting, the latter had been lost. The Indian had perhaps killed buffalo with his rifle, but he was in no humor to be communicative in his language of signs; so nothing was ever known of his adventures. One thing seemed pretty certain, that they were all cured of the buffalo fever.

On the night after the first buffalo scamper, we encamped upon a woodless ravine and were obliged to resort to buffalo chips (dry ordure) for fuel. It is amusing to witness the bustle which generally takes place in collecting this offal. In dry weather it is an excellent substitute for wood, than which it even makes a hotter fire; but when moistened by rain, the smouldering pile will smoke for hours before it condescends to burn, if it does at all. The buffalo meat which the hunter roasts or broils upon this fire he accounts more savory than the steaks dressed by the most delicate cooks in civilized life.

# Chapter 10

## AMONG THE COMANCHES

AS it now appeared that we had been forced at least two points north of the course we had originally intended to steer, by the northern bearing of the Canadian, we made an effort to cross a ridge of timber to the south, which after considerable labor proved successful. Here we found a multitude of gravelly, bright-flowing streams, with rich bottoms, lined all along with stately white oak, black walnut, mulberry, and other similar growths, that yielded us excellent materials for wagon repairs, of which the route from Missouri, after passing Council Grove, is absolutely in want.

Although we found the buffalo extremely scarce westward of Spring Valley, yet there was no lack of game; for every nook and glade swarmed with deer and wild turkeys, partridges and grouse. We had also occasion to become acquainted with another species of prairie tenant whose visits generally produced impressions that were anything but agreeable. I allude to a small black insect generally known to prairie travelers as the buffalo-gnat. It not only attacks the face and hands, but even contrives to insinuate itself into those parts which one is most careful to guard against intrusion. Here it fastens itself and luxuriates until completely satisfied. Its bite is so poisonous as to give the face, neck, and hands, or any other part of the person upon which its affectionate caresses have been bestowed, the appearance of a pustulated varioloid. The buffalo-gnat is in fact a much more annoying insect than the mosquito, and also much more frequently met with on the prairies.

We now continued our line of march between the Canadian and the timbered ridge with very little difficulty. Having stopped to noon in a bordering valley, we were quite surprised by the appearance of an Indian with no other protection than his squaw. From what we could gather by their signs, they had been victims of a love scrape. The fellow, whom I found to be a Kiowa, had according to his own account stolen the wife of another and then fled to the thickets, where he purposed to lead a lonely life in hopes of escaping the vengeance of his incensed predecessor. From this it would appear that affairs of gallantry are not evils exclusively confined to civilization. Plausible, however, as the Indian's story seemed to be, we had strong suspicions that others of his band were not far off; and that he, with his better half, had only been skulking about in hopes of exercising their acquisitiveness at our expense; when, on finding themselves discovered, they deemed it the best policy fearlessly to approach us. This singular visit afforded a specimen of that confidence with which civilization inspires even the most untutored savages. They remained with us in the utmost nonchalance till the following morning.

Shortly after the arrival of the visitors we were terribly alarmed at a sudden prairie conflagration. The old grass of the valley in which we were encamped had not been burned off, and one of our cooks having unwittingly kindled a fire in the midst of it, it spread at once with wonderful rapidity; and a brisk wind springing up at the time, the flames were carried over the valley in spite of every effort we could make to check them. Fortunately for us, the fire had broken out to the leeward of our wagons, and therefore occasioned us no damage; but the accident itself was a forcible illustration of the danger that might be incurred by pitching a camp in the midst of dry grass, and the advantages that might be taken by hostile savages in such a locality.

After the fire had raged with great violence for a few hours a cloud suddenly obscured the horizon, which was almost immediately followed by a refreshing shower of rain: a phenomenon often witnessed upon the prairies after an extensive conflagration; and affording a practical exemplification of Professor Espy's celebrated theory of artificial showers.[80]

[80] James Pollard Espy, whose *Philosophy of Storms* was published at Boston and London in 1841.

We now continued our journey without further trouble, except that of being still forced out of our proper latitude by the northern bearing of the Canadian. On the 30th of May, however, we succeeded in doubling the spur of the great North Bend.[81] Upon ascending the dividing ridge again, which at this point was entirely destitute of timber, a prairie expanse once more greeted our view. This and the following day our route lay through a region that abounded in gypsum, from the finest quality down to ordinary plaster. On the night of the 31st we encamped on a tributary of the North Fork, which we called Gypsum Creek,[82] in consequence of its being surrounded with vast quantities of that substance.

Being compelled to keep a reckoning of our latitude, by which our travel was partly governed, and the sun being now too high at noon for the use of the artificial horizon, we had to be guided entirely by observations of the meridian altitude of the moon, planets, or fixed stars. At Gypsum Creek our latitude was 36° 10', being the utmost northing we had made. As we were now about thirty miles

[81] In modern Dewey County, Oklahoma.
[82] There are two Gypsum creeks in modern Oklahoma, one a tributary of the Cimarron in the northwest and the other a tributary of the Red in southwestern Oklahoma. Gregg's Gypsum Creek may have been modern Persimmon Creek, in northern Dewey and southern Woodward counties.

north of the parallel of Santa Fé, we had to steer henceforth a few degrees south of west in order to bring us on our direct course.

The following night we encamped in a region covered with sandy hillocks, where there was not a drop of water to be found:[38] in fact, an immense sand-plain was now before us, somewhat variegated in appearance, being entirely barren of vegetation in some places, while others were completely covered with an extraordinarily diminutive growth which has been called *shin-oak*, and a curious plum-bush of equally dwarfish stature. These singular-looking plants (undistinguishable at a distance from the grass of the prairies) were heavily laden with acorns and plums, which, when ripe, are of considerable size although the trunks of either were seldom thicker than oat-straws, and frequently not a foot high. We also met with the same in many other places on the prairies.

Still the most indispensable requisite, water, was nowhere to be found, and symptoms of alarm were beginning to spread far and wide among us. When we had last seen the Canadian and the North Fork, they appeared to separate in their course almost at right angles, therefore it was impossible to tell at what distance we were from either. At last my brother and myself, who had been scouring the plains during the morning without success,

[83] Probably in eastern Ellis County, Oklahoma.

finally perceived a deep hollow leading in the direction of the Canadian, where we found a fine pool of water and our wagons made port again before midday; thus quieting all alarm.

Although we had encountered but very few buffalo since we left Spring Valley, they now began to make their appearance again, though not in very large droves; together with the deer and the fleet antelope, which latter struck me as being much more tame in this wild section of the prairies than I had seen it elsewhere. The graceful and majestic mustang would also now and then sweep across the naked country, or come curvetting and capering in the vicinity of our little caravan, just as the humor prompted them. But what attracted our attention most were the little dog settlements, or, as they are more technically called, dog-towns, so often alluded to by prairie travelers. As we were passing through their streets, multitudes of the diminutive inhabitants were to be seen among the numerous little hillocks which marked their dwellings, where they frisked about or sat perched at their doors, yelping defiance, to our great amusement—heedless of the danger that often awaited them from the rifles of our party; for they had perhaps never seen such deadly weapons before.

On the 5th of June we found ourselves once more traveling on a firm rolling prairie, about the region, as we supposed, of the boundary between the United States and Mexico;[84] when Lieut. Bowman, in pursuance of his instructions, began to talk seriously of returning.[85] While the wagons were stopped at noon a small party of us, including a few dragoons, advanced a few miles ahead to take a survey of the route. We had just ascended the highest point of a ridge to get a prospect of the country beyond, when we descried a herd of buffalo in motion and two or three horsemen in hot pursuit. "Mexican Ciboleros!" we all exclaimed at once; for we supposed we might now be within the range of the buffalo hunters of New Mexico. Clapping spurs to our horses, we set off towards them at full speed. As we might have expected, our precipitate approach frightened them away and we soon lost sight of them altogether. On reaching the spot where they had last been seen we found a horse and two mules saddled, all tied to the carcass of

[84] From subsequent observations, this point appears to have been some miles west of the 100th degree of longitude. Gregg.

[85] The treaty of 1819 defined the boundary between the United States and Spain's American possessions by a line running from the Gulf of Mexico up the Sabine River to latitude 32°; thence by a north line to Red River; thence up Red River to the 100° meridian; thence north to the Arkansas; thence up the Arkansas to its source, and the 42° parallel to the Pacific. In approaching the 100° meridian (the present western boundary of Oklahoma) the party was approaching the boundary between the United States and Spanish America.

a slain buffalo which was partly skinned. We made diligent search in some copses of small growth and among the adjacent ravines, but could discover no further traces of the fugitives. The Indian rigging of the animals, however, satisfied us that they were not Mexicans.

We were just about giving up the pursuit when a solitary Indian horseman was espied upon a ridge about a mile from us. My brother and myself set out towards him, but on seeing us approach he began to manifest some fear, and therefore my brother advanced alone. As soon as he was near enough he cried out "*Amigo!*" to which the Indian replied "*Comantz!*" and giving himself a thump upon the breast, he made a graceful circuit and came up at full speed, presenting his hand in token of friendship. Nothing, however, could induce him to return to his animals with us, where the rest of our party had remained. He evidently feared treachery and foul play. Therefore we retraced our steps to the wagons, leaving the Indian's property just as we had found it, which, we subsequently discovered, was taken away after our departure.

In the afternoon of the same day five more Indians (including a squaw) made their appearance, and having been induced by friendly tokens to approach us, they spent the night at our encampment. The next morning we expressed a desire, by signs, to be conducted to the nearest point on our route where good pasturage and water might be found. A sprightly young chief, armed only with his bow and arrows, at once undertook the task, while his comrades still traveled along in our company. We had not progressed far before we found ourselves in the very midst of another large dog-town.

The task of describing the social and domestic habits of these eccentric little brutes has been so graphically and amusingly executed by the racy and popular pen of G. Wilkins Kendall that any attempt by me would be idle; and I feel that the most agreeable service I can do my readers is to borrow a paragraph from his alluring *Narrative*, describing a scene presented by one of these prairie commonwealths.

"In their habits they are clannish, social, and extremely convivial, never living alone like other animals, but, on the contrary, always found in villages or large settlements. They are a wild, frolicsome, madcap set of fellows when undisturbed, uneasy and ever on the move, and appear to take especial delight in chattering away the time, and visiting from hole to hole to gossip and talk over each other's affairs—at least so their actions would indicate. . . . On several occasions I crept close to their villages without being observed, to watch their movements. Directly in the center of one of them I particularly noticed a very large dog sitting in front of the door or entrance to his burrow, and by his own actions and those of his neighbors it really seemed as though he was the president, mayor, or chief—at all events, he was the big dog of the place. For at least an hour I secretly watched the operations in this community. During that time the large dog I have mentioned received at least a dozen visits from his fellow-dogs, which would stop and chat with him a few moments and then run off to their domiciles. All this while he never left his post for a moment, and I thought I could discover a gravity in his deportment not discernible in those by which he was surrounded. Far is it from me to say that the visits he received were upon business, or had anything to do with the local government of the village; but it certainly appeared so. If any animal has a system of laws regulating the body politic, it is certainly the prairie dog."

As we sat on our horses, looking at these "village transactions," our Comanche guide drew an arrow for the purpose of cutting short the career of a little citizen that sat yelping most doggedly in the mouth of his hole, forty or fifty paces distant. The animal was almost entirely concealed behind the hillock which encompassed the entrance of his apartment, so that the dart could not reach it in a direct line; but the Indian had resort to a maneuver which caused the arrow to descend with a curve, and in an instant it quivered in the body of the poor little quadruped. The slayer only smiled at his feat, while we were perfectly astounded. There is nothing strange in the rifleman's being able to hit his mark with his fine-sighted barrel; but the accuracy with which these savages learn to shoot their feathered missiles, with such random aim, is almost incomprehensible. I had at the same time drawn one of my Colt's repeating pistols, with a view of paying a similar compliment to another dog; when, finding that it excited the curiosity of the chief, I fired a few shots in quick succession as an explanation of its virtues. He seemed to comprehend the secret instantly, and, drawing his bow once more, he discharged a number of arrows with the same rapidity, as a palpable intimation that he could shoot as fast with his instrument as we could with our patent fire-arms. This was not merely a vain show: there was more of reality than of romance in his demonstration.

Shortly after this we reached a fresh brook, a tributary of the North Fork, which wound its silent course in the midst of a picturesque valley, surrounded by romantic hills and craggy knobs. Here we pitched our camp: when three of our visitors left us for the purpose of going to bring all the "capitanes" of their tribe, who were said to be encamped at no great distance from us.

Our encampment, which we designated as Camp Comanche, was only five or six miles from the North Fork, while to the southward the main Canadian was but a little more distant.[86]

After waiting anxiously for the arrival of the Comanche chiefs until our patience was well nigh exhausted, I ascended a high knoll just behind our camp, in company with the younger of the two chiefs who had remained with us, to see if anything could be discovered. By and by the Comanche pointed anxiously towards the northwest, where he espied a party of his people, though at such a great distance that it was some time before I could discern them. With what acuteness of vision are these savages endowed! Accustomed to the open plains, and like the eagle to look out for their prey at immense distances, their optical perception is scarcely excelled by that of the king of birds.

The party, having approached still nearer, assembled upon an eminence as if for the purpose of reconnoitering; but our chief upon the knoll hoisting his blanket, which seemed to say, come ahead, they advanced slowly and deliberately—very unlike the customary mode of approach among all the prairie tribes.

The party consisted of about sixty warriors, at the head of whom rode an Indian of small stature and agreeable countenance, verging on

[86] The party had now entered the northern extension of Texas; the camp was probably in southern Lipscomb County.

the age of fifty. He wore the usual Comanche dress, but instead of moccasins he had on a pair of long white cotton hose, while upon his bare head waved a tall red plume, a mark of distinction which proclaimed him at once the *capitan mayor*, or principal chief. We addressed them in Spanish, inquiring if they had brought an interpreter, when a lank-jawed, grum-looking savage announced his readiness to officiate in that capacity. "*Sabes hablar en Español, amigo?*" (Can you talk Spanish, friend?) I inquired. "*Si*" (yes), he gruffly replied. "Where are your people?" "Encamped just above on yonder creek." "How many of you are there?" "Oh, a great many—nearly all the Comanche nation; for we are *en junta* to go and fight the Pawnees." "Well, can you tell us how far it is to Santa Fé?" But the surly savage cut short my inquiries by observing—"*Ahi platicaremos despues*"—"We will talk about that hereafter."

We then showed them a spot a few rods from us where they might encamp so as not to intermix their animals with ours; after which all the *capitanes* were invited to our camp to hold a big talk. In a very short time we had ten chiefs seated in a circle within our tent, when the pipe, the Indian token of peace, was produced: but doubting, perhaps, the sincerity of our professions, they at first refused to smoke. The interpreter, however, remarked as an excuse for their conduct that it was not their custom to smoke until they had received

some presents: but a few Mexican cigarritos
being produced, most of them took a whiff, as
if under the impression that to smoke cigars
was no pledge of friendship.

Lieut. Bowman now desired us to broach
the subject of peace and amity betwixt the
Comanches and our people, and to invite them
to visit the Capitan Grande at Washington
and enter into a perpetual treaty to that effect;
but they would not then converse on the subject. In fact, the interpreter inquired, "Are
we not at war?—how can we go to see the
Capitan Grande?" We knew they held themselves at war with Mexico and Texas, and probably had mistaken us for Texans, which had
no doubt caused the interpreter to speak so
emphatically of their immense numbers. Upon
this we explained to them that the United
States was a distinct government and at peace
with the Comanches. As an earnest of our
friendly disposition we then produced some
scarlet cloth, with a small quantity of vermillion, tobacco, beads, etc., which being distributed among them they very soon settled
down into a state of placidness and content-
ment. Indeed, it will be found that with wild
Indians presents are always the corner-stone
of friendship. "We are rejoiced," at last said
the elder chief with a ceremonious air, "our
hearts are glad that you have arrived among us:
it makes our eyes laugh to see Americans walk
in our land. We will notify our old and young

men—our boys and our maidens—our women
and children—that they may come to trade
with you. We hope you will speak well of us to
your people, that more of them may hunt the
way of our country, for we like to trade with
the white man." This was delivered in Comanche, but translated into Spanish by the
interpreter, who although a full Indian had
lived several years among the Mexicans and
spoke their language tolerably well. Our big
talk lasted several hours, after which the
Indians retired to sleep. The next morning,
after renewing their protestations of friendship,
they took their departure, the principal chief
saying, "Tell the Capitan Grande that when
he pleases to call us we are all ready to go to
see him."

The project of bringing some of the chiefs of
these wild prairie tribes to Washington City
has been entertained, but never yet carried
into effect. The few who have penetrated as
far as Fort Gibson, or perhaps to a frontier
village, have probably left with more unfavor-
able impressions than they had before. Believing the former to be our great Capital, and
the most insignificant among the latter our
largest cities, they have naturally come to the
conclusion that they surpass us in numbers and
power if not in wealth and grandeur. I have
no doubt that the chiefs of the Comanches and
other prairie tribes, if rightly managed, might
be induced to visit our veritable Capitan Grande

and our large cities, which would doubtless have a far better effect than all the treaties of peace that could be concluded with them for an age to come. They would then see with their own eyes and hear with their own ears the magnificence and power of the whites, which would inspire them at once with respect and fear.

This was on the 7th of June. About noon, Lieut. Bowman and his command finally took leave of us, and at the same time we resumed our forward march. This separation was truly painful: not so much on account of the loss we were about to experience, in regard to the protection afforded us by the troops (which, to say the truth, was more needed now than it had ever been before), as for the necessity of parting with a friend who had endeared himself to us all by his affable deportment, his social manners, and accommodating disposition. Ah! little did we think then that we should never see that gallant officer more! So young, so robust, and so healthy, little did we suspect that the sound of that voice which shouted so vigorously in responding to our parting salute in the desert would never greet our ears again! But such was Fate's decree! Although he arrived safely at Fort Gibson, in a few short weeks he fell a victim to disease.

There were perhaps a few timid hearts that longed to return with the dragoons, and ever and anon a wistful glance would be cast back at the receding figures in the distance. The idea of a handful of thirty-four men having to travel without guide or protection through a dreary wilderness peopled by thousands of savages, who were just as likely to be hostile as friendly, was certainly very little calculated to produce agreeable impressions. Much to the credit of our men, however, the escort was no sooner out of sight than the timorous regained confidence, and all seemed bound together by stronger ties than before. All we feared were ambuscades or surprise; to guard against which, it was only necessary to redouble our vigilance.

On the following day, while we were enjoying our noon's rest upon a ravine of the Canadian, several parties of Indians, amounting altogether to about three hundred souls, including women and children, made their appearance. They belonged to the same band of Comanches with whom we had had so agreeable an intercourse, and had brought several mules in the expectation of driving a trade with us. The squaws and papooses were so anxious to gratify their curiosity; and so very soon began to give such striking manifestations of their pilfering propensities, that at the request of the chiefs we carried some goods at a little distance, where a trade was opened in hopes of attracting their attention. One woman, I observed, still lingered among the wagons, who, from certain peculiarities of features, struck me very forcibly as not being an Indian. In accordance with this impression I addressed her in Spanish, and was soon confirmed in all my suspicions. She was from the neighborhood of Matamoros, and had been married to a Comanche since her captivity. She did not entertain the least desire of returning to her own people.

Similar instances of voluntary captivity have frequently occurred. Dr. Sibley, in a communication to the War Department in 1805, relates an affecting case, which shows how a sensitive female will often prefer remaining with her masters, rather than encounter the horrible ordeal of ill-natured remarks to which she would inevitably be exposed on being restored to civilized life. The Comanches, some twenty years previous, having kidnaped the daughter of the Governor-General of Chihuahua, the latter transmitted $1,000 to a trader to procure her ransom. This was soon effected, but to the astonishment of all concerned, the unfortunate girl refused to leave the Indians. She sent word to her father that they had disfigured her by tattooing; that she was married and perhaps *enceinte;* and that she would be more unhappy by returning to her father under these circumstances than by remaining where she was.

My attention was next attracted by a sprightly lad ten or twelve years old, whose nationality could scarcely be detected under his Indian guise. But, though quite Indianized, he was exceedingly polite. I inquired of him in Spanish, "Are you not a Mexican?" "Yes, sir,—I once was." "What is your name?" "Bernardino Saenz, sir, at your service." "When and where were you taken?" "About four years ago, at the Hacienda de las Animas, near Parral." "Shan't we buy you and take you to your people?—we are going thither." At this he hesitated a little, and then answered in an affecting tone, "*No, señor; ya soy demasiado bruto para vivir entre los Cristianos*" (O, no, sir; I am now too much of a brute to live among Christians); adding that his owner was not there, and that he knew the Indian in whose charge he came would not sell him.

The Hacienda de las Animas is in the department of Chihuahua, some fifteen miles from the city of Parral, a much larger place than Santa Fé. Notwithstanding this, about three hundred Comanches made a bold inroad into the very heart of the settlements—laid waste the unfortunate hacienda, killing and capturing a considerable number—and remained several days in the neighborhood, committing all sorts of outrages. This occurred in 1835. I happened to be in Chihuahua at the time and very well remember the bustle and consternation that prevailed. A thousand volunteers were raised, commanded by the Governor himself, who "hotly pursued" the enemy during their tardy retreat; but returned with the usual report—"*No les pudimos alcanzar*" (we could not overtake them).

Out of half a dozen Mexican captives that happened to be with our new visitors, we only met with one who manifested the slightest inclination to abandon Indian life. This was a stupid boy about fifteen years of age, who had probably been roughly treated on account of his laziness. We very soon struck a bargain with his owner, paying about the price of a mule for the little outcast, whom I sent to his family as soon as we reached Chihuahua. Notwithstanding the inherent stupidity of my protégé, I found him abundantly grateful—much to his credit be it spoken—for the little service I had been able to render him.

We succeeded in purchasing several mules, which cost us between ten and twenty dollars worth of goods apiece. In Comanche trade the main trouble consists in fixing the price of the first animal. This being settled by the chiefs, it often happens that mule after mule is led up and the price received without further cavil. Each owner usually wants a general assortment; therefore the price must consist of several items, as a blanket, a looking-glass, an awl, a flint, a little tobacco, vermillion, beads, etc.

Our trade with the new batch of Comanches being over, they now began to depart as they had come, in small parties, without bidding us adieu or even informing us of their intention, it being the usual mode of taking leave among Indians to depart *sans cérémonie,* and as silently as possible.

The Santa Fé caravans have generally avoided every manner of trade with the wild Indians for fear of being treacherously dealt with during the familiar intercourse which necessarily ensues. This I am convinced is an erroneous impression; for I have always found that savages are much less hostile to those with whom they trade than to any other people. They are emphatically fond of traffic, and, being anxious to encourage the whites to come among them, instead of committing depredations upon those with whom they trade they are generally ready to defend them against every enemy.

# Chapter 11

THE Comanches having all disappeared, we resumed our march and soon emerged into an open plain or *mesa* which was one of the most monotonous I had ever seen, there being not a break, not a hill nor valley, nor even a shrub to obstruct the view. The only thing which served to turn us from a direct course pursued by the compass was the in- numerable ponds which bespeckled the plain, and which kept us at least well supplied with water. Many of these ponds seem to have grown out of buffalo wallows, a term used on the prairies to designate a sink made by the buffalo's pawing the earth for the purpose of obtaining a smooth dusty surface to roll upon.

After three or four days of weary travel over this level plain the picturesque valley of the Canadian burst once more upon our view, presenting one of the most magnificent sights I had ever beheld. Here rose a perpendicular cliff in all the majesty and sublimity of its desolation; there another sprang forward as if in the very act of losing its balance and about to precipitate itself upon the vale below; a little farther on, a pillar with crevices and cornices so curiously formed as easily to be mistaken for the work of art; while a thousand other objects grotesquely and fantastically arranged and all shaded in the sky-bound perspective by the blue ridge-like brow of the *mesa* far beyond the Canadian constituted a kind of chaotic space where nature seemed to have indulged in her wildest caprices. Such was the confusion of ground-swells and eccentric cavities that it was altogether impossible to determine whereabouts the channel of the Canadian wound its way among them.

It would seem that these mesas might once have extended up to the margin of the stream, leaving a *cañon* or chasm through which the river flowed, as is still the case in some other places. But the basis of the plain not having been sufficiently firm to resist the action of the waters, these have washed and cut the bordering *cejas* or brows into all the shapes they now present. The buffalo and other animals have no doubt assisted in these transmutations. Their deep-worn paths over the brows of the plains form channels for the descending rains; which are soon washed into the size of ravines —and even considerable creeks. The beds of these continue to be worn down until veins of lasting water are opened, and constant-flowing streams thus established. Numerous were the embryo rivulets which might be observed forming in this way along the borders of those streams. The frequent isolated benches and mounds, whose tabular summits are on a level

with the adjacent plains and appear entirely
of a similar formation, indicate that the intermediate earth has been washed away or removed by some other process of nature—all
seeming to give plausibility to our theory.

It was somewhere in this vicinity that a
small party of Americans experienced a terrible
calamity in the winter of 1832–33, on their way
home; and as the incident had the tendency to
call into play the most prominent features of
the Indian character, I will digress so far here
as to relate the facts.

The party consisted of twelve men, chiefly
citizens of Missouri. Their baggage and about
ten thousand dollars in specie were packed
upon mules. They took the route of the Canadian River, fearing to venture on the northern
prairies at that season of the year. Having left
Santa Fé in December, they had proceeded
without accident thus far, when a large body
of Comanches and Kiowas were seen advancing
towards them. Being well acquainted with the
treacherous and pusillanimous disposition of
those races, the traders prepared at once for
defense; but the savages having made a halt
at some distance, began to approach one by one
or in small parties, making a great show of
friendship all the while, until most of them had
collected on the spot. Finding themselves
surrounded in every direction, the travelers
now began to move on in hopes of getting rid of
the intruders: but the latter were equally ready

for the start; and, mounting their horses, kept jogging on in the same direction. The first act of hostility perpetrated by the Indians proved fatal to one of the American traders named Pratt, who was shot dead while attempting to secure two mules which had become separated from the rest. Upon this, the companions of the slain man immediately dismounted and commenced a fire upon the Indians, which was warmly returned, whereby another man of the name of Mitchell was killed.

By this time the traders had taken off their packs and piled them around for protection; and now falling to work with their hands, they very soon scratched out a trench deep enough to protect them from the shot of the enemy. The latter made several desperate charges, but they seemed too careful of their own personal safety, notwithstanding the enormous superiority of their numbers, to venture too near the rifles of the Americans. In a few hours all the animals of the traders were either killed or wounded, but no personal damage was done to the remaining ten men, with the exception of a wound in the thigh received by one, which was not at the time considered dangerous.

During the siege the Americans were in great danger of perishing from thirst, as the Indians had complete command of all the water within reach. Starvation was not so much to be dreaded; because, in case of necessity, they could live on the flesh of their slain animals, some of which lay stretched close around them. After being pent up for thirty-six hours in this horrible hole, during which time they had seldom ventured to raise their heads above the surface without being shot at, they resolved to make a bold sortie in the night, as any death was preferable to the fate which awaited them there. As there was not an animal left that was at all in a condition to travel, the proprietors of the money gave permission to all to take and appropriate to themselves whatever amount each man could safely undertake to carry. In this way a few hundred dollars were started with, of which, however, but little ever reached the United States. The remainder was buried deep in the sand, in hopes that it might escape the cupidity of the savages; but to very little purpose; for they were afterwards seen by some Mexican traders making a great display of specie, which was without doubt taken from this unfortunate cache.

With every prospect of being discovered, overtaken, and butchered, but resolved to sell their lives as dearly as possible, they at last emerged from their hiding-place and moved on silently and slowly until they found themselves beyond the purlieus of the Indian camps. Often did they look back in the direction where from three to five hundred savages were supposed to watch their movements, but much to their astonishment no one appeared to be in pursuit. The Indians, believing no doubt

that the property of the traders would come
into their hands, and having no amateur pre-
dilection for taking scalps at the risk of losing
their own, appeared willing enough to let the
spoliated adventurers depart without further
molestation.

The destitute travelers having run themselves short of provisions, and being no longer
able to kill game for want of materials to load
their rifles with, they were very soon reduced
to the necessity of sustaining life upon roots
and the tender bark of trees. After traveling
for several days in this desperate condition, with
lacerated feet and utter prostration of mind
and body, they began to disagree among themselves about the route to be pursued and eventually separated into two distinct parties.
Five of these unhappy men steered a westward course and after a succession of sufferings
and privations which almost surpassed belief
they reached the settlements of the Creek
Indians near the Arkansas River, where they
were treated with great kindness and hospitality. The other five wandered about in the
greatest state of distress and bewilderment,
and only two finally succeeded in getting out
of the mazes of the wilderness. Among those
who were abandoned to their fate and left to
perish thus miserably was a Mr. Schenk, the
same individual who had been shot in the thigh;
a gentleman of talent and excellent family con-
nections, who was a brother, as I am informed,

of the Hon. Mr. Schenk, at present a member of Congress from Ohio.

But let us resume our journey. We had for some days, while traveling along the course of the Canadian, been in anxious expectation of reaching a point from whence there was a cart-road to Santa Fé, made by the Ciboleros; but being constantly baffled and disappointed in this hope, serious apprehensions began to be entertained by some of the party that we might after all be utterly lost. In this emergency one of our Mexicans, who pretended to be a great deal wiser than the rest, insisted that we were pursuing a wrong direction and that every day's march only took us farther from Santa Fé. There appeared to be so much plausibility in his assertion, as he professed a perfect knowledge of all the country around, that many of our men were almost ready to mutiny —to take the command from the hands of my brother and myself and lead us southward in search of the Colorado,[87] into the fearful *Llano Estacado*, where we would probably have perished. But our observations of the latitude, which we took very frequently, as well as the course we were pursuing, completely contradicted the Mexican wiseacre. A few days afterwards we were overtaken by a party of *Comancheros*, or Mexican Comanche traders, when we had the satisfaction of learning that we were in the right track.

[87] That is, the Red River.

# Commerce of the Prairies

These men had been trading with the band of Comanches we had lately met, and learning from them that we had passed on, they had hastened to overtake us so as to obtain our protection against the savages, who, after selling their animals to the Mexicans, very frequently take forcible possession of them again, before the purchasers have been able to reach their homes. These parties of *Comancheros* are usually composed of the indigent and rude classes of the frontier villages, who collect together several times a year and launch upon the plains with a few trinkets and trumperies of all kinds, and perhaps a bag of bread and maybe another of *pinole*, which they barter away to the savages for horses and mules. The entire stock of an individual trader very seldom exceeds the value of twenty dollars, with which he is content to wander about for several months, and glad to return home with a mule or two as the proceeds of his traffic.

These Mexican traders had much to tell us about the Comanches: saying that they were four or five thousand in number, with perhaps a thousand warriors, and that the fiery young men had once determined to follow and attack us; but that the chiefs and sages had deterred them by stating that our cannons could kill to the distance of many miles, and shoot through hills and rocks and destroy everything that happened to be within their range. The main object of our visitors, however, seemed to be

to raise themselves into importance by ex-
aggerating the perils we had escaped from.
That they had considered themselves in great
jeopardy, there could be no doubt whatever,
for in their anxiety to overtake us they came
very near killing their animals.

It was a war-party of this band of Comanches that paid the flying visit to Bent's Fort
on the Arkansas River to which Mr. Farnham
alludes in his trip to Oregon.[88] A band of the
same Indians also fell in with the caravan from
Missouri, with whom they were for a while
upon the verge of hostilities.

The next day we passed the afternoon upon
a ravine where we found abundance of water,
but to our great surprise our animals refused to
drink. Upon tasting the water we found it
exceedingly nauseous and bitter; far more re-
pugnant to some palates than a solution of
Epsom salts. It is true that the water had been
a little impregnated with the same loathsome
substance for several days; but we had never
found it so bad before. The salinous compound
which imparts this savor is found in great
abundance in the vicinity of the table-plain
streams of New Mexico, and is known to the
natives by the name of *salitre*.[89] We had the

[88] The allusion is to Thomas J. Farnham's *Travels
in the Great Western Prairie, the Anahuac and Rocky
Mountains, and in Oregon Territory* (London, 1843).

[89] Literally *saltpetre;* but the *salitre* of New Mexico is a
compound of several other salts besides nitre. Gregg.

good fortune to find in the valley a few sinks filled by recent rains, so that actually we experienced no great inconvenience from the want of fresh water. As far as our own personal necessities were concerned, we were abundantly supplied; it being an unfailing rule with us to carry in each wagon a five-gallon keg always filled with water, in order to guard against those frightful contingencies which so frequently occur on the prairies. In truth, upon leaving one watering-place, we never knew where we would find the next.

On the 20th of June we pitched our camp upon the north bank of the Canadian or Colorado, in latitude 35° 24′ according to a meridian altitude of Saturn. On the following day I left the caravan, accompanied by three Comancheros, and proceeded at a more rapid pace towards Santa Fé. This was rather a hazardous journey, inasmuch as we were still within the range of the Pawnee and Comanche war-parties, and my companions were men in whom I could not repose the slightest confidence, except for pilotage; being fully convinced that in case of meeting with an enemy they would either forsake or deliver me up, just as it might seem most conducive to their own interest and safety. All I had to depend upon were my firearms, which could hardly fail to produce an impression in my favor; for, thanks to Mr. Colt's invention, I carried thirty-six charges ready loaded, which I could easily fire at the rate of a dozen per minute. I do not believe that any band of those timorous savages of the western prairies would venture to approach even a single man under such circumstances. If, according to an old story of the frontier, an Indian supposed that a white man fired with both his tomahawk and scalping knife, to account for the execution done by a brace of pistols, thirty-six shots discharged in quick succession would certainly overawe them as being the effect of some great medicine.

As we jogged merrily along I often endeavored to while away the time by catechising my three companions in relation to the topography of the wild region we were traversing; but I soon found that, like the Indians, these ignorant rancheros have no ideas of distances, except as compared with time or with some other distance. They will tell you that you may arrive at a given place by the time the sun reaches a certain point: otherwise, whether it be but half a mile or half a day's ride to the place inquired for, they are as apt to apply *esto cerquita* (it is close by), or *esta lejos* (it is far off), to the one as to the other, just as the impression happens to strike them, when compared with some other point more or less distant. This often proves a source of great annoyance to foreign travelers, as I had an opportunity of experiencing before my arrival. In giving directions these people—in fact, the lower classes of Mexicans generally—are also in the habit of using very odd gesticulations, altogether peculiar to themselves. Instead of pointing with their hands and fingers they generally employ the mouth, which is done by thrusting out the lips in the direction of the spot or object which the inquirer wishes to find out—accompanied by *aqui* or *alli esta*. This habit of substituting labial gestures for the usual mode of indicating has grown from the use of the *sarape*, which keeps their hands and arms perpetually confined.

*Giving directions*

From the place where we left the wagons, till we reached the *Angostura*, or narrows[90] (a distance of 60 miles), we had followed a plain cart-road, which seemed everywhere passable for wagons. Here, however, we found the point of a table-plain projecting abruptly against the river, so as to render it impossible for wagons to pass without great risk. The huge masses of solid rock which occur in this place, and the rugged cliffs or brows of the table-lands which rise above them, appear to have been mistaken by a detachment of the Texan Santa Fé Expedition for spurs of the Rocky Mountains; an error which was rational enough, as they not unfrequently tower to the height of two thousand feet above the valley; and are often as rocky and rough as the rudest heaps of trap-rock can make them. By ascending the main summit of these craggy promontories, however, the eastern ridge of

[90] In eastern San Miguel County, New Mexico.

the veritable Rocky Mountains may be seen, still very far off in the western horizon, with a widespread and apparently level table-plain intervening and extending in every direction as far as the eye can reach; for even the deep-cut chasms of the intersecting rivers are rarely visible except one be upon their very brink.

Upon expressing my fears that our wagons would not be able to pass the *Angostura* in safety, my comrades informed me that there was an excellent route, of which no previous mention had been made, passing near the *Cerro de Tucumcari,* a round mound plainly visible to the southward.[91] After several vain efforts to induce some of the party to carry a note back to my brother, and to pilot the caravan through the Tucumcari route, one of them, known as Tio Baca, finally proposed to undertake the errand for a bounty of ten dollars, besides high wages till they should reach the frontier. His conditions being accepted, he set out after breakfast, not, however, without previously recommending himself to the Virgin Guadalupe and all the saints in the calendar, and desiring us to remember him in our prayers. Notwithstanding his fears, however, he arrived in perfect safety, and I had the satisfaction of learning afterward that my brother found the new route everything he could have desired.

[91] In eastern Quay County, New Mexico.

I continued my journey westward with my two remaining companions; but, owing to their being provided with a relay of horses, they very soon left me to make the balance of the travel alone—though yet in a region haunted by hostile savages. On the following day about the hour of twelve, as I was pursuing a horse-path along the course of the Rio Pecos, near the frontier settlements, I met with a shepherd, of whom I anxiously inquired the distance to San Miguel. "O, it is just there," responded the man of sheep. "Don't you see that point of mesa yonder? It is just beyond that." This welcome information cheered me greatly; for owing to the extraordinary transparency of the atmosphere, it appeared to me that the distance could not exceed two or three miles. "*Está cerquita,*" exclaimed the shepherd as I rode off; "*ahora está V. allá*"—"it is close by; you will soon be there."

I set off at as lively a pace as my jaded steed could carry me, confident of taking dinner in San Miguel. Every ridge I turned I thought must be the last, and thus I jogged on, hoping and anticipating my future comforts till the shades of evening began to appear, when I descended into the valley of the Pecos, which, although narrow, is exceedingly fertile and beautifully lined with verdant fields, among which stood a great variety of mud cabins. About eight o'clock I called at one of these cottages and again inquired the distance to San

Miguel; when a swarthy-looking ranchero once more saluted mine ears with *"Está cerquita; ahora está V. allá."* Although the distance was designated in precisely the same words used by the shepherd eight hours before, I had the consolation at least of believing that I was something nearer. After spurring on for a couple of miles over a rugged road, I at last reached the long-sought village.

The next day I hired a Mexican to carry some flour back to meet the wagons; for our party was by this time running short of provisions. In fact, we should long before have been in danger of starvation had it not been for our oxen; for we had not seen a buffalo since the day we first met with the Comanches. Some of our cattle being in good plight, and able, as we were, to spare a few from our teams, we made beef of them when urged by necessity: an extra advantage in ox teams on these perilous expeditions.

On the 25th of June I arrived safely at Santa Fé, but again rode back to meet the wagons, which did not reach the capital till the 4th of July. We did not encounter a very favorable reception from His Majesty, Gov. Armijo. He had just established his arbitrary impost of $500 per wagon, which bore rather heavily upon us; for we had an overstock of coarse articles which we had merely brought along for the purpose of increasing the strength of our company by adding to the number of our wagons.

But these little troubles in a business way were entirely drowned in the joyful sensations arising from our safe arrival, after so long and so perilous an expedition. Considering the character and our ignorance of the country over which we had traveled, we had been exceedingly successful. Instances are certainly rare of heavily-laden wagons having been conducted, without a guide, through an unexplored desert; and yet we performed the trip without any important accident—without encountering any very difficult passes—without suffering for food or for water.

We had hoped that at least a few days of rest and quiet recreation might have been allowed us after our arrival; for relaxation was sorely needed at the end of so long a journey and its concomitant privations: but it was ordered otherwise. We had scarcely quartered ourselves within the town before a grand flare-up took place between Gov. Armijo and the foreigners [92] in Santa Fé, which for a little while bade fair to result in open hostilities. It originated in the following circumstances.

In the winter of 1837–38 a worthy young American named Daley was murdered at the

[92] Among the New Mexicans the terms *foreigner* and *American* are synonymous; indeed, the few citizens of other nations to be found there identify themselves with those of the United States. All foreigners are known there as *Americanos*, but south of Chihuahua they are indiscriminately called *Los Ingleses*, the English. Gregg.

gold mines by a couple of villains, solely for plunder. The assassins were arrested, when they confessed their guilt; but in a short time they were permitted to run at large again, in violation of every principle of justice or humanity. About this time they were once more apprehended, however, by the interposition of foreigners: and at the solicitation of the friends of the deceased a memorial from the Americans in Santa Fé was presented to Armijo representing the injustice of permitting the murderers of their countryman to go unpunished; and praying that the culprits might be dealt with according to law. But the Governor affected to consider the affair as a conspiracy; and collecting his ragamuffin militia attempted to intimidate the petitioners. The foreigners were now constrained to look to their defense, as they saw that no justice was to be expected. Had Armijo persisted, serious consequences might have ensued; but seeing the "conspirators" firm he sent an apology, affecting to have misconstrued their motives and promising that the laws should be duly executed upon the murderers.

Besides the incentives of justice and humanity, foreigners felt a deep interest in the execution of this promise. But a few years previous another person had been assassinated and robbed at the same place; yet the authorities having taken no interest in the matter, the felons were never discovered; and now, should these assassins escape the merited forfeit of their atrocious crime, it was evident there would be no future security for our lives and property. But the Governor's due execution of the laws consisted in retaining them a year or two in nominal imprisonment, when they were again set at liberty: yet by far the greater portion of this time they were merely the *criados sin sueldo* (servants without hire) of the Governor, laboring for him as a remuneration for both the life and liberty which he granted them. Besides these, other foreigners have been murdered in New Mexico with equal impunity.

# Chapter 12

AFTER passing the custom-house ordeal and exchanging some of our merchandise for Eagle Dollars—an operation which occupied us several weeks, I prepared to set out for the Chihuahua market,[93] whither a portion of our stock had been designed. Upon this expedition I was obliged to depart without my brother, who was laboring under the home fever and anxious to return to his family. "He that hath wife and children," says Lord Bacon, "hath given hostages to fortune; for they are impediments to great enterprises, either of virtue or mischief." Men under such bonds are peculiarly unfitted for the chequered life of a Santa Fé trader. The domestic hearth with all its sacred and most endearing recollections is sure to haunt them in the hour of trial, and almost every step of their journey is apt to be attended by melancholy reflections of home and domestic dependencies.

[93] The journey from Santa Fé to Chihuahua, described in the present chapter, was likewise made by Lieutenant Pike in the spring of 1807. For his description of his experiences see *The Southwestern Expedition of Zebulon M. Pike*, 144-70.

Before starting on this new journey I deem it proper to make a few observations relative to the general character of the Chihuahua trade. I have already remarked that much surprise has frequently been expressed by those who are unacquainted with all the bearings of the case that the Missouri traders should take the circuitous route to Santa Fé, instead of steering direct for Chihuahua, inasmuch as the greatest portion of their goods is destined for the latter city. But as Chihuahua never had any port of entry for foreign goods till the last six or eight years, the market of that department had to be supplied in a great measure from Santa Fé. By opening the ports of El Paso and Presidio del Norte[94] the commercial interest was so little affected that when Santa Anna's decree for closing them again was issued the loss was scarcely felt at all.

The mode of transmitting merchandise from the ports to the interior is very different from what it is in the United States. It is not enough to have to pass the tedious ordeal of custom houses on the frontier; we have not only to submit to a supervision and repayment of duty on arriving at our point of destination, but our cargo is subject to scrutiny at every town we have to pass through on our journey. Nor would it be advisable to forsake the main route in order to avoid this tyrannical system

[94] At the mouth of Los Conchos River, in the state of Chihuahua.

of taxation; because, according to the laws of the country, every *cargamento* which is found out of the regular track (except in cases of unavoidable necessity) is subject to confiscation, although accompanied by the necessary custom-house documents.

There are also other risks and contingencies very little dreamed of in the philosophy of the inexperienced trader. Before setting out, the entire bill of merchandise has to be translated into Spanish; when, duplicates of the translation being presented to the custom house, one is retained while the other, accompanied by the *guia* (a sort of clearance or mercantile passport), is carried along with the cargo by the conductor. The trader can have three points of destination named in his *guia*, to either of which he may direct his course, but to no others: while in the drawing up of the *factura* or invoice the greatest care is requisite, as the slightest mistake, even an accidental slip of the pen might, according to the terms of the law, subject the goods to confiscation.[95]

The *guia* is not only required on leaving the ports for the interior, but is indispensable to

[95] In confirmation of this it is only necessary to quote the following from the *Pauta de Comisos*, Cap. II, Article 22:

"*Ni las guias ni las facturas, ni los pasas, en todos los casos de qua trata este decreto, han de contener esmendedura, raspadura,*"—and this under penalty of confiscation. Gregg.

the safe conveyance of goods from one department of the Republic to another: nay, the simple transfer of property from town to town and from village to village in the same department is attended by precisely the same proportion of risk, and requires the same punctilious accuracy in the accompanying documents. Even the produce and manufactures of the country are equally subject to these embarrassing regulations. New Mexico has no internal custom houses and is therefore exempt from this rigorous provision; but from Chihuahua south every village has its revenue officers; so that the same stock of merchandise sometimes pays the internal duty at least half a dozen times before the sale is completed.

Now, to procure this same *guia*, which is the cause of so much difficulty and anxiety in the end, is no small affair. Before the authorities condescend to draw a single line on paper the merchant must produce an endorser for the *tornaguia*, which is a certificate from the custom house to which the cargo goes directed, showing that the goods have been legally entered there. A failure in the return of this document within a prescribed limit of time subjects the endorser to a forfeiture equal to the amount of the impost. Much inconvenience and not a little risk are also occasioned on this score by the irregularity—I may say insecurity—of the mails.

Speaking of mails, I beg leave to observe that there are no conveniences of this kind in

New Mexico, except on the route from Santa Fé to Chihuahua, and these are very irregular and uncertain. Before the Indians had obtained such complete possession of the highways through the wilderness, the mails between these two cities were carried semi-monthly; but now they are much less frequent, being mere expresses, in fact, dispatched only when an occasion offers. There are other causes, however, besides the dread of marauding savages, which render the transportation of the mails in New Mexico very insecure: I mean the dishonesty of those employed in superintending them. Persons known to be inimical to the post-master or to the powers that be, and wishing to forward any communication to the south, most generally either wait for a private conveyance or send their letters to a post office (the only one besides that of Santa Fé in all New Mexico) some eighty miles on the way; thus avoiding an overhauling at the capital. Moreover, as the post-rider often carries the key of the mail-bag (for want of a supply at the different offices) he not unfrequently permits whomsoever will pay him a trifling *douceur* to examine the correspondence. I was once witness to a case of this kind in the Jornada del Muerto, where the entire mail was tumbled out upon the grass that an individual might search for letters, for which luxury he was charged by the accommodating carrier the moderate price of one dollar.

# Commerce of the Prairies

The *derecho de consumo* (the internal or consumption duty) is an impost averaging nearly twenty per cent on the United States cost of the bill. It supplies the place of a direct tax for the support of the departmental government, and is decidedly the most troublesome if not the most oppressive revenue system that ever was devised for internal purposes. It operates at once as a draw-back upon the commercial prosperity of the country and as a potent incentive to fraudulent practices. The country people especially have resort to every species of clandestine intercourse to escape this galling burden; for every article of consumption they carry to market, whether fish, flesh, or fowl, as well as fruit and vegetables, is taxed more or less; while another impost is levied upon the goods they purchase with the proceeds of their sales. This system, so beautifully entangled with corruptions, is supported on the ground that it supersedes direct taxation, which, in itself, is an evil that the free and independent people of Mexico would never submit to. Besides the petty annoyances incidental upon the laxity of custom-house regulations, no one can travel through the country without a passport, which to free-born Americans is a truly insupportable nuisance.

Having at last gone through with all the vexatious preparations necessary for our journey, on the 22d of August we started for

Chihuahua. I fitted out myself but six wagons for this market, yet joining in company with several other traders, our little caravan again amounted to fourteen wagons with about forty men. Though our route lay through the interior of northern Mexico, yet, on account of the hostile savages which infest most of the country through which we had to pass, it was necessary to unite in caravans of respectable strength, and to spare few of those precautions for safety which are required on the prairies.

The road we traveled passes down through the settlements of New Mexico for the first hundred and thirty miles, on the east side of the Rio del Norte. Nevertheless, as there was not an inn of any kind to be found upon the whole route, we were constrained to put up with very primitive accommodations. Being furnished from the outset, therefore, with blankets and buffalo rugs for bedding, we were prepared to bivouac, even in the suburbs of the villages, in the open air; for in this dry and salubrious atmosphere it is seldom that travelers go to the trouble of pitching tents.[96] When traveling alone, however, or with but a comrade or two, I have always experienced a great

[96] How scant soever our outfit of camp comforts might appear, our Mexican muleteers were much more sparsely supplied. The exposure endured by this hardy race is really surprising. Even in the coldest winter weather they rarely carry more than one blanket apiece—the *sarape*, which serves as a cloak during the day, and at night is their only "bed and bedding." Gregg.

deal of hospitality from the rancheros and villageois of the country. Whatever sins these ignorant people may have to answer for, we must accord to them at least two glowing virtues—gratitude and hospitality. I have suffered like others, however, from one very disagreeable custom which prevails among them. Instead of fixing a price for the services they bestow upon travelers, they are apt to answer, "*Lo que guste,*" or "*Lo que le dé la gana*" (whatever you please, or have a mind to give), expecting, of course, that the liberal foreigner will give more than their consciences would permit them to exact.

In about ten days' drive we passed the southernmost settlements of New Mexico, and twenty or thirty miles farther down the river we came to the ruins of Valverde. This village was founded about twenty years ago in one of the most fertile valleys of the Rio del Norte. It increased rapidly in population until it was invaded by the Navajoes, when the inhabitants were obliged to abandon the place after considerable loss and it has never since been repeopled. The bottoms of the valley, many of which are of rich alluvial loam, have lain fallow ever since, and will perhaps continue to be neglected until the genius of civilization shall have spread its beneficent influences over the land. This soil is the more valuable for cultivation on account of the facilities for irrigation which the river affords; as it too frequently happens that the best lands of the settlements remain unfruitful for want of water.

Our next camping place deserving of mention was Fray Cristobal, which, like many others on the route, is neither town nor village, but a simple isolated point on the river-bank— a mere *parage*, or camping-ground. We had already passed San Pascual, El Contadero, and many others, and we could hear Aleman, Robledo, and a dozen such spoken of on the way, leading the stranger to imagine that the route was lined with flourishing villages. The arriero will tell one to hasten—"We must reach San Diego before sleeping." We spur on, perhaps with redoubled vigor, in hopes to rest at a town; but lo! upon arriving we find only a mere watering-place, without open ground enough to graze the *caballada*. Thus every point along these wilderness highways used as a camping-site has received a distinctive name, well known to every muleteer who travels them. Many of these *parages*, without the slightest vestige of human improvement, figure upon most of the current maps of the day as towns and villages. Yet there is not a single settlement (except of very recent establishment) from those before mentioned to the vicinity of El Paso, a distance of near two hundred miles.

We arrived at Fray Cristobal in the evening, but this being the threshold of the famous *Jornada del Muerto*, we deemed it prudent to let our animals rest here until the following afternoon. The road over which we had hitherto been traveling, though it sometimes traverses upland ridges and undulating sections, runs generally near the border of the river, and for the most part in its immediate valley: but here it leaves the river and passes for nearly eighty miles over a table-plain to the eastward of a small ledge of mountains whose western base is hugged by the circuitous channel of the Rio del Norte. The craggy cliffs which project from these mountains render the eastern bank of the river altogether impassable. As the direct route over the plain is entirely destitute of water we took the precaution to fill all our kegs at Fray Cristobal, and late in the afternoon we finally set out. We generally find a great advantage in traveling through these arid tracts of land in the freshness of the evening, as the mules suffer less from thirst and move on in better spirits— particularly in the season of warm weather.

Early the next morning we found ourselves at the *Laguna del Muerto*, or Dead Man's Lake, where there was not even a vestige of water. This lake is but a sink in the plain of a few rods in diameter, and only filled with water during the rainy season. The marshes which are said by some historians to be in this vicinity are nowhere to be found: nothing but the firmest and driest table-land is to be seen in every direction. To procure water for our thirsty

animals it is often necessary to make a halt
here and drive them to the *Ojo del Muerto*
(Dead Man's Spring), five or six miles to the
westward, in the very heart of the mountain
ridge that lay between us and the river. This
region is one of the favorite resorts of the
Apaches, where many a poor arriero has met
with an untimely end. The route which leads
to the spring winds for two or three miles down
a narrow cañon or gorge overhung on either
side by abrupt precipices, while the various
clefts and crags which project their gloomy
brows over the abyss below seem to invite
the murderous savages to deeds of horror and
blood.

There is a tradition among the arrieros from
which it would appear that the only road
known in ancient time about the region of the
*Jornada* wound its circuitous course on the
western side of the river. To save distance an
intrepid traveler undertook to traverse this
desolate tract of land in one day, but having
perished in the attempt, it has ever after borne
the name of *La Jornada del Muerto*, the Dead
Man's Journey, or more strictly, the Day's
Journey of the Dead Man. One thing appears
very certain, that this dangerous pass has cost
the life of many travelers in days of yore; and
when we at last reached Robledo, a camping-
site upon the river, where we found abundance
of wood and water, we felt truly grateful that
the arid *Jornada* had not been productive of

more serious consequences to our party. We now found ourselves within the department of Chihuahua, as the boundary betwixt it and New Mexico passes not far north of Robledo.

We were still some sixty miles above Paso del Norte, but the balance of the road now led down the river valley or over the low bordering hills. During our journey between this and El Paso we passed the ruins of several settlements which had formerly been the seat of opulence and prosperity, but which have since been abandoned in consequence of the marauding incursions of the Apaches.

On the 12th of September we reached the usual ford of the Rio del Norte six miles above El Paso; but the river being somewhat flushed we found it impossible to cross over with our wagons. The reader will no doubt be surprised to learn that there is not a single ferry on this "Great River of the North" till we approach the mouth. But how do people cross it? Why, during three-fourths of the year it is everywhere fordable, and when the freshet season comes on each has to remain on his own side, or swim, for canoes even are very rare. But as we could neither swim our wagons and merchandise nor very comfortably wait for the falling of the waters our only alternative was to unload the vehicles and ferry the goods over in a little dug-out about thirty feet long and two feet wide, of which we were fortunate enough to obtain possession.

We succeeded in finding a place shallow enough to haul our empty wagons across: but for this good fortune we should have been under the necessity of taking them to pieces (as I had before done) and of ferrying them on the small craft before mentioned. Half of a wagon may thus be crossed at a time by carefully balancing it upon the canoe, yet there is, of course, no little danger of capsizing during the passage.

This river, even when fordable, often occasions a great deal of trouble, being, like the Arkansas, embarrassed with many quicksand mires. In some places, if a wagon is permitted to stop in the river but for a moment it sinks to the very body. Instances have occurred where it became necessary not only to drag out the mules by the ears and to carry out the loading package by package, but to haul out the wagon piece by piece—wheel by wheel.

On the 14th we made our entrance into the town of *El Paso del Norte*,[97] which is the northernmost settlement in the department of Chihuahua. Here our cargo had to be examined by a stern, surly officer, who, it was feared,

[97] This place is often known among Americans as "The Pass." It has been suggested in another place that it took its name from the *passing* thither of the refugees from the massacre of 1680; yet many persons very rationally derive it from the *passing* of the river (*el paso del Rio del Norte*) between two points of mountains which project against it from each side, just above the town. Gregg.

would lay an embargo on our goods upon the slightest appearance of irregularity in our papers; but notwithstanding our gloomy forebodings, we passed the ordeal without any difficulty.

The valley of El Paso is supposed to contain a population of about four thousand inhabitants, scattered over the western bottom of the Rio del Norte to the length of ten or twelve miles. These settlements are so thickly interspersed with vineyards, orchards, and cornfields as to present more the appearance of a series of plantations than of a town: in fact, only a small portion at the head of the valley where the *plaza publica* and parochial church are located would seem to merit this title. Two or three miles above the *plaza* there is a dam of stone and brush across the river, the purpose of which is to turn the current into a dike or canal, which conveys nearly half the water of the stream, during a low stage, through this well-cultivated valley for the irrigation of the soil. Here we were regaled with the finest fruits of the season: the grapes especially were of the most exquisite flavor. From these the inhabitants manufacture a very pleasant wine, somewhat resembling Malaga. A species of *aguardiente* (brandy) is also distilled from the same fruit, which, although weak, is of very agreeable flavor. These liquors are known among Americans as "Pass wine" and "Pass whiskey," and constitute a profitable article of trade, supplying the markets of Chihuahua and New Mexico.[98]

As I have said before, the road from Santa Fé to El Paso leads partly along the margin of the Rio del Norte or across the bordering hills and plains; but the *sierra* which separates the waters of this river and those of the Rio Pecos was always visible on our left. In some places it is cut up into detached ridges, one of which is known as *Sierra Blanca* in consequence of its summit's being covered with snow till late in the spring and having all the appearance of a glittering white cloud. There is another still more picturesque ridge farther south called *Los Organos*, consisting of an immense cliff of basaltic pillars which bear some resemblance to the pipes of an organ, whence the mountain derived its name. Both these sierras are famous as being the strongholds of the much-dreaded Apaches.

The mountains from El Paso northward are mostly clothed with pine, cedar, and a dwarfish species of oak. The valleys are timbered with cottonwood and occasionally with *mezquite*, which, however, is rarely found higher up

[98] There is very little wine or legitimate *aguardiente* manufactured in New Mexico. There was not a distillery, indeed, in all the province until established by Americans some fifteen or twenty years ago. Since that period considerable quantities of whiskey have been made there, particularly in the vicinity of Taos—distilled mainly from wheat, as this is the cheapest grain the country affords. Gregg.

than the lower settlements of New Mexico. In the immediate vicinity of El Paso there is another small growth called tornillo (or screwwood), so denominated from a spiral pericarp, which, though different in shape, resembles that of the mezquite in flavor. The plains and highlands generally are of a prairie character and do not ·differ materially from those of all northern Mexico, which are almost everywhere completely void of timber.

One of the most useful plants to the people of El Paso is the *lechuguilla*, which abounds on the hills and mountain-sides of that vicinity, as well as in many other places from thence southward. Its blades, which resemble those of the palmilla, being mashed, scraped, and washed, afford very strong fibers like the common Manilla sea-grass, and equally serviceable for the manufacture of ropes and other purposes.

After leaving El Paso our road branched off at an angle of about two points to the westward of the river, the city of Chihuahua being situated nearly a hundred miles to the west of it. At the distance of about thirty miles we reached Los Medanos, a stupendous ledge of sand-hills, across which the road passes for about six miles. As teams are never able to haul the loaded wagons over this region of loose sand, we engaged an *atajo* of mules at El Paso upon which to convey our goods across. These Medanos consist of huge hillocks and ridges of pure sand, in many places without a vestige of vegetation. Through the lowest gaps between the hills, the road winds its way.

What renders this portion of the route still more unpleasant and fatiguing is the great scarcity of water. All that is to be found on the road for the distance of more than sixty miles after leaving El Paso consists in two fetid springs, or pools, whose water is only rendered tolerable by necessity. A little farther on, however, we very unexpectedly encountered, this time, quite a superabundance of this necessary element. Just as we passed Lake Patos we were struck with astonishment at finding the road ahead of us literally overflowed by an immense body of water with a brisk current, as if some great river had suddenly been conjured into existence by the aid of supernatural arts. A considerable time elapsed before we could unravel the mystery. At last we discovered that a freshet had lately occurred in the streams that fed Lake Patos and caused it to overflow its banks, which accounted for this unwelcome visitation. We had to flounder through the mud and water for several hours before we succeeded in getting across.

The following day we reached the *acequia* below Carrizal, a small village with only three or four hundred inhabitants, but somewhat remarkable as being the site of a *presidio* (fort) at which is stationed a company of troops to protect the country against the ravages of the

Apaches, who, notwithstanding, continue to lay waste the ranchos in the vicinity and to depredate at will within the very sight of the fort.

About twelve miles south of Carrizal there is one of the most charming warm springs called Ojo Caliente, where we arrived the next day. It forms a basin some thirty feet long by about half that width, and just deep and warm enough for a most delightful bath at all seasons of the year. Were this spring (whose outlet forms a bold little rivulet) anywhere within the United States, it would doubtless soon be converted into a place of fashionable resort. There appears to be a somewhat curious phenomenon connected with this spring. It proceeds, no doubt, from the little river of Carmen, which passes within half a mile and finally discharges itself into the small lake of Patos before mentioned. All the water of this stream disappears in the sand some miles above the spring; and what medium it traverses in its subterranean passage to impart to it so high a temperature before breaking out in this fountain would afford to the geologist an interesting subject of inquiry.

After fording the Rio Carmen, which, though usually without a drop of water in its channel, we now found a very turbulent stream, we did not meet with any object particularly worthy of remark until we reached the *Laguna de Encinillas*. This lake is ten or twelve miles long by two or three in width and seems to have no outlet even during the greatest freshets, though fed by several small constantly-flowing streams from the surrounding mountains. The water of this lake during the dry season is so strongly impregnated with nauseous and bitter salts as to render it wholly unpalatable to man and beast. The most predominant of these noxious substances is a species of alkali, known there by the title of *tequesquite*. It is often seen oozing out from the surface of marshy grounds about the table-plains of all northern Mexico, forming a grayish crust, and is extensively used in the manufacture of soap and sometimes by the bakers even for raising bread. Here we had another evidence of the alarming effects of the recent flood, the road for several miles along the margin of the lake being completely inundated. It was, however, in the city of Chihuahua itself that the disastrous consequences of the freshet were most severely felt. Some inferior houses of *adobe* were so much soaked by the rains that they tumbled to the ground, occasioning the loss of several lives.

The valley of Encinillas is very extensive and fertile, and is the locale of one of those princely estates which are so abundant farther south, and known by the name of *Haciendas*. It abounds in excellent pasturage and in cattle of all descriptions. In former times, before the Apaches had so completely devastated the country, the herds which grazed in this beautiful valley presented much the appearance of the buffalo of the plains, being almost as wild and generally of dark color. Many of the proprietors of these princely haciendas pride themselves in maintaining a uniformity in the color of their cattle: thus some are found stocked with black, others red, others white —or whatsoever shade the owner may have taken a fancy to.

As we drew near to Chihuahua our party had more the appearance of a funeral procession than of a band of adventurers about to enter into the full fruition of dancing hopes and the realization of golden dreams. Every one was uneasy as to what might be the treatment of the revenue officers. For my own part, I had not quite forgotten sundry annoyances and trials of temper I had been made to experience in the season of 1837, on a similar occasion. Much to our surprise, however, as well as delight, we were handled with a degree of leniency by the custom-house deities, on our arrival, that was almost incomprehensible. But the charm which operated in our favor, when understood, was very simple. A caravan had left Chihuahua direct for the United States the spring previous and was daily expected back. The officers of the custom house were already compromised by certain cogent arguments to receive the proprietors of this caravan with striking marks of favor, and the *Señor Administrador de Rentas*, Zuloaga himself, was expecting an *ancheta* of goods. Therefore, had they treated us with their wonted severity the contrast would have been altogether too glaring.

We arrived at Chihuahua on the first of October, after a trip of forty days, with wagons much more heavily laden than when we started from the United States. The whole distance from Santa Fé to Chihuahua is about 550 miles, being reckoned 320 to Paso del Norte and 230 from thence to Chihuahua. The road from El Paso south is mostly firm and beautiful, with the exception of the sand-hills before spoken of; and is only rendered disagreeable by the scarcity and occasional ill-savor of the water. The route winds over an elevated plain among numerous detached ridges of low mountains—spurs, as it were, of the main Cordilleras, which lie at a considerable distance to the westward. Most of these extensive intermediate plains, though in many places of fertile-looking soil, must remain wholly unavailable for agricultural purposes on account of their natural aridity and a total lack of water for irrigation.

# Chapter 13

A VISIT TO AGUASCALIENTES

THE patient reader who may have accompanied me thus far without murmuring at the dryness of some of the details will perhaps pardon me for presenting here a brief account of a trip which I made to Aguascalientes in the interior of northern Mexico in the year 1835, and which the arrangement I have adopted has prevented me from introducing before in its chronological order.

The trade to the south constitutes a very important branch of the commerce of the country, in which foreigners as well as natives are constantly embarking. It is customary for most of those who maintain mercantile establishments in Chihuahua to procure assortments of Mexican fabrics from the manufactories of Leon, Aguascalientes, and other places of the same character in the more southern districts of the Republic. At certain seasons of the year there are held regular *ferias*, at which the people assemble in great numbers, as well of sellers as of purchasers. There are some eight or ten of these annual fairs held in the Republic, each of which usually lasts a week or more. It was about as much, however, from a desire to behold the sunny districts of the south as for commercial purposes that I undertook this expedition in 1835; and as my engagements have not permitted me to revisit this section since, the few notes of interest I was then able to collect seem to come more appropriately in this part of my work than in any other place that I could readily select.

I set out from Chihuahua on the 26th of February, 1835. My party consisted of four men (including myself) and two empty wagons—not a very formidable escort to protect our persons as well as specie and bullion (the only transmissible currency of the country) against the bands of robbers which at all times infest that portion of our route that lay south of Durango. From Chihuahua to that city the road was rendered still more perilous by the constant hostilities of the Indians. On the 7th of March, however, we arrived without accident at the town of Cerro Gordo, the northernmost settlement in the department of Durango; and the following day we reached La Zarca, which is the principal village of one of the most extensive haciendas in the north. So immense is the amount of cattle on this estate that, as it was rumored, the proprietor once offered to sell the whole hacienda, stock, etc., for the consideration alone of fifty cents for each head of cattle found on the estate; but that no person has ever yet been able or willing to muster sufficient capital to take up the offer. It is very likely, however, that if such a proposition was ever made the proprietor intended to include all his stock of rats and mice, reptiles and insects—in short, every genus of "small cattle" on his premises. This estate covers a territory of perhaps a hundred miles in length, which comprises several flourishing villages.

In two days more we reached Rio Nazas, a beautiful little river that empties itself into Lake Cayman.[99] Rio Nazas has been celebrated for the growth of cotton, which, owing to the mildness of the climate, is sometimes planted fresh only every three or four years. The light frosts of winter seldom destroy more than the upper portion of the stalk, so that the root is almost perennial. About twenty-five miles farther we stopped at the mining village of La Noria, where we were obliged to purchase water for our mules—a novel expense to the American traveler, but scarcely to be complained of, inasmuch as the water had to be drawn from wells with a great deal of labor. It is not unusual, also, for the proprietors of haciendas to

[99] The numerous little lakes throughout the interior of Mexico, without outlet, yet into which rivers are continually flowing, present a phenomenon which seems quite singular to the inhabitants of our humid climates. But the wastage in the sand, and still greater by evaporation in those elevated, dry regions, is such that there are no important rises in the lakes except during unusual freshets. Gregg.

demand remuneration for the pasturage on the open plains consumed by the animals of travelers—a species of exaction which one never hears of in the north of Mexico.

Our next stopping-place was Cuencamé, which may well be called the Village of Churches: for, although possessing a very small population, there are five or six edifices of this description. As I had business to transact at Durango, which is situated forty or fifty miles westward of the main southern road, I now pursued a direct route for that city, where I arrived on the 16th of March.

Durango is one of the handsomest cities in the north, with a population of about 20,000. It is situated in a level plain, surrounded in every direction by low mountains. It presents two or three handsome squares with many fine edifices and some really splendid churches. The town is supplied with water for irrigating the gardens and for many other ordinary purposes by several open aqueducts, which lead through the streets from a large spring a mile or two distant; but as these are kept filthy by the offal that is thrown into them, the inhabitants who are able to buy it procure most of their water for drinking and culinary purposes from the *aguadores*, who pack it on asses, usually in large jars, from the spring.

This is the first northern city in which there is to be found any evidence of that variety of tropical fruits for which southern Mexico is so justly famed. Although it was rather out of season, yet the market actually teemed with all that is most rich and exquisite in this kind of produce. The *maguey*, from which is extracted the popular beverage called *pulque*,[100] is not only cultivated extensively in the fields but grows wild everywhere upon the plains. This being the height of the pulque season, a hundred shanties might be seen loaded with jugs and goblets filled with this favorite liquor, from its sweetest unfermented state to the grade of hard cider; while the incessant cries of "Pulque! pulque dulce bueno!" added to the shrill and discordant notes of the fruit venders, created a confusion of sounds amidst which it was impossible to hear oneself talk.

Durango is also celebrated as being the headquarters, as it were, of the whole scorpion family. During the spring, especially, so much

[100] Also, from the *pulque* is distilled a spirituous liquor called *mezcal*. The *maguey* (*Agave Americana*) is besides much used for hedging. It here performs the double purpose of a cheap and substantial fence, and of being equally valuable for *pulque*. When no longer serviceable in these capacities, the pulpy stalk is converted by roasting into a pleasant item of food, while the fibrous blades, being suitably dressed, are still more useful. They are manufactured into ropes, bags, etc., which resemble those made of the common sea-grass, though the fibers are finer. There is one species (which does not produce *pulque*, however) whose fibers, known in that country as *pita*, are nearly as fine as dressed hemp, and are generally used for sewing shoes, saddlery, and similar purposes. Gregg.

are the houses infested by these poisonous insects that many people are obliged to have resort to a kind of mosquito-bar in order to keep them out of their beds at night. As an expedient to deliver the city from this terrible pest, a society has actually been formed which pays a reward of a *cuartilla* (three cents) for every *alacran* (or scorpion) that is brought to them. Stimulated by the desire of gain, the idle boys of the city are always on the lookout: so that in the course of a year immense numbers of this public enemy are captured and slaughtered. The body of this insect is of the bulk of a medium spider, with a jointed tail one to two inches long, at the end of which is a sting whose wounds are so poisonous as often to prove fatal to children, and are very painful to adults.

The most extraordinary peculiarity of these scorpions is that they are far less dangerous in the north than in the south, which in some manner accounts for the story told Capt. Pike, that even those of Durango lose most of their venom as soon as they are removed a few miles from the city.

Although we were exceedingly well armed, yet so many fearful stories of robberies said to be committed almost daily on the southern roads reached my ears that before leaving Durango I resolved to add to my weapons of defense one of those peculiarly terrible dogs which are sometimes to be found in this

country, and which are very serviceable to
travelers situated as I was. Having made my
wishes known to a free negro from the United
States, named George, he recommended me to
a custom-house officer, and a very particular
friend of his, as being possessed of the very
article I was in search of. I accordingly called
at the house of that functionary, in company
with my sable informant, and we were ushered
into a handsome parlor, where two or three
well-dressed señoritas sat discussing some of the
fruitful topics of the day. One of them—the
officer's wife, as it appeared, and a very comely
dame she was—rose immediately, and with a
great deal of ceremonious deference saluted
*Señor Don Jorge*, inviting him at the same time
to a seat, while I was left to remain perfectly
unnoticed in my standing position. George
appeared considerably embarrassed, for he had
not quite forgotten the customs and manners
of his native country, and was even yet in the
habit of treating Americans not only with
respect but with humility. He, therefore, declined the tendered distinction, and remarked
that *el señor* had only come to purchase their
dog. Upon this the lady pointed to a kennel
in a corner, when the very first glimpse of the
ferocious animal convinced me that he was
precisely the sort of a customer I wanted for a
companion. Having therefore paid down six
dollars, the stipulated sum of purchase, I bowed
myself out of the presence of the ladies, not a

little impressed with my own insignificance in the eyes of these fair *doñas*, contrasted with the grandeur of my sable companion. But the popularity of negroes in northern Mexico has ceased to be a matter of surprise to the traveler.

With regard to *Don Jorge*, if I was surprised at the marks of attention paid him by a white lady, I had cause to be much more astonished shortly after. As the sooty don was lounging about my wagons, a clever-visaged youth approached and placed in his hands a satin stock with the compliments of his sister (the officer's wife), hoping that he would receive that trifle, wrought by her own hand, as a token of her particular regard! But notwithstanding these marks of distinction (to apply no harsher epithet) George was exceedingly anxious to engage in my employ in whatsoever capacity I might choose to take him; for he discovered that such honors were far from affording him a livelihood: yet I did not then need his services, and have never heard of him since.

On the 22d we left Durango, and after a few days' march found ourselves once more in the *camino real* that led from Chihuahua to Zacatecas. All the frightful stories I had heard about robbers now began to flash upon my memory, which made me regard every man I encountered on the road with a very suspicious eye. As all travelers go armed, it is impossible to distinguish them from banditti;[101] so that the unsuspecting traveler is very frequently set upon by the very man he had been consorting with in apparent good-fellowship, and either murdered on the spot or dragged from his horse with the lazo and plundered of all that is valuable about him.

I have heard it asserted that there is a regular bandit trade organized throughout the country, in which some of the principal officers of state (and particularly of the judicial corps) are not unfrequently engaged. A capital is made up by shares, as for any other enterprise, bandits are fitted out and instructed where to operate, and at stated periods of the year a regular dividend is paid to the stockholders. The impunity which these gentlemen of the order almost everywhere enjoy in the country is, therefore, not to be marveled at. In Durango, during my sojourn there, a well-dressed caballero was frequently in the habit of entering our *meson*, whom mine host soon pointed out to me as a notorious brigand. "Beware of him," said the honest publican; "he is prying into your affairs"—and so it turned out; for my muleteer informed me that the fellow had been trying to pump from him all the particulars

[101] Travelers on these public highways not only go armed to the teeth, but always carry their weapons exposed. Even my wagoners carried their guns and pistols swung upon the pommels of their saddles. At night, as we generally camped out, they were laid under our heads or close by our sides. Gregg.

in regard to our condition and destination. Yet this worthy was not only suffered to prowl about unmolested by the authorities, but appeared to be on familiar terms with many of the principal dignitaries of the city. Notwithstanding all our apprehensions, however, we arrived at our place of destination without even the novelty of an incident to swell our budget of gossip.

The city of Aguascalientes is beautifully situated in a level plain and would appear to contain about twenty thousand inhabitants, who are principally engaged in the manufacture of *rebozos* and other textures mostly of cotton. As soon as I found myself sufficiently at leisure I visited the famous warm spring (*ojo caliente*) in the suburbs, from which the city derives its euphonious name. I followed up the *acequia* that led from the spring—a ditch four or five feet wide, through which flowed a stream three or four feet in depth. The water was precisely of that agreeable temperature to afford the luxury of a good bath, which I had hoped to enjoy; but every few paces I found men, women, and children submerged in the acequia; and when I arrived at the basin it was so choked up with girls and full-grown women, who were paddling about with all the nonchalance of a gang of ducks, that I was forced to relinquish my long-promised treat.

It had been originally my intention to continue on to Leon, another manufacturing town, some seventy or eighty miles from Aguas-calientes; but hearing that Santa Anna had just arrived there with a large army on his way to Zacatecas to quell an insurrection, I felt very little curiosity to extend my rambles farther. Having, therefore, made all my purchases in the shortest possible time, in a few days I was again in readiness to start for the north.

That my mules might be in condition for the hard travel before me it was necessary to have them shod: a precaution, however, which is seldom used in the north of Mexico, either with mules or horses. Owing a little to the peculiar breed, but more still, no doubt, to the dryness of the climate, Mexican animals have unusually hard hoofs. Many will travel for weeks and even months over the firm [102] and often rocky roads of the interior (the pack-mules carrying their huge loads) without any protection whatever to the feet save that which nature has provided. But most of mine being a little tender-footed, I engaged Mexican *herreros* to fit them out in their own peculiar style. Like almost everything else of their manufacturing, their mule-shoes are of a rather primitive model—broad, thin plates tacked on with large club-headed nails. But the expertness

[102] Some of these table-plain highways, though of but a dry, sandy, and clayey soil, are as firm as a brick pavement. In some places, for miles, I have remarked that the nail-heads of my shod animals would hardly leave any visible impression. Gregg.

of the shoers compensated in some degree for the defects of the *herraduras*. It made but little odds how wild and vicious the mule— an assistant would draw up his foot in an instant, and soon place him *hors de combat;* and then fixing a nail, the shoer would drive it to the head at a single stroke, standing usually at full arm's length, while the assistant held the foot. Thus in less than half the time I had ever witnessed the execution of a similar job before, they had completely shod more than twenty of the most unruly brutes—without once resorting to the expedient, so usual in such cases, of throwing the animals upon the ground.

Just as the process of shoeing my mules had been completed, a person who proved to be a public officer entered the *corral*, and pointing to the mules, very politely informed me that they were wanted by the government to transport troops to Zacatecas. "They will be called for tomorrow afternoon," he continued; "let them not be removed!" I had, of course, to bow acquiescence to this imperative edict, well knowing that all remonstrance would be vain; yet fully determined to be a considerable distance on the road northward before that morrow should be very far advanced.

But a new difficulty now presented itself. I must procure a *guia* or passport for my cargo of merchandise, with a responsible endorser, an additional imposition I was wholly unprepared for, as I was then ignorant of any law to that effect being in force and had not a single acquaintance in the city. I was utterly at a loss what to do: under any other circumstances I might have left the amount of the *derecho de consumo* in deposit, as others have been obliged to do on similar occasions; but unfortunately I had laid out the last dollar of my available means.

As I left the custom house brooding over these perplexities, one of the principal clerks of the establishment slipped a piece of paper into my hand containing the following laconic notice: *"Aguárdeme afuera"* (wait for me without); an injunction I passively obeyed, although I had not the least idea of its purport. The clerk was soon with me and remarked: "You are a stranger in the city and ignorant of our severe revenue laws: meet me in an hour from this at my lodgings and we will devise some remedy for your difficulties." It may be well supposed that I did not fail to be punctual. I met the obliging officer in his room with a handful of blank custom-house *pases*. It should be understood that a *pase* only differs from a *guia* in requiring no endorser, but they can only be extended for amounts of goods not exceeding fifty dollars. Taking my bill, he very soon filled me up a *pase* for every package, directing each to a different point in the north. "Now," observed my amiable friend, "if you are disposed to do a little smuggling these will secure your safety, if you avoid the borders of Chihuahua: if not, you may have a friend on the way who will endorse your *guia*." I preferred the latter alternative. I had formed an acquaintance with a worthy German merchant in Durango, who, I felt convinced, would generously lend his signature to the required document.

As the revenue officers of northern Mexico are not celebrated for liberality and disinterestedness, I took it for granted that my friend of the custom house was actuated by selfish motives and therefore proffered him a remuneration for the trouble he had taken on my account; but to my surprise he positively refused accepting anything, observing that he held it the duty of every honest man to assist his fellow creatures in case of difficulty. It is truly a pleasant task to bear record of such instances of disinterestedness in the midst of so many contaminating influences.

While speaking of *guias* I may as well remark that they are also frequently required for specie and always for bullion. This is often very annoying to the traveler, not only because it is sometimes inconvenient to find an endorser, but because the robbers are thus enabled to obtain precise and timely information of the funds and route of every traveler; for they generally have their agents in all the principal cities, who are apt to collude with some of the custom-house clerks and thus procure regular reports of the departures, with the amounts of valuables conveyed.

I was not long in taking leave of Aguascalientes and heard nothing more of the impressment of my mules. It was not my good fortune, however, to remain for any length of time out of trouble. Being anxious to take the city of Zacatecas in my route without jeopardizing my goods, I took passage by the *diligencia*, while my wagons continued on in the *camino real* or main road. On my arrival at Zacatecas I very soon discovered that by leaving my bed and board behind with the wagons I had doomed myself to no small inconvenience and privation. It was with the greatest difficulty I could obtain a place to lie upon and clean victuals with which to allay my hunger. I could get a room, it is true, even for a *real* per day, in one of those great barn-like *mesones* which are to be met with in all these cities, but not one of them was at all furnished. There is sometimes in a corner a raised platform of mud, much resembling a common blacksmith's hearth, which is to supply the place of a bedstead, upon which the traveler may spread his blankets if he happen to have any. On this occasion I succeeded in borrowing one or two of the stage-driver, who was a Yankee, and so made out pretty comfortably in the sleeping way. These *mesones* are equally ill-prepared to furnish food for the traveler, unless he is willing to put up with a dish of *frijoles* and *chile guisado* with *tortillas*, all served up in the most filthy manner. I therefore sought out a public *fonda* kept by an Italian, where I procured an excellent supper. Fondas, however, are mere *restaurants*, and consequently without accommodations for lodging.

Strange as the fact may appear, one may travel fifteen hundred miles and perhaps more on the main public highway through northern Mexico without finding a single tavern with general accommodations. This, however, may be accounted for by taking into consideration the peculiar mode of traveling of the country, which renders resorts of this kind almost unnecessary. *Arrieros* with their *atajos* of pack-mules always camp out, being provided with their cooks and stock of provisions, which they carry with them. Ordinary travelers generally unite in little caravans for security against robbers and marauders; and no caballero ever stirs abroad without a train of servants and a pack-mule to carry his *cantinas* (a pair of large wallets or leathern boxes) filled with provisions, on the top of which is lashed a huge machine containing a mattress and all the other fixings for bed furniture. Thus equipped, the caballero snaps his fingers at all the *hotels garnis* of the universe, and is perfectly independent in every movement.

The city of Zacatecas, as my readers are doubtless aware, is celebrated for its mining interests. Like all other Mexican towns of the same class, it originated in small, insignificant settlements on the hillsides in the immediate vicinity of the mines, until it gradually grew up to be a large and wealthy city with a population of some 30,000 inhabitants. Its locale is a deep ravine formed among rugged mountain ridges; and as the houses are mostly built in rows overtopping one another along the hillsides, some portions of the city present all the appearance of a vast amphitheater. Many of the streets are handsomely paved and two of the squares are finely ornamented with curiously carved *jets-d'eau*, which are supplied with water raised by mule power from wells among the adjacent hills. From these the city is chiefly furnished with water.

I have already mentioned that General Santa Anna was at this time marching against Zacatecas with a large force. It may be remembered that after the General's accession to the supreme authority of Mexico (upon the establishment of *Centralismo*) he deemed it expedient to issue a decree abolishing the state militia, known as Civicos, as being dangerous to the liberties of——the dictator. Zacatecas, so far from obeying this despotic mandate, publicly called on the Civicos to defend their rights, and Santa Anna was now descending upon them with an army double that which the city could raise, to enforce their obedience. The *Zacatecanos*, however, were not idle. The militia was pouring in from the surrounding villages and a degree of enthusiasm prevailed throughout the city which seemed to be the presage of a successful defense. In fact, the city itself, besides being from its location almost impregnable, was completely protected by artificial fortifications. The only accessible point was by the main road, which led from the south immediately up the narrow valley of the ravine. Across this a strong wall had been erected some years before, and the road passed through a large gate, commanded by a bastion upon the hillside above, whence a hundred men well supplied with arms and ammunition might easily cut off thousands upon thousands as fast as they advanced. The city was therefore deemed impregnable, and being supplied with provisions for a lengthy siege, the patriots were in high spirits. A foreign engineer or two had been engaged to superintend the fortifications.

Santa Anna reached Zacatecas a few days after my departure. As he had no idea of testing the doubtful mettle of his army by an attempt to storm the place, which presented so formidable an appearance, he very quietly squatted himself down at the village of Guadalupe, three miles below. From this point he commenced his operations by throwing missiles into the city—not of lead, or cast-iron, or any such cruel agents of warfare, but *bombs of paper*, which fell among the besieged and burst with gentle overtures to their commanding officers. This novel artillery of the dictator produced a perfectly electric effect; for the valor of the commandant of the Civicos rose to such a pitch that he at once marched his forces out of the fortifications to attack the besiegers in the open field—face to face, as true bravery required. But on the very first onset this valiant officer, by some mysterious agency which could not be accounted for, was suddenly seized with a strange panic and, with all his forces, made a precipitate retreat, fleeing helter-skelter, as if all the engines of destruction that were ever invented had been brought to bear upon them; when the victorious army of Santa Anna marched into the city without further opposition.

This affair is a pretty just sample of most of the successful battles of this great general. The treacherous collusion of the principal Zacatecas officers was so apparent that they deemed it prudent to fly the city for safety, lest the wrath of their incensed fellow-citizens should explode upon them. Meanwhile, the soldiery amused themselves by sacking the city and by perpetrating every species of outrage that their mercenary and licentious appetites could devise. Their savage propensities were particularly exercised against the few foreigners that were found in the place.

By this time, I was journeying very leisurely towards Durango, where I arrived on the 21st of April. As the main wagon road to the north does not pass through that city, it was most convenient and still more prudent for me to leave my wagons at a distance: their entrance would have occasioned the confiscation of my goods for the want of the necessary documents, as already alluded to. But I now procured a *guia* without further difficulty; which was indeed a principal object of my present visit to that city.

Before leaving Durango I witnessed one of those civil broils which are so common in Mexico. I was not even aware that any difficulty had been brewing till I was waked on the morning of the 25th by a report of firearms. Stepping out to ascertain what was the matter, I perceived the *azotea* of the parochial church occupied by armed men, who seemed to be employed in amusing themselves by discharging their guns at random upon the people in the streets. These *bravos*, as I was afterwards informed, belonged to the bishop's party, or that of the *Escoceses*, which was openly at war with the liberalists, anti-hierarchists, or *Yorkinos*, and were resorting to this summary mode of proceeding in order to bring about a change of affairs; for at this time the liberal party had the ascendency in the civil government of Durango.

Being somewhat curious to have a nearer view of what was going on, I walked down past the church towards a crowd which was assembled in a *plaza* beyond. This movement on my part was rather inconsiderate: for foreigners were in extremely bad odor with the belligerents; nor had I mingled with the multitude many minutes before a sober-looking citizen plucked me by the sleeve and advised me if I valued my two ears and did not wish to have my career of usefulness cut short prematurely to stay within doors. Of course I needed no further persuasion, and returned at once to my lodgings, where I made immediate preparations for a speedy departure. As I was proceeding through the streets soon afterward with a cargo of goods I received, just after leaving the custom house, a very warm salutation from the belligerents, which made the dust start from almost under my very feet. The *cargadores* who were carrying my packages were no doubt as much frightened as myself. They supposed the reason of their shooting at us to be because they imagined we were carrying off the *parque* (ammunition) of the government, which was deposited in the building we had just left.

We were soon under way and very little regret did I feel when I fairly lost sight of the city of scorpions. But I was not yet wholly beyond the pale of difficulties. Owing to the fame of the Indian hostilities in the north it was almost impossible to procure the services of Mexican muleteers for the expedition. One I engaged took the first convenient opportunity to escape at night, carrying away a gun with which I had armed him; yet I felt grateful that he did not also take a mule, as he had the whole *caballada* under his exclusive charge: and soon after, a Mexican wagoner was frightened back by the reports of savages.

After a succession of such difficulties, and still greater risks from the Indians that infested the route, I was, of course, delighted when I reached Chihuahua on the 14th of May in perfect safety.[103]

[103] The distance from Chihuahua to Durango is about five hundred miles, and from thence to Aguascalientes it is nearly three hundred upon the route we traveled, which was very circuitous. All the intermediate country resembles, in its physical features, that lying immediately north of Chihuahua, which has already been described. Gregg.

# Chapter 14

**B**EFORE resuming my regular narrative I trust the reader will pardon me for introducing here a brief account of an excursion which I made in the fall of the year 1835 to the mining town of Jesus Maria, one of the most important mineral districts in the department of Chihuahua, situated about a hundred and fifty miles west of the city in the very heart of the great Cordilleras.

I had long been desirous of visiting some of the mining establishments of Mexico, and seeing a favorable opportunity of embarking in a profitable enterprise I set out from Chihuahua on the 15th of October. My party consisted of but one American comrade with a Mexican muleteer—and three or four mules freighted with specie to be employed in the silver trade: a rather scanty convoy for a route subject to the inroads both of savages and robbers. For transportation, we generally pack our specie in sacks made of raw beef hide, which shrinks upon drying and thus presses the contents so closely as to prevent friction. A pair of these packages, usually containing between one and two thousand dollars each, constitutes an ordinary mule-load on the mountain routes.

The road in this direction leads through the roughest mountain passes; and in some places it winds so close along the borders of precipices that by a single mis-step an animal might be precipitated several hundred feet. Mules, however, are very sure-footed; and will often clamber along the most craggy cliffs with nearly as much security as the goat. I was shown the projecting edge of a rock over which the road had formerly passed. This shelf was perhaps thirty feet in length by only two or three in width. The road which leads into the town of Jesus Maria from the west side of the mountain is also extremely perilous and steep and seems almost to overhang the houses below. Heavily-laden mules have sometimes slipped off the track and tumbled headlong into the town. This place is even more pent up between ridges than Zacatecas: the valley is narrower and the mountains much higher; while, as is the case with that remarkable city, the houses are sometimes built in successive tiers, one above another; the *azoteas* of the lower ones forming the yard of those above.

The first mine I visited consisted of an immense horizontal shaft cut several hundred feet into a hill-side a short distance below the town of Jesus Maria, upon which the proprietors had already sunk, in the brief space of one year, the enormous sum of one hundred and twenty thousand dollars! Such is often the fate of the speculative miner, whose vocation is closely allied to gaming, and equally precarious.

The most important mine of Jesus Maria at this time was one called Santa Juliana, which had been the means of alternately making and sinking several splendid fortunes. This mine had then reached a depth of between eight and nine hundred feet, and the operations were still tending downwards. The materials were drawn up by mule power applied to a windlass: but as the rope attached to it only extended half way down, another windlass had been erected at the distance of about four hundred feet from the mouth of the cavern, which was also worked by mules and drew the ores, etc., from the bottom. On one occasion as I was standing near the aperture of this great pit, watching the ascent of the windlass rope, expecting every moment the appearance of the large leathern bucket which they employ for drawing up the minerals as well as the rubbish and water[104] from the bottom, what should greet my vision but a mule, puffing and writhing, firmly bound to a huge board constructed for the purpose, and looking about as demure upon the whole as a sheep under the shears. On being untied the emancipated brute suddenly sprang to his feet and looked around him at

[104] Water has sometimes accumulated so rapidly in this mine as to stop operations for weeks together. Gregg.

the bright scenes of the upper world with as much astonishment as Rip Van Winkle may be supposed to have felt after waking up from his twenty years' sleep.

The ore which is obtained from these mines, if sufficiently rich to justify the operation, is transferred to the smelting furnaces, where the pure metal is melted down and extracted from the virgin fossil. If, on the contrary, the ore is deemed of inferior quality, it is then submitted to the process of amalgamation.

The *moliendas* or crushing-mills (*arrastres*, as called at some mines) employed for the purpose of grinding the ores are somewhat singular machines. A circular (or rather annular) cistern of some twenty or thirty feet in diameter is dug in the earth and the sides as well as the bottom are lined with hewn stone of the hardest quality. Transversely through an upright post which turns upon its axis in the center of the plan, passes a shaft of wood, at each end of which are attached by cords one or two grinding-stones with smooth flat surfaces, which are dragged (by mules fastened to the extremities of the shaft) slowly around upon the bottom of the cistern, into which the ore is thrown after being pounded into small pieces. It is here ground, with the addition of water, into an impalpable mortar by the constant friction of the dragging stones against the sides and bottom of the cistern. A suitable quantity of quicksilver is perfectly mixed with the mortar; to which are added some muriates, sulphates, and other chemical substances to facilitate the amalgamation. The compound is then piled up in small heaps and not disturbed until this process is supposed to be complete, when it is transferred to the washing-machine. Those I have observed are very simple, consisting of a kind of stone tub into which a stream of water is made to flow constantly so as to carry off all the lighter matter, which is kept stirred up by an upright studded with pegs that revolves in the center, while the amalgamated metals sink to the bottom. Most of the quicksilver is then pressed out and the silver submitted to a burning process, by which the remaining portion of mercury is expelled.

The silver which is taken from the furnace generally contains an intermixture of gold averaging from ten to thirty per cent; but what is extracted by amalgamation is mostly separated in the washing. While in a liquid state the gold, from its greater specific gravity, mostly settles to the bottom: yet it usually retains a considerable alloy of silver. The compound is distinguished by the name of *oroche*. The main portion of the silver generally retains too little gold to make it worth separating.

Every species of silver is moulded into *barras* or ingots, weighing from fifty to eighty pounds each, and usually worth between one and two thousand dollars. These are assayed by an authorized agent of the government and stamped with their weight and character, which enables the holder to calculate their value by a very simple rule. When the bullion is thus stamped it constitutes a species of currency, which is much safer for remittances than coin. In case of robbery the *barras* are easily identified, provided the robbers have not had time to mould them into some other form. For this reason people of wealth frequently lay up their funds in ingots; and the cellars of some of the *ricos* of the south are often found teeming with large quantities of them, presenting the appearance of a winter's supply of fuel.

As the charge for parting the gold and silver at the Mexican mints is generally from one to two dollars, and coinage about fifty cents, per pound, this assayed bullion yields a profit upon its current value of nearly ten per cent at the United States mint; but if unassayed, it generally produces an advance of about double that amount upon the usual cost at the mines. The exportation of bullion, however, is prohibited, except by special license from the general government. Still, a large quantity is exported in this way, and considerable amounts smuggled out through some of the ports.

A constant and often profitable business in the silver trade is carried on at these mines. As the miners rarely fail being in need of ready money they are generally obliged to sell their bullion for coin, and that often at a great sacrifice, so as to procure available means to prosecute their mining operations. To profit by this trade, as is already mentioned, was a principal object of my present visit. Having concluded my business transactions and partially gratified my curiosity, I returned to Chihuahua, where I arrived November 24, 1835, without being molested either by robbers or Indians, though the route is sometimes infested by both these classes of independent gentry.

But as it is now high time I should put an end to this digression I will once more resume my narrative where it was interrupted at my arrival in Chihuahua on the first of October, 1839.

It is usual for each trader upon his arrival in that city to engage a store-room and to open and exhibit his goods, as well for the purpose of disposing of them at wholesale as retail. His most profitable custom is that of the petty country merchants from the surrounding villages. Some traders, it is true, continue in the retail business for a season or more, yet the greater portion are transient dealers, selling off at wholesale as soon as a fair bargain is offered.

The usual mode of selling by the lot in Chihuahua is somewhat singular. All such cottons as calicoes and other prints, bleached, brown, and blue domestics both plain and twilled, stripes, checks, etc., are rated at two

or three *reales*[105] per *vara*, without the least
reference to quality or cost, and the general
assortment at 60 to 100 per cent upon the bills
of cost, according to the demand. The *varage*
is usually estimated by adding eight per cent
to the yardage, but the *vara* being thirty-three
inches (nearly), the actual difference is more
than nine. In these sales, cloths—indeed all
measurable goods except ribands and the like,
sometimes enter at the *varage* rate. I have
heard of some still more curious contracts in
these measurement sales, particularly in Santa
Fé during the early periods of the American
trade. Everything was sometimes rated by the
vara—not only all textures, but even hats,
cutlery, trinkets, and so on! In such cases
very singular disputes would frequently arise
as to the mode of measuring some particular
articles: for instance, whether pieces of riband
should be measured in bulk, or unrolled and
yard by yard; looking-glasses, cross or length-
wise; pocket-knives, shut or open; writing-
paper, in the ream, in the quire, or by the
single sheet; and then, whether the longer
or shorter way of the paper; and so of many
others.

Before the end of October, 1839, I had an
opportunity of selling out my stock of goods to
a couple of English merchants, which relieved

[105] A footnote table of monetary values appended by
Gregg at this point conveys the information that eight
*reales* make one *peso* or dollar.

me from the delays, to say nothing of the inconveniences, attending a retail trade: such, for instance, as the accumulation of copper coin, which forms almost the exclusive currency in petty dealings. Some thousands of dollars' worth are frequently accumulated upon the hands of the merchant in this way and as the copper of one department is worthless in another, except for its intrinsic value, which is seldom more than ten per cent of the nominal value, the holders are subjected to a great deal of trouble and annoyance.

With regard to the city, there is but little to be said that is either very new or unusually interesting. When compared with Santa Fé and all the towns of the north, Chihuahua might indeed be pronounced a magnificent place; but compared with the nobler cities of *tierra afuera*, it sinks into insignificance. According to Capt. Pike, the city of Chihuahua was founded in 1691. The ground-plan is much more regular than that of Santa Fé, while a much greater degree of elegance and classic taste has been exhibited in the style of the architecture of many buildings; for though the bodies be of *adobe*, all the best houses are cornered with hewn stone and the doors and windows are framed in the same. The streets, however, remain nearly in the same state as nature formed them, with the exception of a few roughly-paved side-walks. Although situated about a hundred miles east of the main chain of the Mexican Cordilleras, Chihuahua is surrounded on every side by detached ridges of mountains, but none of them of any great magnitude. The elevation of the city above the ocean is between four and five thousand feet; its latitude is 28° 36′; and its entire population numbers about ten thousand souls.

The most splendid edifice in Chihuahua is the principal church, which is said to equal in architectural grandeur anything of the sort in the Republic. The steeples, of which there is one at each front corner, rise over a hundred feet above the *azotea*. They are composed of very fancifully-carved columns; and in appropriate niches of the frontispiece, which is also an elaborate piece of sculpture, are to be seen a number of statues as large as life, the whole forming a complete representation of Christ and the twelve Apostles. This church was built about a century ago by contributions levied upon the mines (particularly those of Santa Eulalia, fifteen or twenty miles from the city), which paid over a per centage on all the metal extracted therefrom; a *medio*, I believe, being levied upon each *marco* of eight ounces. In this way about a million of dollars was raised and expended in some thirty years, the time employed in the construction of the building. It is a curious fact, however, that notwithstanding the enormous sums of money expended in outward embellishments, there is not a church from thence southward, perhaps, where the interior arrangements bear such striking marks of poverty and neglect. If, however, we are not dazzled by the sight of those costly decorations for which the churches of southern Mexico are so much celebrated we have the satisfaction of knowing that the turrets are well provided with bells, a fact of which every person who visits Chihuahua very soon obtains auricular demonstration. One, in particular, is so large and sonorous that it has frequently been heard, so I am informed, at the distance of twenty-five miles.

A little below the *Plaza Mayor* stands the ruins (as they may be called) of San Francisco —the mere skeleton of another great church of hewn stone, which was commenced by the Jesuits previous to their expulsion in 1767, but never finished. By the outlines still traceable amid the desolation which reigns around it would appear that the plan of this edifice was conceived in a spirit of still greater magnificence than the Parroquia which I have been describing. The abounding architectural treasures that are mouldering and ready to tumble to the ground bear sufficient evidence that the mind which had directed its progress was at once bold, vigorous, and comprehensive.

This dilapidated building has since been converted into a sort of state prison, particularly for the incarceration of distinguished prisoners. It was here that the principals of the famous

Texan Santa Fé Expedition were confined when they passed through the place on their way to the city of Mexico. This edifice has also acquired considerable celebrity as having received within its gloomy embraces several of the most distinguished patriots who were taken prisoners during the first infant struggles for Mexican independence. Among these was the illustrious ecclesiastic, Don Miguel Hidalgo y Costilla, who made the first declaration at the village of Dolores, September 16, 1810. He was taken prisoner in March, 1811, some time after his total defeat at Guadalaxara; and being brought to Chihuahua, he was shot on the 30th of July following in a little square back of the prison, where a plain white monument of hewn stone has been erected to his memory. It consists of an octagon base of about twenty-five feet in diameter, upon which rises a square, unornamented pyramid to the height of about thirty feet. The monument, indeed, is not an unapt emblem of the purity and simplicity of the curate's character.

Among the few remarkable objects which attract the attention of the traveler is a row of columns supporting a large number of stupendous arches, which may be seen from the heights long before approaching the city from the north. This is an aqueduct of considerable magnitude which conveys water from the little river of Chihuahua to an eminence above the town, whence it is passed through a succession of pipes to the main public square, where it empties itself into a large stone cistern; and by this method the city is supplied with water. This and other public works to be met with in Chihuahua and in the southern cities are glorious remnants of the prosperous times of the Spanish empire. No improvements on so exalted a scale have ever been made under the republican government. In fact, everything in this benighted country now seems to be on the decline and the plain honest citizen of the old school is not unfrequently heard giving vent to his feelings by ejaculating, "*Ojalá pro los dias felices del Rey!*" Oh, for the happy days of the King! In short, there can be no doubt that the common people enjoyed more ease—more protection against the savages—more security in their rights and property—more *liberty*, in truth, under the Spanish dynasty than at present.

No better evidence can be found of the extensive operations which have been carried on in this the greatest mining district of northern Mexico than in the little mountains of *scoria* which are found in the suburbs of the city. A great number of poor laborers make a regular business of hammering to pieces these metallic excrescences, from which they collect silver enough to buy their daily bread. An opinion has often been expressed by persons well acquainted with the subject that a fair business might be done by working this same *scoria* over again.

There are still in operation several furnaces in the city, where silver ores extracted from the mines of the surrounding mountains are smelted. There is also a rough mint in Chihuahua (as there is indeed in all the mining departments), yet most of its silver and all of its gold have been coined in the cities farther south.

When I arrived at Chihuahua in 1839 a great fête had just come off for the double purpose of celebrating the anniversary of the Emperor Iturbide's birthday (Sept. 27, 1783) and that of his triumphal entrance into the city of Mexico in 1821. It will be remembered that after Mexico had been struggling for independence several years General Iturbide, who had remained a faithful officer of the crown and an active agent in persecuting the champions of Mexican liberty, finding himself about the close of 1820 at the head of a large division of the royal army sent against the patriot Guerero, suddenly turned over his whole force to the support of the republican cause, and finally succeeded in destroying the last vestige of Spanish authority in Mexico. How he was afterwards crowned emperor and subsequently dethroned, outlawed by a public decree, and eventually executed is all matter of history. But it is not generally known, I believe, that this unfortunate soldier has since received the honors of the Father of the Republic, a dignity to which he was probably as much entitled as any one else—absurd

though the adoption of such a hero as the
champion of liberty may appear to republicans
of the Jefferson school. A *grande fête d'hila-
rité* takes place annually in honor of his political canonization, which comes off at the date
already mentioned. To this great ball, however, no Americans were invited, with the exception of a Mexicanized denizen or two whose
invitation tickets informed the honored party
that the price of admission to this famous feast—
a ball given by the Governor and other magnates of the land in honor of the hero of independence—was twenty-five dollars.

Balls or reunions of this kind, however, seem
not as frequent in Chihuahua as in New Mexico:
and to those we hear of, claiming the title of
fashionable, Americans are very rarely invited.
There is, in fact, but little social intercourse
between foreigners and the natives except in a
business way, or with a certain class of the
former at the gambling-table. This want of
hospitable feelings is one of the worst traits
in the character of the Chihuahuenos, and when
placed in contrast with the kind and courteous
treatment those who visit the United States
invariably experience from the lawgivers of
fashion among us, their illiberality will appear
a hundred-fold more ungracious. These exclusive laws are the more severely felt in
Chihuahua because in that city there are no
*cafés* nor reading rooms, nor in short any
favorite public resorts except of a gambling

character at which gentlemen can meet to lounge or amuse themselves.

Besides the cock-pit, the gaming-table and the *Alameda*, which is the popular promenade for the wealthy and the indolent, one of the most favorite pastimes of the females generally is shopping; and the most fashionable time for this is by candle-light, after they have partaken of their chocolate and their *cigarritos*. The streets and shops are literally filled from dusk till nine or ten o'clock; and many a time have I seen the counter of a store actually lined till a late hour with the fairest and most fashionable señoritas of the city. On such occasions it is not a little painful as well as troublesome to be compelled to keep a strict eye to the rights of property, not that the dealers are all dishonest but because there never fail to be some present who are painfully afflicted with the self-appropriating mania, even among the fairest-looking señoritas. This, with other purposes no less culpable, has no doubt tended to establish the custom of night-shopping.

It may already be generally known, perhaps, that the predominant party in Mexico (and particularly in the north) is decidedly anti-Masonic. During my stay in Chihuahua I had an opportunity to test their antipathy for that mysterious brotherhood. This was evinced in the seizure of a dozen or two cotton handkerchiefs which, unknown to myself, happened to bear the stamp of the Masonic carpet. These obnoxious articles having attracted the attention of some lynx-eyed friars, one day much to my consternation my store was suddenly invaded by the alcalde and some ecclesiastics. The handkerchiefs were seized without ceremony and by an *auto de fe* condemned to be publicly burned.

# Chapter 15

HAVING closed all my affairs in Chihuahua and completed my preparations for
departing, I took my leave of that city
for the north on the 31st of October, 1839. I
was accompanied by a caravan consisting of
twenty-two wagons (all of which save one belonged to me) and forty-odd men armed to the
teeth and prepared for any emergency we
might be destined to encounter: a precaution
altogether necessary in view of the hordes of
hostile savages which at all times infested the
route before us.

We also set out provided with an ample
stock of bread and other necessaries; for from
the suburbs of Chihuahua to the village of
Carrizal, a distance of nearly a hundred and
fifty miles, there are no settlements on the
route from whence to procure supplies. To
furnish the party with meat, I engaged twenty
sheep, to be delivered a few miles on the way,
which were to be driven along for our daily
consumption. But the contractor having
failed, we found ourselves entering the wilderness without a morsel of meat. The second
day our men began to murmur—it was surely
dry living upon mere bread and coffee: in fact,

by the time we entered the territory of the Hacienda de Encinillas, spoken of in another chapter, they were clearly suffering from hunger. I was therefore under the necessity of sending three Mexican muleteers of our party to *lazo* a beef from a herd which was grazing at some distance from where we had pitched our camp; being one of those buffalo-like droves which run so nearly wild upon this extensive domain. It had been customary from time immemorial for travelers, when they happened to be distressed for meat, to supply their wants out of the wild cattle which nominally belonged to the hacienda, reserving to themselves the privilege of paying a reasonable price afterwards to the proprietor for the damage committed. I must say, however, that although I had traveled over the same road nine times I had never before resorted to this summary mode of procuring food; nor should I on the present occasion have deviated from my regular practice, though thus partially authorized by a custom of the country, but for the strait in which we found ourselves and the fact that I was confident I should meet either with a mayordomo or some of the vaqueros to whom I could pay the value of the beef before passing beyond the purlieus of the hacienda, upon the lands of which we had yet to travel for sixty or eighty miles.

The muleteers had just commenced giving chase to the cattle when we perceived several horsemen emerge from behind a contiguous eminence and pursue them at full speed. Believing the assailants to be Indians, and seeing them shoot at one of the men, chase another, and seize the third, bearing him off prisoner, several of us prepared to hasten to the rescue, when the other two men came running in and informed us that the aggressors were Mexican vaqueros. We followed them, notwithstanding, to the village of Torreon, five or six miles to the westward, where we found a crowd of people already collected around our poor friend, who was trembling from head to foot as though he had really fallen into the hands of savages. I immediately inquired for the mayordomo, when I was informed that the proprietor himself, Don Angel Trias, was present. Accordingly I addressed myself to *su señoría*, setting forth the innocence of my servant and declaring myself solely responsible for whatever crime had been committed. Trias, however, was immovable in his determination to send the boy back to Chihuahua to be tried for robbery, and all further expostulation only drew down the grossest and coarsest insults upon myself as well as my country, of which he professed no inconsiderable knowledge.[106]

[106] Trias, while yet a youth, was dispatched by his adopted father to take the tour of Europe and the United States. He was furnished for pocket money (as I have been told) with nearly a hundred *barras de plata*, each worth a thousand dollars or upwards. This

# Commerce of the Prairies

The altercation was at first conducted solely in Spanish; but the princely señor growing weary of hearing so many unpalatable truths told of himself in the vernacular of his own humble and astounded menials, he stepped out from among the crowd and addressed me in English—a language in which he had acquired some proficiency in the course of his travels. The change of language by no means altered his views nor abated his pertinacity. At last, finding there was nothing to be gained by this war of words, I ordered the boy to mount his horse and rejoin the wagons. "Beware of the consequences!" vociferated the enraged Trias. "Well, let them come," I replied; "here we are." But we were suffered to depart in peace with the prisoner.

That the reader may be able to form some idea of the pusillanimity of this lordly *haciendro,* it is only necessary to add that when the altercation took place we were inside of the fortifications, from which our egress might easily have been prevented by simply closing the outer gate. We were surrounded by the whole population of the village, besides a small detachment of regular troops whose commandant took a very active part in the controversy and

money he easily got rid of during his travels, but retained most of his innate bigotry and self-importance; and with his knowledge of the superiority of the people among whom he journeyed, grew his hatred for foreigners. Gregg.

fought most valiantly with his tongue. But the valor of the illustrious Señor Don Angel knew a much safer course than to vent itself where there was even a remote chance of personal risk. His influence could not fail to enlist the public in his behalf and he thought, no doubt, that his battles might just as well be fought by the officers of justice as by himself.

Yet, ignorant of his designs and supposing the matter would end at this, we continued our march the next day and by the time night approached we were full twenty miles from the seat of our late troubles. While at breakfast on the following morning we were greatly surprised by the appearance of two American gentlemen direct from Chihuahua, who had ridden thus far purposely to apprise us of what was brewing in the city to our detriment. It appeared that Trias had sent an express to the Governor accusing me of rescuing a culprit from the hands of justice by force of arms, and that great preparations were accordingly being made to overtake and carry me back. That the reader may be able to understand the full extent and enormity of my offense, he has only to be informed that the proprietor of an hacienda is at once governor, justice of the peace, and everything besides which he has a mind to fancy himself—a perfect despot within the limits of his little dominion. It was, therefore, through contempt for *his* excellency that I had insulted the majesty of the laws!

Having expressed my sentiments of gratitude to my worthy countrymen for the pains they had taken on my account, we again pursued our journey, determined to abide the worst. This happened on the 3d of November: on the 5th we encamped near the Ojo Caliente, a hundred and thirty miles from Chihuahua. About eleven o'clock at night a large body of men were seen approaching. They very soon passed us and quietly encamped at a distance of several hundred yards. They were over a hundred in number.

Nothing further occurred till next morning, when just as I had risen from my pallet a soldier approached and inquired if I was up. In a few minutes he returned with a message from *El Señor Capitan* to know if he could see me. Having answered in the affirmative, a very courteous and agreeable personage soon made his appearance, who, after bowing and scraping until I began to be seriously afraid that his body would break in two, finally opened his mission by handing me a packet of letters, one of which contained an order from the Governor for my immediate presence in Chihuahua, together with the three muleteers whom I had sent after the cattle; warning me at the same time not to give cause, by my resistance, for any other measure which might be unpleasant to my person. The next document was from Señor Trias himself, in which he expressed his regret at having carried the matter to such an extreme and ended with the usual offer of his services to facilitate an adjustment. Those, however, which most influenced my course, were from Don José Artalejo (*Juez de Hacienda*, Judge of the Customs of Chihuahua), who offered to become responsible for a favorable issue if I would peaceably return; and another from a Mr. Sutton, with whom I had formerly been connected in business. The manly and upright deportment of this gentleman had inspired me with the greatest confidence, and therefore caused me to respect his opinions. But, besides my obligation to submit to a mandate from the government, however arbitrary and oppressive, another strong motive which induced me to return, in obedience to the Governor's order, was a latent misgiving lest any hostile movement on my part, no matter with what justice or necessity, might jeopardize the interests if not the lives of many of my countrymen in Chihuahua.

With regard to ourselves and our immediate safety, we would have found but very little difficulty in fighting our way out of the country. We were all well-armed, and many appeared even anxious to have a brush with the besiegers. However, I informed the captain that I was willing to return to Chihuahua with the three "criminals" provided we were permitted to go armed and free, as I was not aware of having committed any crime to justify an arrest. He rejoined that this was precisely in accordance with his orders and politely tendered me an escort of five or six soldiers, who should be placed under my command, to strengthen us against the Indians that were known to infest our route. Thanking him for his favor, I at once started for Chihuahua, leaving the wagons to continue slowly on the journey and the amiable captain with his band of *valientes* to retrace their steps at leisure towards the capital.

Late on the evening of the third day I reached the city and put up at the American Fonda, where I was fortunate enough to meet with my friend Artalejo, who at once proposed that we should proceed forthwith to the Governor's house. When we found ourselves in the presence of His Excellency my valued friend began by remarking that I had returned according to orders and that he would answer for me with his person and property; and then, without even waiting for a reply, he turned to me and expressed a hope that I would make his house my residence while I remained in the city. I could not, of course, decline so friendly an invitation, particularly as I thought it probable that, being virtually my bail, he might prefer to have me near his person. But as soon as we reached the street he very promptly removed that suspicion from my mind. "I invite you to my house," said he, "as a friend, and not as a prisoner. If you have any business to transact, do not hold yourself under the least restraint. Tomorrow I will see the affair satisfactorily settled."

The *Junta Departamental* or State Council, of which Señor Artalejo was an influential member, was convened the following day. Meanwhile every American I met expressed a great deal of surprise to see me at liberty, as from the excitement which had existed in the city they expected I would have been lodged in the safest calabozo. I was advised not to venture much into the streets as the rabble were very much incensed against me; but, although I afterwards wandered about pretty freely, no one offered to molest me; in fact, I must do the sovereigns of the city the justice to say, that I was never more politely treated than during this occasion. Others suggested that as Trias was one of the most wealthy and influential citizens of Chihuahua I had better try to pave my way out of the difficulty with *plata*, as I could stand no chance in law against him. To this, however, I strenuously objected. I felt convinced that I had been ordered back to Chihuahua mainly for purposes of extortion, and I was determined that the *oficiales* should be disappointed. I had unbounded confidence in the friendship and integrity of Don José Artalejo, who was quite an exception to the general character of his countrymen. He was liberal, enlightened, and honorable and I shall ever remember with gratitude the warm interest he took in my affair, when he could have had no other motive in befriending me except what might spring from the consciousness of having performed a generous action.

At first when the subject of my liberation was discussed in the *Junta Departamental* the symptoms were rather squally, as some bigoted and unruly members of the Council seemed determined to have me punished, right or wrong. After a long and tedious debate, however, my friend brought me the draft of a petition which he desired me to copy and sign, and upon the presentation of which to the Governor it had been agreed I should be released. This step, I was informed, had been resolved upon because after mature deliberation the Council came to the conclusion that the proceedings against me had been extremely arbitrary and illegal, and that if I should hereafter prosecute the Department I might recover heavy damages. The wholesome lesson which had so lately been taught the Mexicans by France was perhaps the cause of the fears of the Chihuahua authorities. A clause was therefore inserted in the petition wherein I was made to renounce all intention on my part of ever troubling the Department on the subject, and became myself a suppliant to have the affair considered as concluded.

This petition I would never have consented to sign had I not been aware of the arbitrary power which was exercised over me. Imprisonment, in itself, was of but little consequence;

but the total destruction of my property, which might have been the result of further detention, was an evil which I deemed it necessary to ward off, even at a great sacrifice of feeling. Moreover, being in duress, no forced concession would, of course, be obligatory upon me after I resumed my liberty. Again, I felt no very great inclination to sue for redress where there was so little prospect of procuring anything. I might certainly have represented the matter to the Mexican government and even have obtained, perhaps, the acknowledgment of my claims against Chihuahua for damages; but the payment would have been extremely doubtful. As to our own government, I had too much experience to rely for a moment upon her interposition.

During the progress of these transactions I strove to ascertain the character of the charges made against me; but in vain. All I knew was that I had offended a *rico* and had been summoned back to Chihuahua at his instance; yet whether for high treason, for an attempt at robbery, or for contempt to his *señoria* I knew not. It is not unusual, however, in that "land of liberty," for a person to be arrested and even confined for weeks without knowing the cause. The writ of *habeas corpus* appears unknown in the judicial tribunes of northern Mexico.

Upon receipt of my petition the Governor immediately issued the following decree, which

I translate for the benefit of the reader, as being not a bad specimen of Mexican grand eloquence:

"In consideration of the memorial which you have this day directed to the Superior Government, His Excellency, the Governor, has been pleased to issue the following decree:

"That, as Don Angel Trias has withdrawn his prosecution, so far as relates to his personal interests, the Government, using the equity with which it ought to look upon faults committed without a deliberate intention to infringe the laws, which appears presumable in the present case, owing to the memorialist's ignorance of them, the grace which he solicits is granted to him; and, in consequence, he is at liberty to retire when he chooses: to which end, and that he may not be interrupted by the authorities, a copy of this decree will be transmitted to him.

"In virtue of the above, I inclose the said decree to you, for the purposes intended.

"God and Liberty. Chihuahua, Nov. 9, 1839.

"AMADO DE LA VEGA, Sec.

"To DON JOSIAH GREGG."

Thus terminated this momentous affair. The moral of it may be summed up in a few words. A citizen of the United States who, under the faith of treaties, is engaged in his business, may be seized and harassed by the arbitrary authorities of Chihuahua with perfect impunity because experience has proved that the American government winks at almost every individual outrage, as utterly unworthy of its serious consideration. At the same time the Indians may enter, as they frequently do, the suburbs of the city, rob, plunder, and destroy life, without a single soldier being raised or an effort made to bring the savage malefactors within the pale of justice. But a few days before the occasion of my difficulty at Torreon, the Apaches had killed a ranchero or two in the immediate neighborhood of the same village; and afterwards, at the very time such a bustle was being made in Chihuahua to raise troops for my special benefit, the Indians entered the cornfields in the suburbs of the city and killed several *labradores* who were at work in them. In neither of these cases, however, were there any troops at command to pursue and chastise the depredators—though a whole army was in readiness to persecute our party. The truth is, they felt much less reluctance to pursue a band of civil traders, who, they were well aware, could not assume a hostile attitude, than to be caught in the wake of a band of savages, who would as little respect their lives as their laws and their property.

Early on the morning of the 10th I once more and for the last time, and with anything but regret, took my leave of Chihuahua with my companions in trouble. Toward the afternoon we met my old friend, the captain, with his valiant followers, whom I found as full of urbanity as ever—so much so, indeed, that he never even asked to see my passport.

On the evening of the next day, now in the heart of the savage haunts, we were not a little alarmed by the appearance of a large body of horsemen in the distance. They turned out, however, to be *Pasenos*, or citizens of the Paso del Norte. They were on their way to Chihuahua with a number of pack-mules laden with apples, pears, grapes, wine, and *aguardiente*—proceeds of their productive orchards and vineyards. It is from El Paso that Chihuahua is chiefly supplied with fruits and liquors, which are transported on mules or in carretas. The fruits, as well fresh as in a dried state, are thus carried to the distant markets. The grapes, carefully dried in the shade, make excellent *pasas* or raisins, of which large quantities are annually prepared for market by the people of that delightful town of vineyards and orchards, who, to take them altogether, are more sober and industrious than those of any other part of Mexico I have visited; and are happily less infested by the extremes of wealth and poverty.

On the 13th I overtook my wagons a few miles south of El Paso, whence our journey was continued without any additional casualty and on the 6th of December we reached Santa Fé in fine health and spirits.

# Chapter 16

ABOUT the beginning of February, 1840, and just as I was making preparations to return to the United States, the small-pox broke out among my men in a manner which at first occasioned at least as much astonishment as alarm. One of them who had traveled in a neighboring district where there were some cases of smallpox complained of a little fever, which was followed by slight eruptions but so unlike true variolous pustules that I treated the matter very lightly; not even suspecting a varioloid. These slight symptoms having passed off nothing more was thought of it until eight or ten days after, when every unvaccinated member of our company was attacked by that fell disease, which soon began to manifest very malignant features. There were no fatal cases, however; yet much apprehension was felt lest the disease should break out again on the route; but to our great joy we escaped this second scourge.

A party that left Santa Fé for Missouri soon afterward was much more unfortunate. On the way several of their men were attacked by the smallpox: some of whom died; and others retaining the infection till they approached the

304

Missouri frontier, they were compelled to undergo a quarantine in the bordering prairie, before they were permitted to enter the settlements.

On the 25th of February we set out from Santa Fé; but owing to some delays we did not leave San Miguel till the 1st of March. As the pasturage was yet insufficient for our animals we here provided ourselves with over six hundred bushels of corn to feed them on the way. This time our caravan consisted of twenty-eight wagons, two small cannons, and forty-seven men, including sixteen Mexicans and a Comanche Indian, who acted in the capacity of guide.[107] Two gentlemen of Baltimore, Messrs. S. Wethered and J. R. Ware, had joined our caravan with one wagon and three men, making up the aggregate above mentioned. We had also a *caballada* of more than two hundred mules, with nearly three hundred sheep and goats. The sheep were brought

---

[107] Manuel *el Comanche* was a full Indian, born and bred upon the great prairies. Long after having arrived at the state of manhood, he accompanied some Mexican *Comancheros* to the frontier village of San Miguel, where he fell in love with a Mexican girl, married her, and has lived in that place, a sober, civilized citizen for the last ten or twelve years, endowed with much more goodness of heart and integrity of purpose than a majority of his Mexican neighbors. He had learned to speak Spanish quite intelligibly, and was therefore an excellent Comanche interpreter; and being familiar with every part of the prairies, he was very serviceable as a guide. Gregg.

along partially to supply us with meat in case of emergency: the surplusage, however, could not fail to command a fair price in the United States.

Instead of following the trail of the year before, I determined to seek a nearer and better route down the south side of the Canadian River, under the guidance of the Comanche; by which movement we had again to travel a distance of four hundred miles over an entirely new country.[108] We had just passed the Laguna Colorada, where the following year a division of Texan volunteers under General McLeod surrendered to Col. Archuleta, when our fire was carelessly permitted to communicate with the prairie grass. As there was a head-wind blowing at the time we very soon got out of reach of the conflagration: but the next day, the wind having changed, the fire was again perceived in our rear, approaching us at a very brisk pace. The terror which these prairie conflagrations are calculated to inspire when the grass is tall and dry, as was the case in the present instance, has often been described, and though the perils of these disasters are not

[108] The route followed by Gregg on this return journey from Santa Fé to Van Buren, Arkansas, was substantially the same route taken by many of the goldseekers in their rush to California in 1849 and subsequent years. An account of it is given by Ralph P. Bieber in his "Southwestern Trails to California in 1849," published in the *Mississippi Valley Historical Review* for December, 1925 (Volume XII, 342 ff.).

unfrequently exaggerated, they are sometimes sufficient to daunt the stoutest heart. Mr. Kendall relates a frightful incident of this kind which occurred to the Texan Santa Fé Expedition; and all those who have crossed the prairies have had more or less experience as to the danger which occasionally threatens the caravans from these sweeping visitations. The worst evil to be apprehended with those bound for Santa Fé is from the explosion of gun powder, as a keg or two of twenty-five pounds each is usually to be found in every wagon. When we saw the fire gaining so rapidly upon us we had to use the whip very unsparingly; and it was only when the lurid flames were actually rolling upon the heels of our teams that we succeeded in reaching a spot of short-grass prairie, where there was no further danger to be apprehended.

The headway of the conflagration was soon after checked by a small stream which traversed our route; and we had only emerged fairly from its smoke on the following day (the 9th) when our Comanche guide returned hastily from his accustomed post in advance and with a beaming countenance informed us that he had espied three buffaloes not far distant. These were the first we had met with, and being already heartily tired of the dried beef with which we had provided ourselves, we were delighted at the prospect of a change. He said he preferred to hunt on horseback and with his bow and arrow; and believing my riding-horse the fleetest in company (which, by the by, was but a common pony, and thin in flesh withal), I dismounted and gave him the bridle with many charges to treat him kindly as we still had a long journey before us. "Don't attempt to kill but one—that will serve us for the present!" I exclaimed, as he galloped off. The Comanche was among the largest of his tribe—bony and muscular—weighing about two hundred pounds: but once at his favorite sport he very quickly forgot my injunction as well as the weakness of my little pony. He soon brought down two of his game, and shyly remarked to those who followed in his wake that had he not feared a scolding from me he would not have permitted the third to escape.

On the evening of the 10th our camp was pitched in the neighborhood of a ravine in the prairie and as the night was dark and dreary the watch tried to comfort themselves by building a rousing fire, around which they presently drew and commenced spinning long yarns about Mexican fandangoes and black-eyed damsels. All of a sudden the stillness of the night was interrupted by a loud report of firearms and a shower of bullets came whizzing by the ears of the heedless sentinels. Fortunately, however, no one was injured; which must be looked upon as a very extraordinary circumstance when we consider what a fair mark our men thus huddled around a blazing fire presented to the rifles of the Indians. The savage yells which resounded from every part of the ravine bore very satisfactory testimony that this was no false alarm; and the Pawnee whistle which was heard in every quarter at once impressed us with the idea of its being a band of that famous prairie banditti.

Every man sprang from his pallet with rifle in hand; for upon the prairies we always sleep with our arms by our sides or under our heads. Our Comanche seemed at first very much at a loss what to do. At last, thinking it might possibly be a band of his own nation, he began a most boisterous harangue in his vernacular tongue, which he continued for several minutes; when finding that the enemy took no notice of him and having become convinced, also, from an occasional Pawnee word which he was able to make out, that he had been wasting breath with the mortal foes of his race, he suddenly ceased all expostulations and blazed away with his rifle with a degree of earnestness which was truly edifying, as if convinced that that was the best he could do for us.

It was now evident that the Indians had taken possession of the entire ravine, the nearest points of which were not fifty yards from our wagons: a warning to prairie travelers to encamp at a greater distance from whatsoever might afford shelter for an enemy. The banks of the gully were low but still they formed a very good breastwork, behind which the enemy lay ensconced, discharging volleys of balls upon our wagons, among which we were scattered. At one time we thought of making an attempt to rout them from their fortified position; but being ignorant of their number and unable to distinguish any object through the dismal darkness which hung all around, we had to remain content with firing at random from behind our wagons, aiming at the flash of their guns or in the direction whence any noise appeared to emanate. Indeed, their yelling was almost continuous, breaking out every now and then in the most hideous screams and vociferous chattering, which were calculated to appall such timorous persons as we may have had in our caravan. All their screeching and whooping, however, had no effect—they could not make our animals break from the enclosure of the wagons in which they were fortunately shut up; which was no doubt their principal object for attacking us.

I cannot forbear recording a most daring feat performed by a Mexican muleteer named Antonio Chavez during the hottest of the first onset. Seeing the danger of my two favorite riding-horses, which were tethered outside within a few paces of the savages, he rushed out and brought safely in the most valuable of the two, though fusil-balls were showering around him all the while. The other horse broke his halter and made his escape.

Although sundry scores of shots had been fired at our people we had only two men wounded. One, a Mexican, was but slightly injured in the hand, but the wound of the other, who was an Italian, bore a more serious aspect and deserves especial mention. He was a short, corpulent fellow, and had been nick-named "Dutch"—a loquacious, chicken-heart-ed *fainéant*, and withal in the daily habit of gorging himself to such an enormous extent that every alternate night he was on the sick list. On this memorable occasion Dutch had foundered again, and the usual prescription of a double dose of Epsom salts had been his supper portion. The skirmish had continued for about an hour and although a frightful groaning had been heard in Dutch's wagon for some time, no one paid any attention to it as it was generally supposed to be from the effects of his dose. At length, however, some one cried out, "Dutch is wounded!" I immediately went to see him and found him writhing and twisting himself as if in great pain, crying all the time that he was shot. "Shot!—where?" I inquired. "Ah! in the head, sir." "Pshaw! Dutch, none of that; you've only bumped your head in trying to hide yourself." Upon lighting a match, however, I found that a ball had passed through the middle of his hat, and that, to my consternation, the top of his head was bathed in blood. It turned out upon subse-quent examination that the ball had glanced upon the skull, inflicting a serious-looking wound, and so deep that an inch of sound skin separated the holes at which the bullet had entered and passed out. Notwithstanding I at first apprehended a fracture of the skull, it very soon healed, and Dutch was up and about again in the course of a week.

Although teachers not unfrequently have cause to deplore the thickness of their pupils' skulls, Dutch had every reason to congratulate himself upon possessing such a treasure, as it had evidently preserved him from a more serious catastrophe. It appeared he had taken shelter in his wagon at the commencement of the attack, without reflecting that the boards and sheets were not ball-proof: and as Indians, especially in the night, are apt to shoot too high, he was in a much more dangerous situation than if upon the ground.

The enemy continued the attack for nearly three hours, when they finally retired so as to make good their retreat before daylight. As it rained and snowed from that time till nine in the morning, their sign was almost entirely obliterated and we were unable to discover whether they had received any injury or not. It was evidently a foot party, which we looked upon as another proof of their being Pawnees; for these famous marauders are well known to go forth on their expeditions of plunder without horses, although they seldom fail to return well mounted.

Their shot had riddled our wagons considerably: in one we counted no less than eight bullet-holes. We had the gratification to believe, however, that they did not get a single one of our animals: the horse which broke away at the first onset doubtless made his escape; and a mule which was too badly wounded to travel was dispatched by the muleteers, lest it should fall into the hands of wolves; and they deemed it more humane to leave it to be eaten dead than alive. We also experienced considerable damage in our stock of sheep, a number of them having been devoured by wolves. They had been scattered at the beginning of the attack; and in their anxiety to fly from the scene of action had jumped, as it were, into the very jaws of their ravenous enemies.

On the 12th of March we ascended upon the celebrated Llano Estacado and continued along its borders for a few days. The second night upon this dreary plain, we experienced one of the strongest and bleakest northwesters that ever swept across those prairies; during which our flock of sheep and goats, being left unattended, fled over the plain in search of some shelter, it was supposed, from the furious element. Their disappearance was not observed for some time, and the night being too dark to discern anything, we were obliged to defer going in pursuit of them till the following morning. After a fruitless and laborious search during which the effects of the mirage proved a constant source of annoyance and disappointment we were finally obliged to relinquish the pursuit and return to the caravan without finding one of them.

These severe winds are very prevalent upon the great western prairies, though they are seldom quite so inclement. At some seasons they are about as regular and unceasing as the trade winds of the ocean. It will often blow a gale for days and even weeks together without slacking for a moment, except occasionally at night. It is for this reason, as well as on account of the rains, that percussion guns are preferable upon the prairies, particularly for those who understand their use. The winds are frequently so severe as to sweep away both sparks and priming from a flint lock, and thus render it wholly ineffective.

The following day we continued our march down the border of the Llano Estacado. Knowing that our Comanche guide was about as familiar with all those great plains as a landlord with his premises, I began to question him, as we traveled along, concerning the different streams which pierced them to the southward. Pointing in that direction, he said there passed a water-course at the distance of a hard day's ride, which he designated as a *cañada* or valley, in which there was always water to be found at occasional places, but that none flowed in its channel except during the rainy season. This

cañada he described as having its origin in the
Llano Estacado some fifty or sixty miles east
of Rio Pecos and about the same distance
south of the route we came, and that its direction was a little south of east, passing to the
southward of the northern portion of the
Witchita Mountains, known to Mexican Ciboleros and Comancheros as *Sierra Jumanes.* It
was, therefore, evident that this was the principal northern branch of Red River. The false
Washita, or *Rio Negro*, as the Mexicans call it,
has its rise, as he assured me, between the
Canadian and this cañada, at no great distance
to the southeastward of where we were then
traveling.

On the 15th our Comanche guide, being
fearful lest we should find no water upon the
plain, advised us to pursue a more north-
wardly course, so that, after a hard day's ride,
we again descended the *ceja* or brow of the
Llano Estacado, into the undulating lands which
border the Canadian; and on the following day
we found ourselves upon the southern bank of
that stream.

Although but a few days' travel above
where we now were the Canadian runs pent up
in a narrow channel scarcely four rods across,
we here found it spread out to the width of
from three to six hundred yards and so full of
sand bars (only interspersed with narrow rills)
as to present the appearance of a mere sandy
valley instead of the bed of a river. In fact,

during the driest seasons the water wholly disappears in many places. Captain Boone,[109] of the U. S. Dragoons, being upon an exploring expedition in the summer of 1843, came to the Canadian about the region of our western boundary, where he found the channel perfectly dry. Notwithstanding it presents the face of one of the greatest rivers of the West during freshets, yet even then it would not be navigable on account of its rapidity and shallowness. It would appear almost incredible to those unacquainted with the prairie streams that a river of about 1,500 miles in length, and whose head wears a cap of perennial snow (having its source in the Rocky Mountains), should scarcely be navigable for even the smallest craft over fifty miles above its mouth.

We pursued our course down the same side of the river for several days, during which time we crossed a multitude of little streams which flowed into the Canadian from the adjoining plains, while others presented nothing but dry beds of sand. One of these was so remarkable,

[109] Captain Nathan Boone was the youngest son of Daniel Boone, the famous Kentucky pioneer. Nathan was born in Kentucky in 1780. In early manhood he migrated to Missouri, where he became a man of considerable local prominence. He served in the War of 1812 and in the Black Hawk War of 1832. In the latter year he entered the regular army as a captain of rangers, and during the next two decades he saw much active service on the southwestern frontier. In 1850 he became lieutenant colonel; three years later he resigned from the army, and in 1857 he died at his home in Missouri.

on account of its peculiarity and size, that we named it Dry River. The bed was at least 2,000 yards wide, yet without a vestige of water; notwithstanding, our guide assured us that it was a brisk-flowing stream some leagues above: and from the drift-wood along its borders it was evident that even here it must be a considerable river during freshets.

While traveling down the course of the Canadian, we sometimes found the buffalo very abundant. On one occasion two or three hunters who were a little in advance of the caravan, perceiving a herd quietly grazing in an open glade, crawled upon them after the manner of the still hunters. Their first shot having brought down a fine fat cow, they slipped up behind her and, resting their guns over her body, shot two or three others without occasioning any serious disturbance or surprise to their companions; for, extraordinary as it may appear, if the buffalo neither see nor smell the hunter they will pay but little attention to the crack of guns or to the mortality which is being dealt among them.

The slaughter of these animals is frequently carried to an excess, which shows the depravity of the human heart in very bold relief. Such is the excitement that generally prevails at the sight of these fat denizens of the prairies that very few hunters appear able to refrain from shooting as long as the game remains within reach of their rifles; nor can they ever permit a fair shot to escape them. Whether the mere pleasure of taking life is the incentive of these excesses I will not pretend to decide; but one thing is very certain, that the buffalo killed yearly on these prairies far exceeds the wants of the traveler or what might be looked upon as the exigencies of rational sport.[110]

But in making these observations I regret that I cannot give to my precepts the force of my own example: I have not always been able wholly to withstand the cruel temptation. Not long after the incident alluded to as I was pioneering alone, according to my usual practice, at a distance of a mile or two ahead of the wagons in search of the best route, I perceived in a glade a few rods in front of me several protuberances, which at first occasioned me no little fright, for I took them, as they loomed dimly through the tall grass, for the tops of Indian lodges. But I soon discovered they were the huge humps of a herd of buffalo, which were quietly grazing.

I immediately alighted and approached unobserved to within forty or fifty yards of the unsuspecting animals. Being armed with one of Cochran's nine-chambered rifles, I took aim at one that stood broad-side, and blazed

[110] The same barbarous propensity is observable in regard to wild horses. Most persons appear unable to restrain this wanton inclination to take life when a mustang approaches within rifle-shot. Many a stately steed thus falls a victim to the cruelty of man. Gregg.

away. The buffalo threw up their heads and looked about, but seeing nothing (for I remained concealed in the grass) they again went on grazing as though nothing had happened. The truth is, the one I had shot was perhaps but little hurt; for, as generally happens with the inexperienced hunter—and often with those who know better, the first excitement allowing no time for reflection—I no doubt aimed too high, so as to lodge the ball in the hump. A buffalo's heart lies exceedingly low, so that to strike it the shot should enter not over one-fourth of the depth of the body above the lower edge of the breast bone.

The brutes were no sooner quiet than I took another and more deliberate aim at my former victim, which resulted as before. But believing him now mortally wounded, I next fired in quick succession at four others of the gang. It occurred to me by this time that I had better save my remaining three shots; for it was possible enough for my firing to attract the attention of strolling savages, who might take advantage of my empty gun to make a sortie upon me—yet there stood my buffalo, some of them still quietly feeding.

As I walked out from my concealment a party of our own men came galloping up from the wagons, considerably alarmed. They had heard the six shots and not recollecting my repeating rifle, supposed I had been attacked by Indians, and therefore came to my relief.

Upon their approach the buffalo all fled, except three which appeared badly wounded—one indeed soon fell and expired. The other two would doubtless have followed the example of the first, had not a hunter, anxious to dispatch them more speedily, approached too near; when, regaining strength from the excitement, they fled before him and entirely escaped, though he pursued them for a considerable distance.

A few days after this occurrence Mr. Wethered returned to the camp one evening with seven buffalo tongues (the hunter's usual trophy) swung to his saddle. He said that in the morning one of the hunters had ungenerously objected to sharing a buffalo with him; whereupon Mr. W. set out, vowing he would kill buffalo for himself, and no thanks to any one. He had not been out long when he spied a herd of only seven bulls, quietly feeding near a ravine; and slipping up behind the banks, he shot down one and then another until they all lay before him; and their seven tongues he brought in to bear testimony of his skill.

Not long after crossing Dry River we ascended the high grounds, and soon found ourselves upon the high ridge which divides the waters of the Canadian and False Washita, whose breaks could be traced descending from the Llano Estacado far to the southwest.

By an observation of an eclipse of one of Jupiter's satellites on the night of the 25th of

March, in latitude 35° 51′ 30″, I found that we were near the 100th degree of longitude west from Greenwich. On the following day, therefore, we celebrated our entrance into the United States territory. Those who have never been beyond the purlieus of the land of their nativity can form but a poor conception of the joy which the wanderer in distant climes experiences on treading once more upon his own native soil! Although we were yet far from the abodes of civilization, and farther still from home, nevertheless the heart within us thrilled with exhilarating sensations; for we were again in our own territory, breathed our own free atmosphere, and were fairly out of reach of the arbitrary power which we had left behind us.

As we continued our route upon this narrow dividing ridge we could not help remarking how nearly these streams approach each other: in one place they seemed scarcely five miles apart. On this account our Comanche guide, as well as several Mexicans of our party who had acquaintance with these prairies, gave it as their opinion that the Washita or *Rio Negro* was in fact a branch of the Canadian; for its confluence with Red River was beyond the bounds of their peregrinations.

As the forest of Cross Timbers was now beginning to be seen in the distance, and fearing we might be troubled to find a passway through this brushy region south of the Canadian, we forded this river on the 29th, without the slightest trouble, and very soon entered our former trail, a little west of Spring Valley. This gave a new and joyful impulse to our spirits; for we had been traveling over twenty days without even a trail, and through a region of which we knew absolutely nothing, except from what we could gather from our Comanche pilot. This trail, which our wagons had made the previous summer, was still visible, and henceforth there was an end to all misgivings.

If we take a retrospective view of the country over which we traveled we shall find but little that can ever present attractions to the agriculturist.[111] Most of the low valleys of the Canadian for a distance of five hundred miles are either too sandy or too marshy for cultivation; and the upland prairies are, in many places, but little else than sand-hills. In some parts, it is true, they are firm and fertile,

[111] The present-day Oklahoman would be disposed to take issue with this judgment. Such erroneous observations as that of Gregg in the present instance are common to the literature of travel and exploration, nor, indeed, are they confined to such limits. Thus, in 1847 Horace Greeley made an excursion into northern Illinois and informed the readers of the New York *Tribune* that "deficiency of water" was "the great, formidable, permanent drawback on the eligibility of the prairie region for settlement," a deficiency which he could not see would ever be remedied. About the same time debaters in the Wisconsin Constitutional Convention

but wholly destitute of timber, with the exception of a diminutive branch of the Cross Timbers which occupies a portion of the ridge betwixt the Canadian and the North Fork. The Canadian River itself is still more bare of timber than the upper Arkansas. In its whole course through the plains there is but little except cottonwood, and that very scantily scattered along its banks—in some places, for leagues together, not a stick is to be seen. Except it be near the mountains, where the valleys are more fertile, it is only the little narrow bottoms which skirt many of its tributary rivulets that indicate any amenity. Some of these are rich and beautiful in the extreme, timbered with walnut, mulberry, oak, elm, hackberry, and occasionally cedar about the bluffs.

We now continued our journey without encountering any further casualty, except in crossing the Arkansas River, where we lost several mules by drowning; and on the 22d

were describing the country between the Wisconsin River and modern St. Paul as a wilderness "uninhabited and uninhabitable." Pike, in 1806, crossed northeastern Kansas and ventured the opinion that it might some day be habitable for goats; while Daniel Webster in his great speech on the Compromise of 1850 would not needlessly reënact a law of nature by excluding slavery from California. Even today Vilhjalmur Stefansson is combating, without much apparent success, the practically universal conception concerning the Arctic region, which he affirms to have no foundation in fact.

of April we made our entrance into Van Buren. This trip was much more tedious and protracted than I had contemplated—owing, in the first part of the journey, to the inclemency of the season and a want of pasturage for our animals; and towards the conclusion, to the frequent rains, which kept the route in a miserable condition.

Concerning this expedition I have only one or two more remarks to offer. As regards the two different routes to Santa Fé, although Missouri, for various reasons which it is needless to explain here, can doubtless retain the monopoly of the Santa Fé trade, the route from Arkansas possesses many advantages. Besides its being some days' travel shorter,[112] it is less intersected with large streams; there are fewer sandy stretches, and a greater variety of wood-skirted brooks, affording throughout the journey very agreeable camping-places. Also, as the grass springs up nearly a month earlier than in upper Missouri, caravans could start sooner and the proprietors would have double the time to conduct their mercantile transactions. Moreover, the return companies would find better pasturage on their way back, and reach their homes before the

[112] The latitude of Independence, Missouri, is 39° 8', while that of Van Buren is 35° 26'—within a few miles of the parallel of Santa Fé; and being on about the same meridian as Independence, the distance, of course, is considerably shorter. Gregg.

season of frost had far advanced. Again, such as should desire to engage in the stock trade would at once bring their mules and horses into a more congenial climate—one more in accordance with that of their nativity; for the rigorous winters of Missouri often prove fatal to the unacclimated Mexican animals.

This was my last trip across the plains, though I made an excursion during the following summer among the Comanche Indians and other wild tribes living in the heart of the prairies, but returned without crossing to Mexico. The observations made during this trip will be found incorporated in the notices, which are to follow, of the prairies and their inhabitants.[113]

Since that time I have striven in vain to reconcile myself to the even tenor of civilized life in the United States; and have sought in its amusements and its society a substitute for those high excitements which have attached me so strongly to prairie life. Yet I am almost ashamed to confess that scarcely a day passes without my experiencing a pang of regret that I am not now roving at large upon those western plains. Nor do I find my taste peculiar; for I have hardly known a man who has ever become familiar with the kind of life which I have led for so many years, that has not relinquished it with regret.

[113] These observations fall in chapters which are not reprinted in the present volume.

There is more than one way of explaining this apparent incongruity. In the first place, the wild, unsettled, and independent life of the prairie trader makes perfect freedom from nearly every kind of social dependence an absolute necessity of his being. He is in daily, nay, hourly exposure of his life and property, and in the habit of relying upon his own arm and his own gun both for protection and support. Is he wronged? No court or jury is called to adjudicate upon his disputes or his abuses save his own conscience; and no powers are invoked to redress them save those with which the God of Nature had endowed him. He knows no government—no laws, save those of his own creation and adoption. He lives in no society which he must look up to or propitiate. The exchange of this untrammeled condition—this sovereign independence, for a life in civilization, where both his physical and moral freedom are invaded at every turn by the complicated machinery of social institutions, is certainly likely to commend itself to but few—not even to all those who have been educated to find their enjoyments in the arts and elegancies peculiar to civilized society; as is evinced by the frequent instances of men of letters, of refinement and wealth, voluntarily abandoning society for a life upon the prairies or in the still more savage mountain wilds.

A tour on the prairies is certainly a dangerous experiment for him who would live a quiet contented life at home among his friends and relatives: not so dangerous to life or health, as prejudicial to his domestic habits. Those who have lived pent up in our large cities know but little of the broad, unembarrassed freedom of the great western prairies. Viewing them from a snug fireside, they seem crowded with dangers, with labors, and with sufferings; but once upon them, and these appear to vanish— they are soon forgotten.

There is another consideration, which, with most men of the prairies, operates seriously against their reconciliation to the habits of civilized life. Though they be endowed naturally with the organs of taste and refinement, and though once familiar with the ways and practices of civilized communities, yet a long absence from such society generally obliterates from their minds most of those common laws of social intercourse which are so necessary to the man of the world. The awkwardness and the *gaucheries* which ignorance of their details so often involves are very trying to all men of sensitive temperaments. Consequently, multitudes rush back to the prairies merely to escape those criticisms and that ridicule which they know not how to disarm.

It will hardly be a matter of surprise then, when I add that this passion for prairie life, how paradoxical soever it may seem, will be very apt to lead me upon the plains again, to spread my bed with the mustang and the

buffalo, under the broad canopy of heaven—
there to seek to maintain undisturbed my
confidence in men by fraternizing with the
little prairie dogs and wild colts and the still
wilder Indians—the *unconquered Sabaeans* of
the Great American Deserts.[114]

[114] This forecast was substantially fulfilled; see our
sketch of Gregg's later years and death in the historical
introduction to the present volume.

# Index

# Index

ABREU, Ramon, imprisons official, 123.

Abreu, Santiago, slain, 124.

Aguascalientes, Gregg visits, 251–72; described, 260.

Alarid, Jesus Maria, slain, 124.

Angostura (Narrows), Gregg reaches, 223–24.

Antelope, traders encounter, 196.

Apache Indians, expedition against, 175; waylay travelers, 240; resort of, 244.

Arapaho Indians, plunder traders, 12–13.

Arbuckle, Matthew, career sketched, 178.

Archuleta, Colonel, captures Texans, 306.

Arkansas, route via, 171–72; advantages of, to Santa Fé, 324–25.

Arkansas River, traders plundered, 14–15; reach, 46–47; cross, 161, 173, 323; freshets of, 54; as boundary, 197.

Armijo, Governor, imposes customs duties, 104–105; plots counter-revolution, 127–29; levies duties, 226; dispute with traders, 227–29.

Artalejo, José, befriends Gregg, 296–99.

Atole, article of diet, 147.

BANDITS, prevalence of in Mexico, 256, 258–60.

Barras, silver ingots, described, 277–78.

Battle Ground, story of fight at, 75–76.

Beard, ———, expedition to Santa Fé, 5–6; attacked by Indians, 56–57.

Becknell, Capt., expeditions to Santa Fé, 6–9.

Benton, Thomas H., bill for road to New Mexico, 12.

Bent, Charles, career sketched, 62.

Bent, George, career sketched, 62.

Bent, William, career sketched, 62.

Bent's Fort, location, 62; Indians visit, 220.

Blackfeet Indians, traders encounter, 72, 85.

Boggs, Governor, shot, 169.

# Index

Boone, Nathan, career sketched, 316.

Bowman, Lieut., escorts traders, 180; terminates escort, 197, 206; negotiates with Comanches, 204–205; death, 206.

Broadus, ———, surgical operation on, 47–49.

Buffaloes, water procured from stomach, 9; traders encounter, 42–43, 53, 187–90, 307–308; numbers, 91–92; habitat, 162, 191, 196; slaughtered, 317–18.

Buffalo chips, used for fuel, 189–90.

Buffalo-gnats, attacks of, 191–92.

Buffalo-grass, habitat, 87.

Buffalo wallows, described, 212.

Burial, on plains, described, 13.

CABALLERO, Captain, in Mexican revolution, 127.

Caballeroes, equipment for traveling, 266.

Caches, route via, 8; story of origin, 56–58.

California, Gregg joins in gold rush, xvii–xix; route of gold seekers, 306.

Camp Comanche, on Canadian River, 201–205.

Camp Holmes, traders camp at, 180.

Canadian River (Rio Colorado, Red River), traders reach, 96–97, 174, 322; course of, 174, 191, 194; valley described, 212–14; traders plundered, 214–18; route via, 306; characterized, 316.

Cannon, used by traders, 34, 74–75, 157, 177, 305; traders saluted by discharge, 98.

Captives, among Indians, 207–210.

Carmen River, described, 247.

Carrizal, described, 246–47.

Cattle, of Chihuahua, 248–49; at La Zarca, 252–53; dispute over, 291–301.

Cerro de Tucumcari, route via, 224.

Cerro Gordo, traders pass, 252.

Chambers, ———, expedition to Santa Fé, 5–6; attacked by Indians, 56–57.

Chavez, Antonio, bravery of, 310.

Cherokee Indians, method of collecting debts, 173–74.

Chihuahua, Gregg visits, 230–50; road from to El Paso characterized, 250; departure of traders, 252; city described, 281–89; Gregg arrested, 294–301.

Chile, article of diet, 147.
Chouteau, Auguste Pierre, attacked by Indians, 15–16; career sketched, 180–81; death, 182.
Chouteau's Fort, route via, 181; traders leave, 184.
Chouteau's Island, origin of name, 15–16.
Chuly, Creek Indian, joins Gregg's party, 174–75; hunts buffaloes, 189.
Churches, of Chihuahua, described, 282–84.
Ciboleros, traders encounter, 80–81, 85; characterized, 86; road made by, 218, 223.
Cimarron River, traders plundered on, 12–13; reach, 66–69, 159.
Claverigo, Francisco Xavier, history cited, 146.
Clay County, Mormons locate in, 168; expelled, 169.
Colorado River. See Canadian River.
Comanche Indians, slay traders, 81–83, 187; and first settler of Taos, 139–40; hold council, 180; traders encounter, 181–84, 197–211; raid Mexicans, 209; ideas of trade, 210; plunder traders, 214–18; Mexicans fear, 219–20; as guide, 305–24; Gregg visits, 325.
Comancheros, Gregg encounters, 218–25.
Conestoga wagons, predecessors of Santa Fé wagons, 22.
Connelley, William E., biographer of Josiah Gregg, xii–xiii; estimate of, xix–xxi, xxxi.
Cooke, Capt. Philip St. George, guards Santa Fé traders, 17; career sketched, 18.
Cooper, Colonel, expedition to Santa Fé, 7.
Cooper's Fort, destroyed by Indians, xiv.
Corn, raised in New Mexico, 146.
Coronado, ———, explores New Mexico, 108.
Cortes, Hernan, conquests, 107–108.
Cotton, indigenous to New Mexico, 149.
Cottonwood River, traders camp on, 40–41.
Cottonwood trees, found in New Mexico, 153.
Coues, Dr. Elliott, praises Gregg's map, xx, xxxi.
Council Grove, as rendezvous of traders, 26; described, 30–31; significance of name, 31–32; departure of traders, 38.
Cow Creek, traders cross, 45.

# Index

Creek Indians, story of Chuly, 174–75; succor traders, 217.
Cross Timbers, traders pass, 180, 321.
Cruzate, Pedro Petrir de, destroys Zia, 120.
Cuencame, traders pass, 254.
Customs, venality of officials, 98, 262–64; inspection at Santa Fé, 103–104; duties levied by Governor Armijo, 226; ports of entry, 231; regulations described, 232–35; conduct of officials at Chihuahua, 249–50.
DALEY, ———, murdered, 227–29.
Diamond Spring, arrival of traders, 40.
Doubloon, value defined, 122.
Dragoons, escort traders, 178, 180.
Dry River, characterized, 317.
Durango, described, 254; fruits, 255; scorpions, 255–56; departure of traders, 258; Gregg visits, 269; civil war in, 270–71.
"Dutch," wounded in Indian affray, 311–12.
ECHU-ELEH-HADJO. See Chuly.
Ellis, Powhatan, receives American demands for indemnity, 125.
Elm Grove. See Round Grove.
El Paso del Norte, founded, 119; port of entry established, 231; origin of name, 119, 242; valley described, 243; wine production, 243–44; trade with Chihuahua, 303.
Encinillas, Hacienda de, Gregg's dispute with proprietor, 290–94.
Espy, James P., theory concerning storms, 193.
FACTURA, term explained, 232.
Fairs, commercial, in Mexico, 251.
Fandangoes, Americans attend, 103.
Fanega, unit of measurement, 145.
Farnham, Thomas J., narrative cited, 220.
Fires, on prairie, encountered, 193, 306–307.
Firearms, varieties carried by traders, 36–37.
Fonda, public house, 266, 297.
Food, of New Mexicans, 145–49.
Fort Gibson, Indians visit, 184.
Fort Zarat, location, 47.

334

# Index

Fourth of July, traders celebrate, 78–79.
France, coerces Mexicans, 126, 171.
Frank, hunts buffaloes, 189.
Franklin, starting-point of Santa Fé trade, 6–7, 19; historical sketch, 19.
Fray Cristobal, traders pass, 238.
Frijoles, article of diet, 147.
Fruits, of New Mexico, described, 150–51; of El Paso del Norte, 243; of Durango, 254–55.
GALISTEO, Indian Pueblo, 116.
Gallinas Creek, traders cross, 100.
George, story of, 257–58.
Glenn, ———, expedition of to Santa Fé, 6.
Gonzalez, Governor, deported, 128; shot, 129.
Grapes, culture of in New Mexico, 150; at El Paso del Norte, 243.
Grass, varieties distinguished, 87; of New Mexico, 153–54.
Greeley, Horace, observations on western tour, 322.
Gregg, David, uncle of Josiah, xiii–xiv.
Gregg, Harmon, father of Josiah, xiii–xiv.
Gregg, Jacob, ancestor of Josiah, xiii.
Gregg, John, member of trading expedition, 176; abandons trading career, 230.
Gregg, Josiah, career sketched, xi–xix; ancestry, xiii–xiv; ill health, xiv–xv, xxvi, 21–22; in Mexican War, xvi–xvii; California career, xvii–xix; characterized, xix–xxi; narrative of, xxviii–xxxii; journey from Santa Fé to Independence, 157–63; resumes prairie life, 171; composition of poetry, 176–77; visit to Aguascalientes, 251–65; purchases dog, 256–57; difficulties with Mexican officials, 262–64, 295–301; visits Durango, 269–71; expedition to Jesus Maria, 273–79; at Chihuahua, 281–89; return to Santa Fé, 290–303; dispute with owner of hacienda, 290–94; journey from Santa Fé to Van Buren, 305–24.
Gregg, William, ancestor of Josiah, xiii.
Gregg, William, uncle of Josiah, xiii; slain by Indians, xiv.
Gros Ventre Indians, encounter traders, 72, 85.

# Index

Guia, customs passport, 232–33, 262–64.
Gypsum, deposits of, xx, 194.
Gypsum Creek, traders pass, 194.
HACIENDA de las Animas, Indians raid, 209.
Hays, ——, death of, 172–73.
Hennepin, Father, narrative cited, 58.
Hidalgo, ——, army of, 122.
Hobbs, Dr. Samuel B., aids Gregg, xxix.
Hoffman, Charles Fenno, *Winter in the West*, xxv.
Horses, method of hoppling, 51–53; follow buffaloes, 53. See also mustangs.
Howard County, Greggs settle in, xiv.
Humboldt, Baron, on geography of New Mexico, 132–33, 141–42.
Humboldt Bay, Gregg leads expedition to, xvii–xix.
INDEPENDENCE, Harmon Gregg settles near, xiv; as Mormon center, 20, 163–70; center of Santa Fé trade, 20–21; trading expedition leaves, 26; returns, 163.
Indians, encounter traders, 11–18, 45–46, 49–50, 61–76, 159–61, 192, 197–211; attack traders, 56–57, 81–85, 214–18, 308–13; Mexicans, 75–76, 302; first sight of wagons, 67; proposal to enslave, 110; to Christianize forcibly, 111–12; revolts against Spanish authority, 113–29; attitude of Mormons, 163–64; negotiations with, 201–11; conception of American people, 205–206; captives among, 207–10.
Inns, scarcity in Mexico, 236, 265–66.
Interpreters, activities at Santa Fé, 103.
Irrigation, in New Mexico, described, 143–45.
Irving, Washington, *Tour on the Prairies*, xxv.
Isleta, Spaniards abandon, 118.
Iturbide, General, celebrations in honor of, 286–87.
JACKSON County, Greggs settle in, xiv; Josiah Gregg practices medicine in, xv. See also Independence.
Jesus Maria, expedition to mines of, 273–79.
*Jornado del Muerto*, traders traverse, 238–40.
Justinani, Colonel, campaign against insurgents, 128–29.
KENDALL, George W., historian of Texan Santa Fé Expedition, xxv–xxvi, xxxi; describes prairie dogs, 199–200.

# Index

Kiowa Indians, encounter traders, 16, 184, 192; plunder, 214–18.

Kirker, James, leader of expedition against Indians, 175.

La Cañada, Indians destroy, 115; insurgent center, 123.

Laguna Colorada, traders pass, 306.

Laguna de Encinillas, described, 247–48.

Laguna del Muerto, traders pass, 239.

Lake Patos, overflows, 246.

Lalande, Baptiste, career, 4.

Langham, ———, burial, 158–59.

Lamme, ———, slain by Indians, 16.

La Noria, traders pass, 253.

Las Vegas, founded, 100.

La Zarca, hacienda of, 252–53.

Lechuguilla, plant described, 245.

Leon, arrival of Santa Anna, 261.

Leyva, Francisco Bonillo de, early settler of New Mexico, 109.

Little Arkansas River, traders cross, 44.

Llano Estacado, traders traverse, 313–15.

Long, Major S. H., expedition of, 97.

Los Medanos, traders pass, 245.

Los Organos, mountains described, 244.

Lynch law, application of, 173–74.

McKnight, ———, expedition to Mexico, 5–6; murdered, 187.

McLeod, General, surrenders party to Mexicans, 306.

McNees, ———, and Monroe, slain by Indians, 13–14.

McNee's Creek, traders reach, 78.

Maguey, uses of plant, 255.

Mails, character of in Mexico, 233–34.

Manuel *el Comanche*, guides party across plains, 305–24.

Mariana, ———, historian of Mexico, 107.

Marmaduke, Colonel, acknowledgments to, 10.

Marryat, Capt. Frederick, as plagiarist, xxx–xxxi.

Mason, Richard B., career sketched, 180.

Masonic Order, antipathy of Mexicans toward, 288–89.

Meat, traders' method of curing, 86–88.

Mesas, of Canadian Valley, described, 212–14.

Meteors, shower of in 1833 interpreted, 167.

# Index

Mexicans, venality of officials, 98, 234, 249–50, 262–64, 294–302; captives of Indians, 207–10; manner of giving directions, 222–23; postal system, 233–34; hardiness of muleteers, 236; hospitality of people, 237; as cattle raisers, 248–49; attitude toward negroes, 257–58; method of shoeing mules, 261–62. See also Comancheros and Mexico.

Mexico, France coerces, 126, 171; trade conditions described, 231–35, 251; scarcity of inns, 236, 265–66; bandits in, 256, 258–60; consequences of independence, 285. See also Mexicans.

Mexico City, captured by Cortes, 107.

Mezquite tree, described, 152.

Minter, ———, slain by Indians, 84.

Mirage, described, 89–91.

Miranda, Guadalupe, aids Gregg, 108.

Mitchell, ———, slain by Indians, 215.

Monroe, ———, and McNees, slain by Indians, 13–14.

Mora River (*Rio de la Mora*), traders cross, 100.

Mormons, career in Missouri, 20, 163–70.

Morrison, William, trading adventure to Santa Fé, 4.

Mules, employed in Santa Fé trade, 22–23; obstinacy, 39; battle with mustang, 55–56; traded, 185; method of shoeing, 261–62; hardiness of drivers, 236; employed in mines, 275; drowned, 323.

Muñoz, Captain, leads charge upon insurgents, 129.

Murray, Charles Augustus, *Travels in the United States*, xxv.

Mustangs, battle with mule, 55–56; traders encounter, 196; slaughter, 318.

Narrows, traders pass, 28–29.

Nauvoo, founded, 169.

Navajo Indians, expedition against, 175.

Neosho River, traders cross Cottonwood Fork, 40.

New Mexico, natives revolt, 62; historical sketch, 107–29; Indian wars, 113–29; geographical description, 130–54; boundaries, 130–31; streams, 131–34; villages, 137–38; fertility of soil, 138–39; climate, 140; population, 141–42; state of agriculture, 142–46, 149–51; timber, 151–53; grasses, 153–59.

North Bend, traders pass, 194.

OCATE Creek, traders reach, 158.

Ojeda, ———, describes torture of priest, 120–21.

Ojo Caliente, spring, described, 247.

Ojo del Muerto (Dead Man's Spring), traders resort to, 240.

Oklahoma, boundary fixed, 197; country described, 322–23.

Oñate, Juan de, founds colony in New Mexico, 108–12.

Otermin, Governor Antonio de, rôle in Indian war, 113–20.

Oxen, employed in Santa Fé trade, 23–24; panic among, 41, 94–95; conduct when thirsty, 61.

PALMILLA (soap-plant), found in New Mexico, 153.

Pando, ———, first settler of Taos Valley, 139.

Paso del Norte. See El Paso del Norte.

Pawnee Indians, lookout station of, 49; attacks on traders, 84, 159–61, 308–13.

Pawnee Rock, significance of name, 49.

Perez, Governor Albino, Indians slay, 122–23.

Persimmon Creek, identified with Gypsum Creek, 194.

Peso, value of, 280.

Pike, Zebulon M., narrative cited, 3–5; journey to Chihuahua, 230; erroneous estimate of country, 323.

Pinole, made from mezquite plant, 152.

Piñon, species of tree, 151–52.

Point of Rocks, traders pass, 96.

Polecat, adventure with, 178–80.

Potatoes, cultivation of in New Mexico, 149.

Prairies, curative properties of, xv–xvi, xxvi–xxvii, 21; described, 47, 59, 91, 195, 212–14; fires on, 193, 306–307; fascination of life on, 325–28.

Prairie dogs, traders encounter, 196; described, 199–200.

Pratt, ———, slain by Indians, 215.

Presidio del Norte, port of entry established, 231.

Pueblo Indians, revolt against Spaniards, 113–29.

Pulque, production of at Durango, 255.

# Index

Pursley, James, adventures of, 3–4.
QUAKERS, Gregg's ancestors belong to, xiii.
RABBIT-EAR Mounds, traders reach, 79.
Rattlesnakes, encountered on plains, 55–56.
Real, value of, 122, 280.
Red River, compared with Canadian, 96–97; as boundary, 197; tributary, 315.
Rich Bar, mining camp, xvii–xviii.
Riley, Major Bennett, career sketched, 15; guards Santa Fé traders, 15–17.
Rio Bravo. See Rio del Norte.
Rio Conchos, tributary of Rio del Norte, 133.
Rio del Norte, claims of Texas to, 130; unnavigable, 131; cañon of, 131–32; tributaries, 133; described, 133–34; route via, 236; fertility of valley, 237; traders cross, 241–42.
Rio Grande. See Rio del Norte.
Rio Nazas, traders pass, 253.
Rio Nutria, affluent of Canadian River, 96.
Rio Pecos, course of, 100; tributary of Rio del Norte, 133.
Rio Puerco, tributary of Rio del Norte, 133.
Robledo, traders reach, 240.
Round (Elm) Grove, traders reach, 26.
Round Mound, traders reach, 88, 91.
SABINE River, as boundary, 197.
St. Vrain, Cerain, in southwest trade, 62.
St. Vrain, Marceline, in southwest trade, 62.
Salt, water impregnated with, 220.
San Miguel, objective of Santa Fé expedition, 10; traders reach, 100, 225–26, 305.
Santa Anna, closes ports of entry, 236; arrival at Leon, 261; campaign against Zacatecas, 267–69.
Santa Fé, Texan Expedition to, xxv–xxvi, xxxi, 284, 307; origin of trade with, 3–18; trading expeditions organized, 19–37; traders reach, 101–103; effects of arrival, 105; character of goods in demand, 105–106; Indians besiege, 115–19; lake near, described, 135–36; city described, 136–37; routes to, 171–90, 324–25.

# Index

Santa Fé Creek, described, 133, 134.
Schenk, ———, death, 217.
Scorpions, of Durango, described, 255–56.
Sheep, flock encountered, 100.
Short grass. See buffalo-grass.
Sibley, Dr. ———, report on captive of Indians, 208.
Sierra Blanca Mountains, described, 244.
Silver, mines visited, 266–67, 273–79; method of purifying ore, 276–77; trade in, 278–79; extent of operations, 285–86.
Sioux Indians, traders encounter party, 63.
Slavery, proposal to reduce Indians to, 110.
Smallpox, traders catch, 304–305.
Smelser, Susannah, mother of Josiah Gregg, xiv.
Smith, Capt. Jedediah S., slain by Indians, 81–85.
Smith, Joseph, and Mormon troubles in Missouri, 166; responsibility for shooting of Governor Boggs, 169.
Spain, boundary defined, 197.
Spring Valley, traders name, 186; trader murdered near, 187; traders pass, 322.
Stanley, Elisha, aids Gregg, xxix; captain of caravan, 33; trials of, 72–73; narrative cited, 135–36.
Stefansson, Vilhjalmur, views of Arctic region, 323.
Storms, traders encounter, 28–29, 72, 313–14; frequency in Colorado River region, 99; theory concerning, 193.
Sublette, Capt. William L., career sketched, 62; sufferings of expedition, 81–85.
Surgery, operation performed on trader, 47–49.
TABBAQUENA, Comanche chief, 182–84, 185–86.
Tagnos Indians, besiege Santa Fé, 116–18.
Taos, objective of Santa Fé expedition, 7, 10; Indians revolt, 115; first settler, 139.
Texans, claim Rio del Norte, 130; boundary proposed, 131; surrender to Mexicans, 306.
Texan Santa Fé Expedition, narrative of, xxv–xxvi, xxxi; members imprisoned at Chihuahua, 284; encounters prairie fire, 307.
Tezuque Creek, source described, 134–36.
Thirst, traders suffer, 8–9, 59–61, 68, 82, 215.

341

Thwaites, Dr. Reuben G., edits Gregg's narrative, xii.

Tobacco, cultivation of in New Mexico, 149–50.

Tortilla, article of diet, 146.

Traders, suffer thirst, 8–9, 59–61, 68, 82, 215; encounters with Indians, 11–18, 45–46, 49–50, 56–57, 61–76, 81–85, 159–61, 192, 197–211, 214–18, 308–13; organization of expedition, 19–37; captain of, 33, 72–73; departure from Council Grove, 38–40; encounter buffaloes, 42–43, 53, 187–90, 307–308; cooking utensils, 43–44; bridge quagmires, 44–45; perform surgical operation, 47–49; order of march, 50, 92–93; plan of encampment, 50–51, 93, 184; method of hoppling horses, 51–53; disputes between wagoners, 52; with Governor Armijo, 227–29; cross swollen streams, 54; encounter rattlesnakes, 55–56; celebrate Fourth of July, 78–79; method of curing meat, 86–88; repair wagons, 95–96; arrival at Santa Fé, 101–103; return to Missouri, 155–57; encounter prairie fires, 193, 306–307; avoid trade with plains Indians, 211; trade conditions encountered in Mexico, 231–35; disposal of goods at Chihuahua, 279–80; afflicted with smallpox, 304–305; slaughter buffaloes, 317–18; fascination of prairie life, 325–28.

Treaty of 1819, boundary provisions, 197.

Trias, Angel, dispute with Gregg, 290–94.

Tuberculosis, plains journey as cure, xv–xvi; recommended to Gregg, xxvi–xxvii.

Turkey Creek, traders cross, 42.

UPPER Spring, traders reach, 77.

VALVERDE, traders reach, 237.

Van Buren, Greggs settle near, xiii; starting-point of Santa Fé trade, 172; traders reach, 324.

Vara, unit of measurement, 145, 280.

Vizcarra, Colonel, fights Indians, 76; salutes traders, 98.

WAGONS, employed in Santa Fé trade, 10, 22–23; amaze Indians, 67; repaired, 95–96; return loads from Santa Fé, 157.

Wagoners, eagerness to begin journey, 38; disputes between, 52; use of whips, 93; entry to Santa Fé, 102–103.

# Index

Waldo, Dr. David, aids Gregg, xxix.

Walnut Creek, traders cross, 47; story of surgical operation, 47–49.

Ware, J. R., member of trading expedition, 305.

Washita (Rio Negro, Faux Ouachita) River, home of Comanches, 186; source, 315; reputed branch of Canadian River, 321.

Webster, Daniel, conception of western country, 323.

Wethered, S., member of trading expedition, 305; kills buffaloes, 320.

Wharton, Captain, escorts traders, 17.

Wheat, raised in New Mexico, 138, 146.

Whiskey, manufactured at El Paso del Norte, 243–44.

Willow Bar, traders encounter Indians, 73–75.

Wine, production of at El Paso del Norte, 243–44.

Witchita Indians, council with, 180.

Wolves, follow traders, 161–62.

Women, on Santa Fé expeditions, 36.

Wood, scarcity of on plains, 37.

ZACATECAS, Gregg visits, 265–66; describes, 266–68; wars against Santa Anna, 267–69.

Zapata, Governor Diego de Vargas, reconquers Indians, 120–21.

Zuloaga, ———, customs official, 249–50.